July 20–21, 2013
Los Angeles, California, USA

**Association for
Computing Machinery**

Advancing Computing as a Science & Profession

SUI'13

Proceedings of the ACM Symposium on
Spatial User Interaction

Sponsored by:
ACM SIGCHI and ACM SIGGRAPH

Association for
Computing Machinery

Advancing Computing as a Science & Profession

The Association for Computing Machinery
2 Penn Plaza, Suite 701
New York, New York 10121-0701

Notice to Past Authors of ACM-Published Articles
ACM intends to create a complete electronic archive of all articles and/or other material previously published by ACM. If you have written a work that has been previously published by ACM in any journal or conference proceedings prior to 1978, or any SIG Newsletter at any time, and you do NOT want this work to appear in the ACM Digital Library, please inform permissions@acm.org, stating the title of the work, the author(s), and where and when published.

ISBN: 978-1-4503-2141-9 (Digital)

ISBN: 978-1-4503-2517-2 (Print)

Additional copies may be ordered prepaid from:

ACM Order Department
PO Box 30777
New York, NY 10087-0777, USA

Phone: 1-800-342-6626 (USA and Canada)
+1-212-626-0500 (Global)
Fax: +1-212-944-1318
E-mail: acmhelp@acm.org
Hours of Operation: 8:30 am – 4:30 pm ET

Printed in the USA

Chairs' Welcome

It is our great pleasure to welcome you to the first *ACM Symposium on Spatial User Interaction – SUI'13*. This new event focuses on the user interface challenges that appear when users interact in the space where the flat, two-dimensional, digital world meets the volumetric, physical, three-dimensional (3D) space we live in. This considers both spatial input as well as output, with an emphasis on the issues around the interaction between humans and systems. The goal of the symposium is to provide an intensive exchange between academic and industrial researchers working in the area of SUI and to foster discussions among participants. The first SUI symposium was held July 20-21, 2013 in Los Angeles, USA.

The call for papers attracted 31 submissions from Asia, Europe, Australia, and North and South America in all areas of Spatial User Interaction research. The international program committee consisting of 15 experts in the topic areas and the two program chairs handled the highly competitive and selective review process. Every submission received at least four detailed reviews, two from members of the international program committee and two or more from external reviewers. The reviewing process was double-blind, where only the program chairs as well as the program committee member, who was assigned to each paper to identify external reviewers, knew the identity of the authors.

In the end, the program committee accepted overall 12 (8 full papers plus 4 short papers) out of 31 submissions, which corresponds to an acceptance rate of 26% for full papers (and 38% in total). Additionally 12 posters and demonstrations will complement the program and appear in the proceedings. The topics range from spatial interaction techniques, vision in 3D space, applications, to interaction with multi-touch technologies and in augmented reality. We hope that these proceedings will serve as a valuable reference for Spatial User Interaction researchers and developers.

Putting together the content for *SUI'13* was a team effort. We first thank the authors for providing the content of the program. Special thanks go to the members of the international program committee, who successfully dealt with the reviewing load. We also thank the external reviewers.

Pablo Figueroa and Rob Teather handled the posters and Anamary Leal and Amy Ulinski the demonstrations. The local organization team, led by the general chair, deserves many thanks for organizing the event. James Stewart from PCS assisted by providing and maintaining the reviewing system. Lisa Tolles from ACM and Sheridan Proceedings Service helped greatly to create the proceedings. Our universities, the University of Würzburg and York University and colleagues supported us in this endeavor. Finally, we thank the sponsoring organizations, the ACM Special Interest Groups on Graphics and Human-Computer Interaction (SIGGRAPH, SIGCHI) for co-sponsoring this event

We hope that you will find this program interesting and thought provoking and that the symposium will provide you with a valuable opportunity to share ideas with other researchers and practitioners from institutions around the world.

Evan Suma
SUI'13 General Chair
University of Southern California

Wolfgang Stuerzlinger
SUI'13 Program Co-Chair
York University, Canada

Frank Steinicke
SUI'13 Program Co-Chair
University of Würzburg, Germany

Table of Contents

Full Papers

Demos & Posters

SUI 2013 Symposium Organization

General Chairs: Evan Suma *(USC Institute for Creative Technologies USA)*

Program Chairs: Wolfgang Stuerzlinger *(York University, Canada)*
Frank Steinicke *(University of Würzburg, Germany)*

Posters Chairs: Pablo Figueroa *(Universidad de los Andes, Colombia)*
Rob Teather *(York University, Canada)*

Demonstrations Chairs: Anamary Leal *(Virginia Tech, USA)*
Amy Ulinski *(University of Wyoming, USA)*

Student Volunteer Chairs: Christina Trejo *(USC Institute for Creative Technologies, USA)*
Peter Khooshabeh *(USC Institute for Creative Technologies, USA)*

Publications Chairs: Kyle Johnsen *(University of Georgia, USA)*
Scott Kuhl *(Michigan Technological University, USA)*

Publicity Chair: Gerd Bruder *(University of Würzburg, Germany)*

Local Arrangements Chair David Krum *(USC Institute for Creative Technologies, USA)*

Web Chair: Jennifer Wohlner *(USC Institute for Creative Technologies, USA)*

Program Committee: Ferran Argelaguet Sanz *(INRIA, France)*
Doug Bowman *(Virginia Tech, USA)*
Gerd Bruder *(Universität Würzburg, Germany)*
Géry Casiez *(INRIA at Villeneuve, France)*
Sabine Coquillart *(INRIA, France)*
Steven K. Feiner *(Columbia University, USA)*
Martin Hachet *(INRIA at Bordeaux, France)*
Jonna Häkkilä *(Soul4Design, Finland)*
Tobias Isenberg *(INRIA, France)*
Victoria Interrante *(University of Minnesota, USA)*
Kiyoshi Kiyokawa *(Osaka University, Japan)*
Joseph LaViola *(University of Central Florida, USA)*
Rob Lindeman *(Worcester Polytechnic Institute, USA)*
Johannes Schöning *(Hasselt University Diepenbeek, Belgium)*
Rob Teather *(York University, Canada)*

Additional reviewers:

Ana Afonso	Baizil Jacob
Amro Al-Akkad	Jacek Jankowski
Elisabeth André	Abhijit Karnik
Bruno Araujo	Nicholas Katzakis
Ferran Argelaguet Sanz	Daniel Keefe
Mark Ashdown	Michael Kipp
Ilhan Aslan	Yoshifumi Kitamura
Ravin Balakrishnan	Kiyoshi Kiyokawa
Frank Biocca	Luv Kohli
Jon Bird	Regis Kopper
Nis Bornoe	Matthias Kranz
Doug Bowman	Sven Kratz
Gerd Bruder	Per Ola Kristensson
François Bérard	Torsten Kuhlen
Géry Casiez	Liisa Kuparinen
Steven Castellucci	Bireswar Laha
Jessica Cauchard	Marc Latoschik
Amira Chalbi	Joseph LaViola
Xiang 'Anthony' Chen	Taehee Lee
Ming Ki Chong	Robert Lindeman
Aurélie Cohé	Anamary Leal
Sabine Coquillart	Ligang LIU
Afsaneh Doryab	Liang LIU
Alexandra Douglass-Bonner	Pengfei Lu
Petros Faloutsos	Markus Löchtefeld
Steven Feiner	Charlotte Magnusson
Bruce Ferwerda	Jean-Claude Martin
Pablo Figueroa	Marian Cristian Mihaescu
Christian Fischer Pedersen	Tomer Moscovich
Morten Fjeld	Miguel Nacenta
Aaron Genest	Quan Nguyen
Giuseppe Ghiani	Ohan Oda
Raphael Grasset	Thomas Olsson
Jens Grubert	Michael Ortega
Martin Hachet	S. Joon Park
Taku Hachisu	Young-Woo Park
Jonna Hakkila	Andriy Pavlovych
Mark Hancock	Sönke Pelzer
Nils Hasler	Simon PERRAULT
Uta Hinrichs	Gert Pfurtscheller
Christina Hochleitner	Francis Quek
Victoria Interrante	Umar Rashid
Tobias Isenberg	Zhimin Ren
Daisuke Iwai	Simon Robinson

Mario Romero
Ricardo Ron Angevín
Daisuke Sakamoto
Nobuchika Sakata
Christian Sandor
Sayan Sarcar
Yann Savoye
Reinhold Scherer
Dieter Schmalstieg
Johann Schrammel
Johannes Schöning
S. Sheppard
Nobutaka Shimada
Sajad Shirali-Shahreza
Leonid Sigal
Frank Steinicke
William Steptoe
Wolfgang Stuerzlinger
Sriram Subramanian
Henrik Sørensen
Kazuki Takashima

Robert Teather
Bruce Thomas
Theophanis Tsandilas
Amy Ulinski
Hahne Uwe
Dimitar Valkov
Robert van Liere
Davy Vanacken
Kiran Varanasi
Radu-Daniel Vatavu
Jo Vermeulen
Chat Wacharamanotham
James Wallace
Phil Wieland
Daniel Wigdor
Chadwick Wingrave
Woontack Woo
Himanshu Zade
Jun Zheng
ZhiYing Zhou

SUI 2013 Sponsors & Supporters

Sponsors:

Supporters:

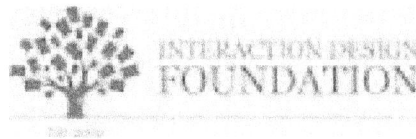

USC Institute for
Creative Technologies

Visualization of Off-Surface 3D Viewpoint Locations in Spatial Augmented Reality

Matt Adcock[*†‡]
matt.adcock@csiro.au

David Feng[*†]
david.feng@csiro.au

Bruce Thomas[‡]
bruce.thomas@unisa.edu.au

[*]CSIRO
Canberra, Australia

[†]Australian National University
Canberra, Australia

[‡]University of South Australia
Mawson Lakes, Australia

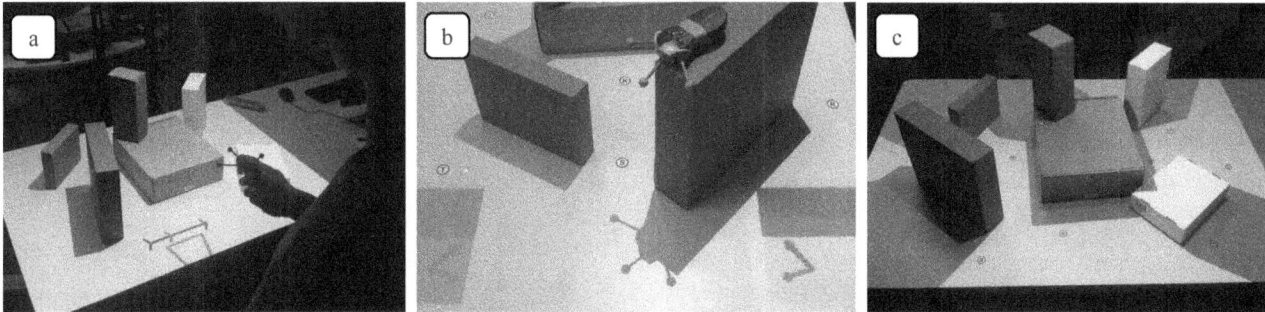

Figure 1. An overview of the techniques we designed to visualize off-surface information. In (a) the red Wedge tracks the location of a user's hand within the display plane and a blue arrow indicates relative height above the surface, in (b) two vectors appear to triangulate the location of the tracked device, and in (c) blue shadows are cast from an Eyelight above the centre of the table.

ABSTRACT

Spatial Augmented Reality (SAR) systems can be used to convey guidance in a physical task from a remote expert. Sometimes that remote expert is provided with a single camera view of the workspace but, if they are given a live captured 3D model and can freely control their point of view, the local worker needs to know what the remote expert can see. We present three new SAR techniques, *Composite Wedge*, *Vector Boxes*, and *Eyelight*, for visualizing off-surface 3D viewpoints and supporting the required workspace awareness. Our study showed that the Composite Wedge cue was best for providing location awareness, and the Eyelight cue was best for providing visibility map awareness.

Categories and Subject Descriptors

H.5.1 [Information interfaces and presentation]: Artificial, augmented, and virtual realities; H.5.2 [Information interfaces and presentation]: User Interfaces – Graphical user interfaces.

Keywords

Spatial Augmented Reality; Spatial User Interfaces; Remote Guidance; Visualization; Off-Surface Rendering.

1. INTRODUCTION

Remote Guidance technologies support distributed collaboration around a physical task and allow expertise in one location to be applied to a task in another location. Typically, this will involve at least one 'worker' who is co-located with the task and one remote 'expert' who will use their expertise to guide the worker through aspects of the task.

Previous research [4, 13, 18] has shown that Remote Guidance technologies are more efficient and effective when they provide

participants with a "common grounding" [2] upon which they can collaborate. One key aspect of this is some awareness for the worker of the remote expert's view of the workspace.

In many Remote Guidance systems developed to date, the worker has an extremely literal awareness of the remote expert's view of the workspace because that viewpoint is physically embodied by the position of a single streaming video camera, but increasingly Remote Guidance systems are employing depth cameras or other sensors to capture and stream real time 3D representations of the physical workspace [12, 20, 24]. These can be rendered in such a way as to provide the remote expert with the ability to independently manipulate their viewpoint within the workspace. We refer to this process as 'free movement'. As Gutwin et al. observed [7], remote collaboration approaches can obscure people's locations, conceal activities and reduce efficiency when they allow users to dynamically alter their viewpoint of the workspace but do not convey this change to others.

Augmented Reality (AR) can be used to depict the location of a virtual object in free space. In application areas such as telemedicine, maintenance and manual assembly it is often undesirable to encumber the worker's head with an HMD, or hands with a tablet device. Spatial Augmented Reality (SAR) systems which project computer graphics directly into the physical environment have been used to convey guidance to the worker while permitting them to maintain a clear and direct view of the task at hand [1, 11]. While SAR has particular benefits in providing task guidance cues on the surface of physical objects, there has been very little success to date in depicting 3D information that does not exist on or near such a surface.

In this paper, we present three new SAR techniques; *Composite Wedge*, *Vector Boxes*, and *Eyelight,* for visualizing off-surface 3D locations and providing a user with an awareness of the portions of the physical work environment that can be seen from the 3D free movement viewport of a remote expert (Figure 1).

In the following sections we review the previous work that pertains to this research problem. We then describe our new techniques and detail our prototype implementations of each of them. We also present a user study that compares the suitability of each of the techniques in terms of their ability to convey the 'viewability map' from an arbitrary floating viewpoint, and their ability to convey the location of an arbitrary off-surface 3D point.

2. RELATED WORK

Gutwin et al. [7] identify and describe four important types of awareness that arise during group work: *Informal Awareness* - a general sense of who's around and what they are up to; *Social Awareness* - information that a person maintains about others in a social context, e.g. their level of interest during a conversation; *Group-Structural Awareness* - knowledge about people's roles and responsibilities in the group; *Workspace Awareness* - maintaining knowledge about other's interactions with the workspace. It is the last of these, Workspace Awareness, which we aim to support with the techniques described in this paper.

In 2D collaborative digital workspaces, previous research has demonstrated a range of techniques for providing Workspace Awareness. The ShrEdit text editing system [3] is an early example of displaying each user's system feedback to all users. Radar Views [7] later showed how small maps representing each user's view of a 2D graphical environment could support Workspace Awareness.

In 3D collaborative virtual environments, Avatars have been often used to represent other users, and even this mimetic representation [10] has been improved by more explicit representations of view frustums and object viewability [9]. In Spatial User Interfaces (SUI), however, visual representations often exist only on the available physical 2D surfaces. Some efforts have been made in previous work to convey task guidance cues to users via SAR [16, 21, 28] but these visual cues use the display surface to convey explicitly authored task goals.

A number of systems have overlaid 'shadows' [15, 23] or video [14, 22] of remote participants' arms and hands directly into the collaborative workspace. The corresponding 3D viewpoint location may be inferred from the assumption they are anatomically human. These systems, however, largely rely on symmetric modes of interaction and become less relevant when the remote worker can choose an arbitrary virtual viewpoint.

Genest et al. [5] presented a technique for representing the height of a finger above a collaborative touch screen. However, their concentric circles visualization was not designed to be linearly mapped to the physical height, nor could it be used within the room surrounding the display surface.

The LightGuide [17] and the LightSpace [27] systems can both display objects at arbitrary 3D locations in a room, however the user must provide their hand or body as a display surface. While these techniques have shown promise in providing gesture guidance and user interaction, they are unsuitable for providing passive visualization of workspace awareness information.

3. VIEWPOINT VISUALIZATION

In this section we describe our three new SAR visualization techniques. These are motivated by application scenarios that include the remote guidance of physical tasks and, as such, we describe the techniques with reference to a table or bench-like display surface, upon which task related objects are placed. A projector then augments the workspace from above. While this arrangement has been used by many researchers to explore visualizations on the table surface, our three new techniques use it to visualize a viewpoint (such as that of a remote expert) that may be effectively 'floating' anywhere in the surrounding room.

3.1 Composite Wedge

The Composite Wedge combines a 2D component and a 1D component to convey the 3D location of the target viewpoint (see Figure 2 and Figure 1a). The 2D component specifies the location of the target point on the plane coincident with the projection surface, and is inspired by the 'Wedge' off-screen point representation technique developed by Gustafson et al. [6] to convey the 2D location of points positioned outside of a small display screen. The Wedge has the shape of an acute isosceles triangle, with the two base corners of the Wedge rendered on-screen, and the (implied) apex of the triangle coinciding with the target point. The user is able to infer the location of the target point by mentally completing the two lines from the base corners to the apex. Gustafson et al. showed that the Wedge technique can out-perform previous off-screen location techniques in both speed and accuracy, especially in the presence of clutter.

The 1D component of the cue is designed to convey the height of the target point to the user. This is achieved through the use of a relative scale, the bottom and top endpoints map to designated physical objects in the scene (such as the tabletop and the projector/ceiling, respectively). The relative height of the target point between these two extremes is rendered on the scale. The scale endpoints and midpoint are rendered as arrows pointing 'up' (in the direction of the upper endpoint, corresponding to the higher reference object) so that the user may easily distinguish the upper and lower endpoints of the scale. When the target viewpoint exists above the display surface, a dot, instead of a wedge is used in combination with this 1D cue.

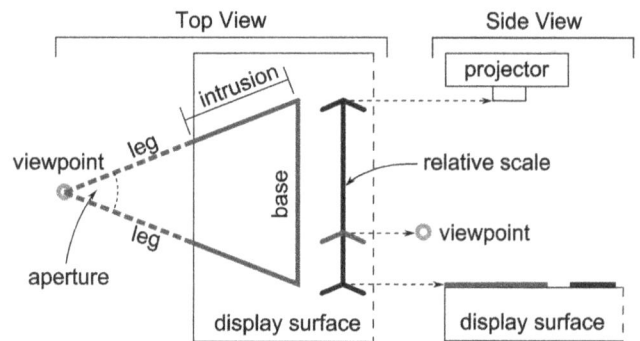

Figure 2. Conceptual diagram of the Composite Wedge cue.

Gustafson et al. describe the main visual components of the wedge as the legs (lines from the base corners to the target point), aperture (angle between the legs), and rotation (the rotation of the Wedge around the target point). Combining these three components give a value called intrusion, defined as the distance of the furthest Wedge base corner from the edge of the screen. Gustafson et al. found that setting intrusion to increase with the distance between the target point and the screen edge gave best results, primarily since it allows more of the legs to be rendered, reducing error for distant target points. They controlled the intrusion through setting the leg length, which is calculated using a non-linear function that levels off for large target point distances. A generalization of Gustafson et al.'s formula for calculating leg length is given by the following equation:

$$leg = dist + \log\left(\frac{dist + A}{B}\right) \times C$$

Where *dist* is the distance from the target point to the display surface, *A* sets the minimum wedge size, *B* controls the rate of change of intrusion relative to *dist*, and *C* linearly adjusts the intrusion of the Wedge into the display surface. All distances are measured in pixels.

Gustafson et al. provide values A=20, B=12 and C=10. However these values were based on a mobile handset's display resolution and typical target distances to the screen. Instead, we use values A=300, B=200 and C=100 which we have found to be more suitable for tabletop size displays. This sets the minimum wedge size as 40mm, and was also found to achieve a good intrusion-clutter balance.

Gustafson et al. map the aperture of each Wedge to the distance of the target from the screen and leg length. Their original formula was found to be suitable for our purposes, and we thus implement it without change.

A rotation of the Wedge occurs when the Wedge is near a corner of the display surface. Gustafson et al. do not provide details of their corner rotation algorithm, and we therefore developed an original algorithm. This algorithm was designed to satisfy two constraints: visual continuity, and preservation of intrusion. Firstly a spatial buffer equal to the minimum wedge size is defined from each display surface edge. Any points on the display surface and outside the buffer are considered part of the inner display surface. If either of the wedge base points is outside the inner display surface, then the Wedge is rotated until both base points are within the inner display surface, increasing leg length as necessary. This rotation, however, modifies intrusion and violates continuity. To address these issues, we modify the leg length by logarithmically interpolating, based on a rotation degree out of 45 degrees, between the non-rotated wedge and the rotated wedge, resulting in a smooth rotation of the Wedge on corners while maintaining appropriate intrusion.

3.2 Vector Boxes

The Vector Boxes method also uses a form of triangulation to perform 3D viewpoint specification (see Figure 3 and Figure 1b). Two or more vectors, all pointing at a common target, are rendered onto the display surface, such that if the vectors were long enough then the target point would coincide with their intersection. These vectors are placed at different locations (e.g. the corners of a tabletop) on the display surface. This cue was inspired, in part, by the '3D Pathlet' vector used by Sodhi et al. [17] to convey off-surface 3D directions using SAR.

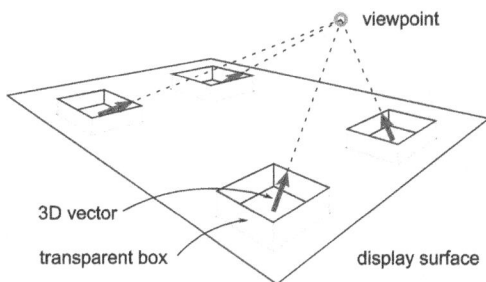

Figure 3. Conceptual diagram of the Vector Boxes cue - the viewer mentally triangulates the vectors to infer the location of the target viewpoint.

Each vector is positioned within a virtual box that appears to be cut-out of the table to the user. This means the arrows appear to the user to be placed below the display surface. By placing the vector below the projection surface we reduce the chance of the vectors apparently being cut off because they exceed the available display surface. Hillinges et al. [8] have previously shown that in a tracked-viewpoint non-stereoscopic system, such as this one,

depth perception can be better when virtual objects appear below or behind the display surface.

3.3 Eyelight

Conceptually, the Eyelight technique works as if a point light has been placed at the physical location of the target point, lighting up the parts of the work environment that are visible from that point, and casting the rest in shadow (see Figure 4 and Figure 1c). In practice this effect is achieved by using a projector to render the lit and shadowed areas into the environment. This cue was inspired by previous work in rendering virtual shadows with SAR, such as the URP system for simulating sunlight conditions for architectural design [26].

Shadows are a part of every person's day-to-day environment and have therefore been explored in previous work as a way to enhance the 'realism' of AR objects. For example, Sugano et al. [19] performed a study using head-mounted video see-though AR, finding that the shadows of virtual objects (a) provide a stronger connection between the real world and virtual objects and so increases virtual object presence, and (b) provide depth cues and so makes three-dimensional perceptions easier for the users of the interface. The converse is also expected to be true; rendering the appropriate virtual shadows within a physical scene would give a good indication of the location of a virtual light source.

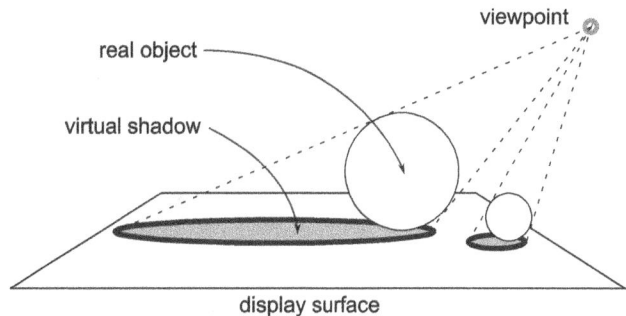

Figure 4. Conceptual diagram of the Eyelight cue - the areas not visible from the target viewpoint are shaded with a virtual shadow.

This cue can be considered to be a quite literal representation of the visibility map of a viewpoint. Areas of the scene which are lit are visible from the light source since by definition they lie on an un-occluded path from the source. Similarly, shadowed areas are not visible from the source.

4. PROTOTYPE IMPLEMENTATION

We constructed a prototype system that implements each of the three techniques described in the previous section. For comparison we also implemented a 'control condition' consisting of a *Screen* showing a simple 'clone' of a real-time 3D view that could be provided to the remote expert. This section describes the main implementation details of the system architecture with calibration process, Vector Boxes, Eyelight and Screen. The Composite Wedge was implemented in OpenGL based on the algorithms described in the previous section.

4.1 System Architecture and Calibration

The hardware utilized in this setup includes a projector with a rigidly attached RGB-D camera (in this case, a Microsoft Kinect) and a tracker system (see Figure 5).

The steps taken to find the pose of each device in a single coordinate system are outlined below:

Projector-Camera: RGBDemo [http://labs.manctl.com/rgbdemo] was used to find the relative pose between the camera and the projector.

Tracker-Camera: Tracking markers were attached to a camera shell, which allows the tracker system to sense the position and orientation of a fixed point on the camera. A custom implementation of Hand-Eye calibration [25] was used to determine the transformation between this 6DOF tracked point and the camera's RGB sensor.

Camera-World: This transformation was computed by manually aligning the virtual display surface with a 3D model of the display surface reconstructed from data from the camera's depth sensor. First, a planar model is fitted to the reconstructed 3D model via the Random Sample Consensus (RANSAC) implementation in the PCL [http://www.pointclouds.org], thereby extracting the dominant plane. The normal of this plane and the virtual plane are then aligned and manual translation and rotation around the now common normal axis is performed until alignment.

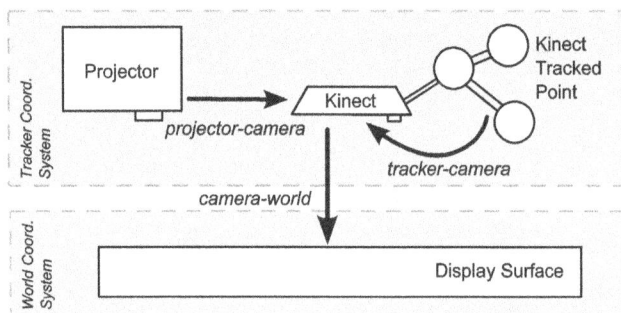

Figure 5. The pair-wise extrinsic relationships computed during calibration. The pose of each device in the world coordinate system can be found by travelling backwards along the arrows from the world coordinate system to the device, and concatenating the poses corresponding to the visited arrows.

4.2 Implementing the Vector Boxes

In this cue, two or more 3D vectors are rendered onto the display surface. Each vector points at the target point, allowing for the user to mentally triangulate the location of this point.

A crucial requirement of this cue is that the vectors appear 3D to the user (Figure 6). In order to achieve perspective-correct rendering, the viewpoint of the user is tracked by having them wear a glasses frame with tracker balls attached (see Figure 7, top right). This allows the approximate location of the user's viewpoint to be streamed from the tracker machine in real time. The streaming was performed using VRPN.

The process for generating the projector-rendered image is now described. A virtual model of the display surface, including the vectors, is rendered from the point of view of the user using a per-frame calculated projection matrix. This projection matrix is computed using the minimum and maximum X, Y and Z values of the display surface corner points transformed to the viewpoint coordinate system, in order to ensure that the display surface fills out the rendered image, thus reducing the aliasing effects that accompany rasterization. The resulting image is temporarily stored in an OpenGL frame buffer object (FBO). The positions of the pixels in the FBO corresponding to the display surface corners are then computed, by applying the projection matrix to each of the 3D corner positions. This information is used to cut out the

portion of the FBO containing the display surface and convert it to a texture. OpenCV was used to perform the perspective warping of this texture, based on the viewpoint of the worker, in order to map it correctly to the virtual display surface. Finally, this texture is applied to the virtual display surface, and rendered onto the physical display surface with the projector.

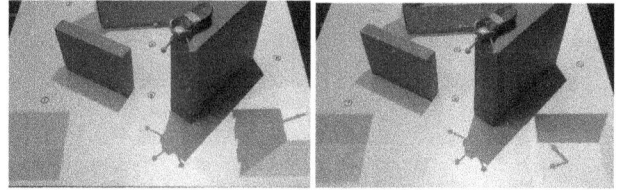

Figure 6. Vector cue viewed from non-user viewpoint in scene (left) and from tracked worker viewpoint (right). In both cases the Vectors are pointing at the 'clicker' on the red box.

Virtual shadows were rendered for each of the virtual vectors and their boxes in this cue, in order to increase the presence of the vectors, and to give the user additional depth cues [19]. The position of the virtual light source used to generate the shadows was selected to be coincident with the physical projector bulb. Shading effects on the vectors were also computed from this light source.

4.3 Implementing the Eyelight

The Eyelight cue functions by 'bathing in light' the portions of a scene which are visible from the target viewpoint and overlaying the rest with 'shadow'. First, a 3D model of the scene is acquired using the Kinect. To minimize the effect of noise in the Kinect sensor, we detected known objects within the obtained point cloud and substituted the respective points with manually created 3D models. Then, the shadows cast within the virtual scene from a given light source are computed using shadow-mapping rendered into the scene with a projector.

Shadow-mapping was implemented using OpenGL, with the aid of the GLEE_ARB extension. Both virtually shadowed and non-shadowed areas within the scene were rendered, in blue and white respectively, in order to distinguish them from real shadows within the scene caused by the projector bulb.

4.4 Control Condition

The non-SAR screen-based technique was also implemented, for comparison. In this method, a virtual camera is placed at the target point, facing the center of the display surface, and the view of the scene from the camera is rendered onto a computer monitor. This essentially shows the same view as a remote expert might see.

The same 3D model that was described in the previous section was rendered to the monitor using OpenGL. In order to aid in distinguishing different objects during the study, each of the real world objects was covered in cardboard of a distinct color, and the corresponding objects in the virtual scene were colored to match.

5. EVALUATIONS

We designed and conducted a user study to compare the relative merits of the new techniques. We investigated both their ability to convey the visibility map for (i.e. what can be seen from) a given point, and also their ability to convey the location in space of a given point.

5.1 Setup

The task environment for the experiment was designed to resemble that of a remote guidance scenario. It involves a table plane where the 'work' is performed, some objects placed on the table, and various optical devices. A list of the equipment utilized in the task environment is as follows (see Figure 7):

1. rectangular tabletop display surface;
2. six color-coded boxes placed on the display surface;
3. fourteen labeled markers placed on the display surface and boxes, for visibility testing;
4. ceiling mounted projector, to render SAR cues onto the display surface;
5. Kinect, for calibration and model generation; and
6. Optitrack infrared tracker system containing six cameras, to obtain the real-time pose of tracked objects in the scene for interaction and calibration.

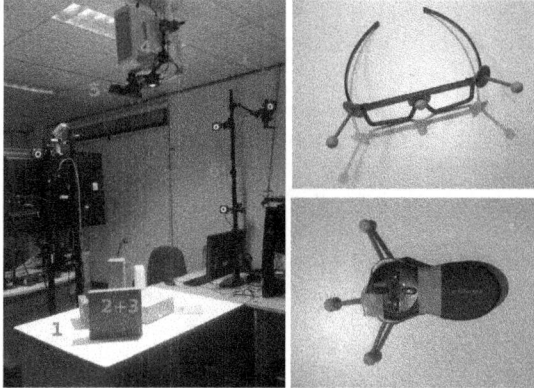

Figure 7. (Left) Task environment setup, includes (1) display surface, (2) box objects for occlusion, (3) markers for visibility testing, (4) projector, (5) Kinect, (6) Optitrack tracker system. (Top Right) The tracked glasses frames (Bottom Right) The 3D tracked 'clicker'.

The cue rendering code was run from a desktop machine with a dual core Intel Xeon E5520 2.26GHz CPU, 3GB RAM, and NVIDIA Quadro FX 4800 GPU, and Windows XP Professional Service Pack 3 (32 bit). Tracking data was obtained and streamed to the rendering machine via Ethernet from a desktop machine with an Intel Core2 Duo E8300 2.83GHz CPU, 2GB RAM, Intel Q35 integrated graphics chipset, and Windows 7 (32 bit).

To facilitate user interaction, a number of tracked objects were utilized in the study. These include a lecture presentation clicker, containing a clickable interaction button, and a pair of glasses, for viewpoint tracking in the Vector Boxes cue. The world coordinate system was defined such that the origin coincided with the center of the display surface, the X and Z axes were parallel to the display surface, and the Y axis was pointing upwards.

5.2 Tasks

5.2.1 Visibility Map Estimation

This task is designed to measure the effectiveness of each cue in conveying a visibility map to the user. During each trial the participant is shown a visual cue, and asked to specify the markers they believe are visible from the viewpoint specified by the cue. User interaction is performed using a pen, a top-down 2D paper diagram of the scene (see Figure 8), and the (for this task, untracked) clicker device. In order to begin a trial, the participant places the clicker over a designated area of the display surface and presses the clicker button to load a viewpoint cue. The participant then circles the corresponding visible markers on the paper diagram. The markers are labeled with letters, both in the scene and on the diagram, in order to ease the mapping between them. The diagram is placed on a clipboard to aid mobility. The

participant presses the clicker again when they are finished, recording the time taken to perform the trial.

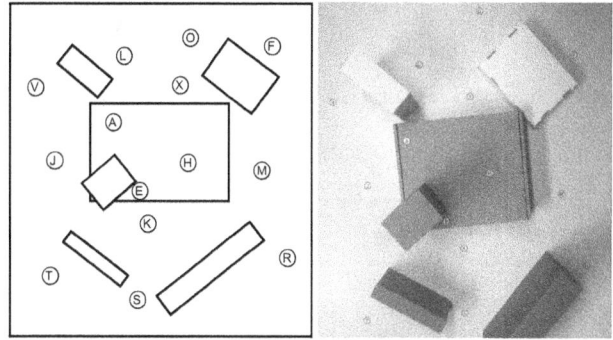

Figure 8. Top-down diagram of the scene provided during the visibility map estimation task (left) and actual top-down view of the scene (right).

5.2.2 Location Estimation

This task is designed to measure the effectiveness of each cue in conveying the 3D location of a viewpoint to a user. For each trial, the participant estimates the location of a target point based on a visual cue rendered in the scene. All user interaction is performed using the tracked clicker device. In order to begin a trial, the participant places the clicker over a designated area of the display surface and presses the clicker button to load a point. This ensures a consistent start position for all trials. The participant is then shown a visual cue corresponding to the trial point, moves the middle ball on the clicker to the 3D position that they believe the cue is conveying, and presses the clicker button once again. On this second button press, the time taken and estimated location are recorded, and the trial is ended.

5.3 Experimental Procedure

A Latin Squares arrangement was used to eliminate ordering effects. With 4 experimental conditions, one for each cue type, 24 participants were recruited to satisfy this arrangement, with each participant experiencing the conditions in a different experiment order. For each participant, the cues, tasks and background were described by the experimenter. The system was then run in 'interactive mode', where the target point is locked to the clicker's position in the physical world, allowing the participant to move the target point around and observe the behavior of the projected cues.

Then, for each of the conditions in the experiment, the participant:

- Is again briefed on the cue corresponding to the condition.
- Performs 5 location estimation practice trials.
- Performs 20 location estimation experimental trials.
- Performs 1 visibility map estimation practice trial.
- Performs 5 visibility map estimation experimental trials.

Every participant was asked to perform each task as quickly and accurately as possible. No feedback on the correctness of guesses made by participants was given during the practice or experimental trials for either task, since no direct feedback would be given in a real world application of this system.

In the location estimation task, a set of 20 fixed target test points, presented in different orderings, were used for all conditions over all participants. The number of points was chosen to be high enough to make it unlikely that participants would notice the same set of points being used each time.

In the visibility map estimation task, due to the much lower number of test trials, it was reasoned that participants would likely notice the re-use of the same five target points across all conditions. Thus four different sets of five target points, all having a similar spread, were created, and each participant experienced these four sets in the same ordering. Due to the Latin Squares arrangement, each condition was applied to each set an equal number of times.

A brief post-experiment survey was performed. This survey asked users to rate their own performance in terms of time and accuracy for each of the tasks.

5.4 Data Collection

Two major quantities were measured during each trial: the cost, which is inversely proportional to accuracy, of the guessed result, and the time taken to complete the task (to millisecond precision). The cost for the point location task is defined as the Euclidean distance between the guessed point and the ground truth, while the cost of the visibility map estimation task is defined as the number of letters labeled incorrectly.

6. RESULTS

6.1 Visibility Estimation Performance

The results of this task indicate the effectiveness of each cue type, in terms of time and cost, at conveying the visibility map of a viewpoint. Timing comes from the manual timer controlled by the participant using the clicker. Cost was measured as the number of incorrect visibility labelings.

6.1.1 Task Completion Time

The Eyelight cue was found to have the shortest completion time for this task, with a mean of 26.30 (SD 9.70) seconds. The Vector Boxes cue appeared to have the longest completion time, with a mean of 35.21 (SD 12.04) seconds (see Figure 9a).

A two-way (condition × trial) repeated measures ANOVA was applied to the time data after a log transformation had been applied. This transform was used to satisfy the assumption of homogeneity in the data. Completion times differed significantly across the four types ($F(3,449)=23.51$, $p<.001$). The analysis also showed that trial number affected completion time ($F(4,449)=6.36$, $p<.001$).

A post-hoc Scheffe test (significance level 0.05) was run on the data, and a significant difference was found between the two fastest cues (Eyelight and Screen) and the two slowest cues (Composite Wedge and Vector Boxes).

6.1.2 Task Cost

Figure 9b shows the total task cost for the visibility map estimation task over all participants and trials for each condition. The Eyelight cue had the lowest number of mislabeled points, followed closely by the Screen cue. The Composite Wedge and Vector Boxes cues had a higher cost, with almost twice the mislabel rate of the previous cues. A Wilcoxon signed-rank test showed all cost differences were significant ($p<0.05$).

6.2 Location Estimation Performance

6.2.1 Task Completion Time

The Composite Wedge cue was found to have the lowest completion time, with a mean of 6.560 (SD 2.671) seconds. The task with the longest completion time is the Screen cue, with a mean of 12.664 (SD 6.789) seconds (see Figure 9c).

A two-way (condition × trial) repeated measures ANOVA was applied to the (also log transformed) time data to test for differences in completion time among the four cue types. Completion times differed significantly across the four types ($F(3,1873)=206.87$, $p<.001$). The analysis also showed that trial number had a minor effect on completion time ($F(19,1873)=8.02$, $p<.001$). Note that there was one outlier in the data, omitted from the calculations, caused by the user accidentally skipping a trial by clicking in quick succession.

Performing the Scheffe post-hoc test (significance level 0.05) on the data revealed that a significant difference exists between the mean of the fastest cue (Composite Wedge) and each of the other cues. Additionally, a significant difference was found to exist between the slowest cue (Screen) and all the other cues.

6.2.2 Task Cost

The Composite Wedge cue had the lowest estimation cost, with a mean of 207.4 (SD 187.2) mm. The Screen cue had the highest cost for this task, with a mean cost of 379.7 (SD 247.6) mm (see Figure 9d).

A two-way (condition × trial) repeated measures ANOVA was used to find that there was a significant difference in task cost between conditions ($F(3,1873)=119.24$, $p<.001$). Additionally, trial number had an effect on task cost ($F(19,1873)=29.22$, $p<.001$). This analysis also omits the outlier mentioned in the previous section.

Applying the Scheffe post-hoc test (significance level 0.05) revealed that there was a significant difference in cost between the most accurate cue (Composite Wedge) and the other cues. The Vector Boxes cue was also found to have a significantly lower cost than the Eyelight and Screen cues.

6.3 Questionnaire

6.3.1 Visibility Estimation

Most participants felt that they performed the visibility map estimation task more quickly using the Eyelight and Screen cues than with the Vector Boxes and Composite Wedge cues (see Figure 10). The majority of participants asserted that, even when using the latter two cues, they performed the task with an above average accuracy.

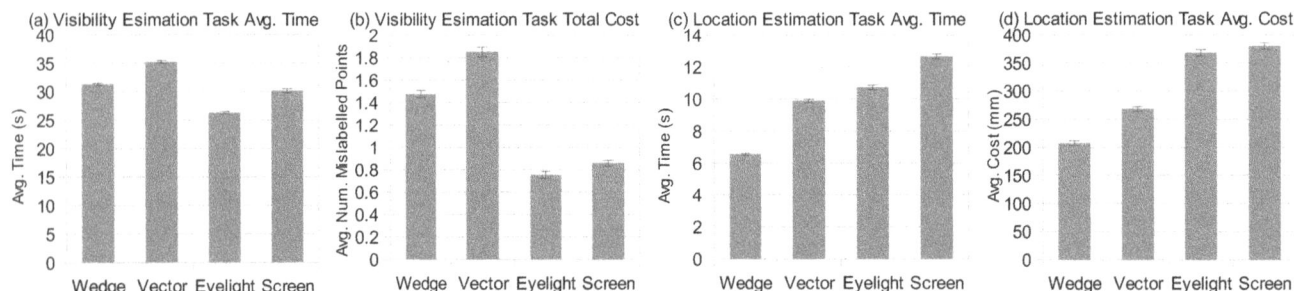

Figure 9. Results for Times and Costs for the Visibility Estimation and Location Estimation tasks. Bars indicate standard error.

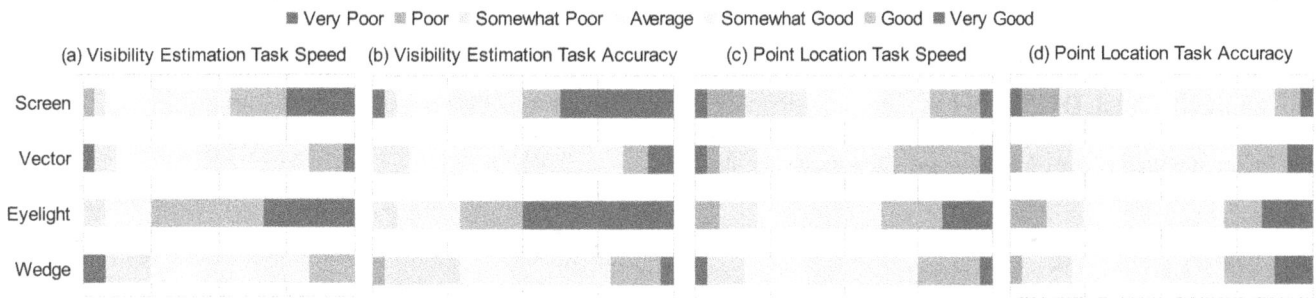

Figure 10. Participant responses to the qualitative survey.

Similarly, the majority of participants perceived that they performed the visibility map estimation task more accurately with the Eyelight and Screen cues than with the Composite Wedge and Vector Boxes cues. Half of the participants felt that the Eyelight cue enabled them to complete the task with the highest possible accuracy.

6.3.2 Location Estimation
The Eyelight, Vector Boxes and Composite Wedge cues had similar perceived task completion times. Participants generally thought they performed slower with the screen cue than the other cues.

Most of the participants believed that they completed the point location task with an above average accuracy using the Eyelight and the Vector Boxes cue. The Screen cue has the lowest overall perceived completion accuracy for this task.

7. DISCUSSION
The results of our study are particularly encouraging and indicate that SAR can indeed be used to visualize off-surface information. No single approach was found to perform better for conveying **both** a visibility map and a point's 3D location: the Composite Wedge is a 'clear winner' in terms of 3D location estimation, while the Eyelight and the Screen cues performed best for the visibility map estimation task. We note that a system could, for example, simultaneously use an Eyelight for workspace awareness and reinforce the visualization with the Composite Wedge depicting the viewpoint's location.

The Vector Boxes cue did not come out on top in either the visibility estimation or the location estimation tasks. We expect this is, in part, because the large separation between arrows needed to reduce uncertainty in triangulation resulted in more 'looking around' in the workspace for the worker.

In the location estimation task, the distance of the target point from the centre of the display surface appears to have an effect on cost, with closer points having a higher mean accuracy. This is unsurprising, since as distance increases, the performance of every cue is expected to degrade. Even the Screen technique shows a smaller image on the scene when the distance is greater.

In the location estimation task, the amount of error in the Y (up) dimension tended to be much greater than that of either the X or Z dimensions for all but the Screen cue, which had a similarly high error in all three dimensions (see Figure 11).

Over half the participants rated themselves as performing the location estimation task with greater than average accuracy using the Eyelight cue, despite having the third highest mean cost during the task. This suggests that the Eyelight cue entailed a false sense of confidence, and in this sense may even be slightly

misleading when no feedback is given. This may stem from the fact that participants frequently experience shadows in the real world, with this constant exposure leading them to believe they are able to perform the task with a high accuracy.

Participants generally perceived themselves as taking longer to perform the location estimation task with the Screen cue than with the other cues. It was noted that numerous participants verbally commented on this fact during the study. One participant commented that the difficulty of this cue was due to a lack of visual feedback for this cue when moving around, since it is not projected into the physical workspace like the others.

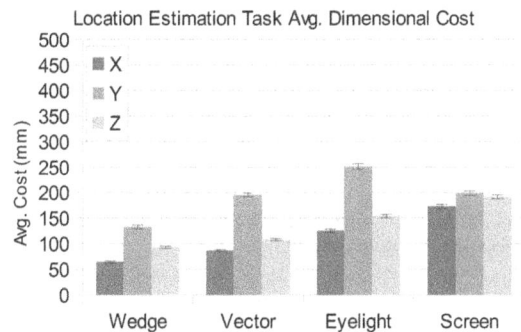

Figure 11. The average cost over all participants in the X, Y and Z dimensions for the location estimation task. Error bars indicate standard error.

8. CONCLUSION AND FUTURE WORK
We have presented the design, implementation and evaluation of three novel techniques of providing viewpoint awareness using SAR visual cues. The user study showed that the Composite Wedge cue was the best for providing location awareness, and the Eyelight cue was the best for providing visibility map awareness. These two cues do not appear to be conflicting or incompatible, so when both types of awareness are likely to be useful, a combination of the Composite Wedge and Eyelight cues should be considered.

The most obvious extension to this work is to consider multiple remote viewers, and their associated viewpoints. Encouragingly, the 2D Wedge has previously been shown to work with multiple instances and we believe a handful of Eyelights, each with different colors, may also prove effective. Future research could also address augmenting the cues presented here with information about the field of view of the viewpoint, as suggested in [9]. There is also scope to reduce the Y-axis (up) errors through modifications to these visualization techniques.

Further studies could more thoroughly investigate the behavior of each of our techniques when conveying a dynamic viewpoint, or when the user's attention is partially invested in a particular task.

There is also much scope to investigate the performance of these visualizations on non-planar surfaces.

9. ACKNOWLEDGMENTS

We sincerely thank: the user study participants, Warren Muller for his expert statistics advice, John Zic and Chris Gunn for their support, and the SUI'13 anonymous reviewers for their comments and feedback.

10. REFERENCES

[1] Adcock, M. and Gunn, C. 2010. Annotating with "sticky" light for remote guidance. *ACM SIGGRAPH ASIA 2010 Posters* (Seoul, South Korea, 2010).

[2] Clark, H.H. and Brennan, S.E. 1991. Grounding in communication. *Perspectives on socially shared cognition.* American Psychological Association.

[3] Dourish, P. and Bellotti, V. 1992. Awareness and coordination in shared workspaces. *Proceedings of the 1992 ACM conference on Computer-supported cooperative work - CSCW '92* (Toronto, Canada, Dec. 1992), 107–114.

[4] Fussell, S., Setlock, L., Yang, J., Ou, J., Mauer, E. and Kramer, A. 2004. Gestures Over Video Streams to Support Remote Collaboration on Physical Tasks. *Human-Computer Interaction.* 19, 3 (Sep. 2004), 273–309.

[5] Genest, A. and Gutwin, C. 2012. Evaluating the effectiveness of height visualizations for improving gestural communication at distributed tabletops. *Proceedings of the ACM 2012 conference on Computer Supported Cooperative Work - CSCW '12* (Seattle, USA, Feb. 2012), 519.

[6] Gustafson, S., Baudisch, P., Gutwin, C. and Irani, P. 2008. Wedge: clutter-free visualization of off-screen locations. *Proceeding of the twenty-sixth annual CHI conference on Human factors in computing systems - CHI '08* (Florence, Italy, Apr. 2008).

[7] Gutwin, C., Greenberg, S. and Roseman, M. 1996. Workspace Awareness in Real-Time Distributed Groupware: Framework, Widgets, and Evaluation. (Jan. 1996), 281–298.

[8] Hilliges, O., Kim, D., Izadi, S., Weiss, M. and Wilson, A. 2012. HoloDesk: Direct 3D Interactions with a Situated See-Through Display. *Proceedings of the 2012 ACM annual conference on Human Factors in Computing Systems - CHI '12* (Austin, USA, May. 2012), 2421.

[9] Hindmarsh, J., Fraser, M., Heath, C., Benford, S. and Greenhalgh, C. 1998. Fragmented interaction: establishing mutual orientation in virtual environments. *Proceedings of the 1998 ACM conference on Computer supported cooperative work - CSCW '98* (Seattle, USA, Nov. 1998), 217–226.

[10] Hutchins, M., Adcock, M., Stevenson, D., Gunn, C. and Krumpholz, A. 2005. The Design of Perceptual Representations for Practical Networked Multimodal Virtual Training Environments. *Proc. HCI International 2005: 11th International Conference on Human-Computer Interaction* (2005).

[11] Iyoda, T., Abe, T., Tokai, K., Sakamoto, S., Shingu, J., Onuki, H., Shi, M., Uchihashi, S., Satoh, S., Nack, F. and Etoh, M. 2008. LightCollabo: Distant Collaboration Support System for Manufacturers. *Advances in Multimedia Modeling* (Berlin, Heidelberg, 2008), 369–379.

[12] Kainz, B., Schmalstieg, D., Hauswiesner, S., Reitmayr, G., Steinberger, M., Grasset, R., Gruber, L., Veas, E., Kalkofen, D. and Seichter, H. 2012. OmniKinect: real-time dense volumetric data acquisition and applications. *Proceedings of the 18th ACM symposium on Virtual reality software and technology - VRST '12* (Toronto, Canada, Dec. 2012), 25.

[13] Kirk, D. and Stanton Fraser, D. 2006. Comparing remote gesture technologies for supporting collaborative physical tasks. *Proceedings of the SIGCHI conference on Human Factors in computing systems - CHI '06.* (2006), 1191.

[14] Kirk, D.S. 2006. *Turn It This Way!: Remote Gesturing in Video-Mediated Communication David Stanley Kirk , BSc (Hons), MSc Thesis submitted to the University of Nottingham for the degree of Doctor of Philosophy.* University of Nottingham.

[15] Robinson, P. and Tuddenham, P. 2007. Distributed Tabletops: Supporting Remote and Mixed-Presence Tabletop Collaboration. *Second Annual IEEE International Workshop on Horizontal Interactive Human-Computer Systems (TABLETOP'07)* (Oct. 2007), 19–26.

[16] Rosenthal, S., Kane, S.K., Wobbrock, J.O. and Avrahami, D. 2010. Augmenting on-screen instructions with micro-projected guides: When it Works, and When it Fails. *Proceedings of the 12th ACM international conference on Ubiquitous computing - Ubicomp '10* (Copenhagen, Denmark, Sep. 2010), 203.

[17] Sodhi, R., Benko, H. and Wilson, A. 2012. LightGuide: projected visualizations for hand movement guidance. *Proceedings of the 2012 ACM annual conference on Human Factors in Computing Systems - CHI '12* (Austin, USA, May. 2012), 179.

[18] Stevenson, D., Li, J., Smith, J. and Hutchins, M. 2008. A collaborative guidance case study. *AUIC '08* (2008).

[19] Sugano, N., Kato, H. and Tachibana, K. 2003. The effects of shadow representation of virtual objects in augmented reality. *The Second IEEE and ACM International Symposium on Mixed and Augmented Reality, 2003. Proceedings.* (2003), 76–83.

[20] Söderholm, H.M., Sonnenwald, D.H., Cairns, B., Manning, J.E., Welch, G.F. and Fuchs, H. 2007. The potential impact of 3d telepresence technology on task performance in emergency trauma care. *Proceedings of the 2007 international ACM conference on Conference on supporting group work - GROUP '07* (Sanibel Island, USA, Nov. 2007), 79.

[21] TSIMERIS, J.A. 2010. *Visual Cues for the Instructed Arrangement of Physical Objects Using Spatial Augmented Reality (SAR).* University of South Australia.

[22] Tang, A., Neustaedter, C. and Greenberg, S. 2006. VideoArms: Embodiments for Mixed Presence Groupware. *The 20th BCS HCI Group Conference* (London, 2006).

[23] Tang, J.C. and Minneman, S. 1991. VideoWhiteboard: Video Shadows to Support Remote Collaboration. *Proceedings of the SIGCHI conference on Human factors in computing systems Reaching through technology - CHI '91* (New Orleans, USA, Mar. 1991), 315–322.

[24] Tecchia, F., Alem, L. and Huang, W. 2012. 3D helping hands: a gesture based MR system for remote collaboration. *Proceedings of the 11th ACM SIGGRAPH International Conference on Virtual-Reality Continuum and its Applications in Industry - VRCAI '12* (Singapore, Dec. 2012), 323.

[25] Tsai, R.Y. and Lenz, R.K. 1989. A new technique for fully autonomous and efficient 3D robotics hand/eye calibration. *IEEE Transactions on Robotics and Automation.* 5, 3 (Jun. 1989), 345–358.

[26] Underkoffler, J. and Ishii, H. 1999. Urp: a luminous-tangible workbench for urban planning and design. *Proceedings of the SIGCHI conference on Human factors in computing systems the CHI is the limit - CHI '99* (Pittsburgh, USA, May. 1999), 386–393.

[27] Wilson, A.D. and Benko, H. 2010. Combining multiple depth cameras and projectors for interactions on, above and between surfaces. *Proceedings of the 23nd annual ACM symposium on User interface software and technology - UIST '10* (New York, New York, USA, Oct. 2010), 273.

[28] Zhou, J., Lee, I., Thomas, B., Menassa, R., Farrant, A. and Sansome, A. 2011. Applying spatial augmented reality to facilitate in-situ support for automotive spot welding inspection. *Proceedings of the 10th International Conference on Virtual Reality Continuum and Its Applications in Industry - VRCAI '11* (Hong Kong, Dec. 2011), 195.

To Touch or not to Touch? Comparing 2D Touch and 3D Mid-Air Interaction on Stereoscopic Tabletop Surfaces

Gerd Bruder
Department of Computer Science
University of Würzburg
gerd.bruder@uni-wuerzburg.de

Frank Steinicke
Department of Computer Science
University of Würzburg
frank.steinicke@uni-wuerzburg.de

Wolfgang Stürzlinger
Department of Computer Science and Engineering
York University
wolfgang@cse.yorku.ca

ABSTRACT

Recent developments in touch and display technologies have laid the groundwork to combine touch-sensitive display systems with stereoscopic three-dimensional (3D) display. Although this combination provides a compelling user experience, interaction with objects stereoscopically displayed in front of the screen poses some fundamental challenges: Traditionally, touch-sensitive surfaces capture only direct contacts such that the user has to penetrate the visually perceived object to touch the 2D surface behind the object. Conversely, recent technologies support capturing finger positions in front of the display, enabling users to interact with intangible objects in mid-air 3D space. In this paper we perform a comparison between such 2D touch and 3D mid-air interactions in a Fitts' Law experiment for objects with varying stereoscopical parallax. The results show that the 2D touch technique is more efficient close to the screen, whereas for targets further away from the screen, 3D selection outperforms 2D touch. Based on the results, we present implications for the design and development of future touch-sensitive interfaces for stereoscopic displays.

Categories and Subject Descriptors

H.5.2 [**Information Interfaces and Presentation**]: User Interfaces – Input Devices and Strategies, Evaluation / Methodology.

Keywords

Touch-sensitive systems, stereoscopic displays, 3D interaction.

1. MOTIVATION

Two different technologies dominated recent exhibitions and the entertainment market: (multi-)touch-sensitive surfaces and 3D stereoscopic displays. These technologies have the potential to provide more intuitive and natural interaction setups for a wide range of areas, including geo-spatial applications, urban planning, architectural design, or collaborative tabletops. These two technologies are orthogonal, as (multi-)touch is about *input* and 3D stereoscopic visualization about *output*. First commercial hardware sys-

tems have recently been launched (e. g., [4]), and interdisciplinary research projects explore interaction with stereoscopic content on 2D touch surfaces (e. g., [1, 2]). Moreover, an increasing number of hardware solutions provide the means to sense hand and finger poses and gestures in 3D space without input devices or instrumentation (e. g., Leap Motion [3]). The combination of these novel technologies provides enormous potential for a variety of new interaction concepts.

Until recently, research in the area of (multi-)touch interaction was mostly focused on monoscopically displayed data. There, the ability to directly touch elements has been shown to be very appealing for novice as well as expert users. Also, passive haptics and multi-touch capabilities have both shown their potential to improve the user experience [7]. Touch surfaces build a consistent and pervasive illusion in perceptual and motor space that two-dimensional graphical elements on the surface can be touched. Yet, three-dimensional data limits this illusion of place and plausibility [31]. 3D data sets are either displayed monoscopically, which has been shown to impair spatial perception in common 3D tasks, or stereoscopically, which can enrich the experience and interaction, but causes objects to appear detached from the touch surface [26, 30].

Stereoscopic display technology has been known for decades. It has recently been revived in the rise of 3D cinema and 3D televisions. With stereoscopic displays, each eye sees a different perspective of the same scene through appropriate technology. This requires showing two distinct images on the display. Objects may be displayed with *negative*, *zero*, or *positive* parallax, corresponding to in front of, at, or behind the screen. Objects with centroid at *zero parallax* appear attached to the screen and are perfectly suited for touch interaction. In contrast, it is more difficult to apply direct-touch interaction techniques to objects that appear in front of or behind the screen [18, 27, 29]. In this paper we focus on the major challenge in this context, namely objects that appear in front of the screen such as a virtual object floating above the surface within the user's personal interaction space [12]. Teather and Stuerzlinger [34] provide a review of interaction techniques for distant objects behind the screen.

Two methodologies can be used for interacting with stereoscopic objects in front of a tabletop display:

1. If the touch-sensitive surface captures only direct contacts, the user has to penetrate the visually perceived object to touch the 2D surface behind the object [36, 37].

2. Alternatively, if finger poses in front of the screen can be captured, the user can directly interact with the intangible object in 3D space [3].

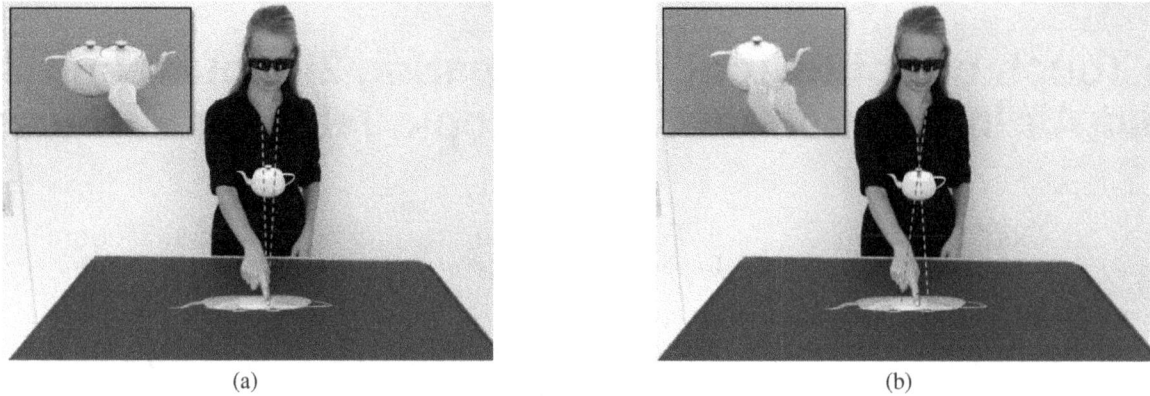

Figure 1: Illustration of the main problem of 2D touch interaction with stereoscopically displayed 3D data: The user is either focused (a) on her finger, which makes the selection ambiguous, or (b) on the object, which disturbs the visual perception of the finger.

Due to the discrepancy between perceptual and motor space and missing haptic feedback, both approaches provide natural feedback only for objects rendered with zero parallax. One question posed by this issue is where users "touch" a stereoscopically displayed intangible object in 3D space, considering the misperception of distances in virtual 3D scenes [22]. Conversely, it also brings up the issue where users "touch" a stereoscopically displayed object on a 2D display surface, considering that there are two distinct projections for each eye [36]. If the user penetrates the object while focusing on her finger, the stereoscopic impression of the object is disturbed, since the user's eyes are not accommodated and converged to the display surface. Thus, the left/right image pairs of the object appear blurred and can potentially not be merged (Figure 1(a)). Yet, focusing on the virtual object causes a disturbance of the stereoscopic perception of the user's finger, since her eyes are converged on the object's 3D position (Figure 1(b)). When the user selects an object in 3D space, by holding her finger in front of the screen, she can see a stereoscopic image while converging to her finger. However, due the vergence-accomodation conflict, the virtual object will appear blurred in comparison to the real finger (Figure 2).

In this paper we address the challenge of how to interact with stereoscopic content in front of a touch-sensitive tabletop surface. We evaluate interaction with touch-sensitive screens to select a 3D object, and compare this approach to systems where the user's finger is tracked in 3D space. We use a Fitts' Law experimental design to determine differences in 3D object selection performance for varying object parallax in front of the screen. The results of this experiment provide guidelines for the choice of touch technologies, as well as the optimal placement and parallax of interactive elements in stereoscopic touch environments.

Our contributions are:

- A direct comparison of the performance of 2D touch and 3D mid-air selection for different spatial configurations of interactive 3D objects.

- Guidelines for designing user interfaces for stereoscopic touch-sensitive tabletop setups.

The remainder of this paper is structured as follows. Section 2 summarizes background information on touch interaction and stereoscopic display. Section 3 describes the experiment we conducted to evaluate and compare 2D/3D interaction performance. Section 4 presents the results, which are discussed in Section 5. Section 6 concludes the paper.

2. BACKGROUND

Recently, many approaches for extending multi-touch interaction techniques to 3D applications with *monoscopic* display have been proposed [18, 25, 28, 29, 41]. In order to extend interaction possibilities with monoscopic 2D surfaces, Hancock et al. [18] presented approaches for 3D interaction within a limited range above the surface. Yet, interaction with stereoscopically displayed scenes introduces new challenges [30], since the displayed objects can float in front of or behind the interactive display surface.

2.1 Interaction with Stereoscopic Objects

In this section we describe work related to interaction with stereoscopically displayed objects. In particular, we discuss 2D touch and 3D mid-air selection techniques.

2.1.1 3D Mid-Air Interaction Techniques

To enable selection of stereoscopically displayed 3D objects in space, 3D tracking technologies capture a user's hand or finger motions in front of the display surface. The kinematics of point and grasp gestures in 3D space and the underlying cognitive functions have been studied [16, 23, 39]. For instance, it has been shown that the arm movement during grasping consists of two distinct phases: (1) an initial, *ballistic phase* during which the user's attention is focused on the object to be grasped (or touched). The motion is essentially controlled by proprioception, and (2) a *correction phase* that reflects refinement and error-correction of the movement, incorporating visual feedback in order to minimize the error between the hand or finger and the target [21]. MacKenzie et al. [23] investigated real time kinematics of limb movements in a Fitts' task and showed that, while Fitts' Law holds for the total limb-movement time, humans decelerate the motion sooner, if the target seems to require more precision in the end phase. The changes of the kinematics and control for reaching tasks within virtual environments have been investigated [14, 38].

Hilliges et al. [19] investigated extending the interaction space beyond the touch surface. They tested two depth-sensing approaches to enrich multi-touch interaction on a tabletop with monoscopic display. Although 3D "mid-air" interaction provides an intuitive technique, it has been shown that touching an intangible object, i. e., *touching the void* [11], leads to confusion and a significant number of overshoot errors. This is due to the fact that depth perception is less accurate in virtual scenes compared to the real world, as well as the introduced double vision and vergence-accommodation conflicts. Bruder et al. [10] investigated the effects

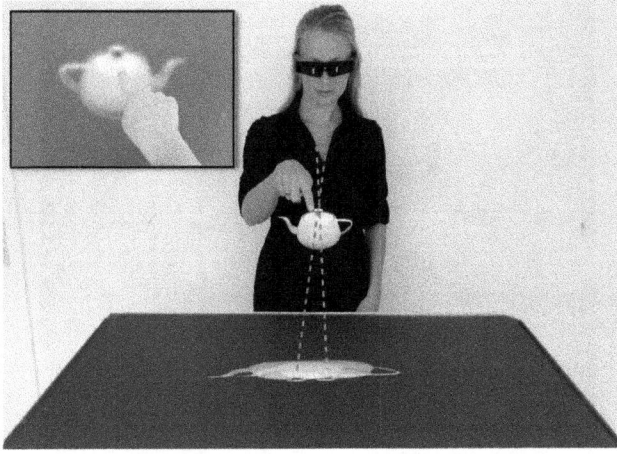

Figure 2: Illustration of the main problem of 3D mid-air interaction with stereoscopically displayed 3D data: The user sees a stereoscopic image while converging to her finger, but due to the vergence-accommodation conflict, the virtual object appears blurred in comparison to the finger.

of visual conflicts on 3D selection performance with stereoscopic tabletop displays. Some devices, such as the CyberGrasp, support haptic feedback when touching objects in space, but require extensive user instrumentation. Other approaches are based on the user moving tangible surfaces in 3D space to align with floating objects, e.g., through transparent props [11], or on controlling the 3D position of a cursor through multiple touch points [5, 32]. Toucheo uses 2D projections to define widget for interaction with objects presented stereoscopically above a multi-touch display [17]. Yet, the projection direction for Toucheo is straight down towards the display surface. This paradigm does not work well for objects that are stacked one above the other, as their projections then conflict.

2.1.2   2D Touch Techniques

Recently, multi-touch devices with non-planar surfaces, such as cubic [13] or spherical [6], were proposed. These can specify 3D axes or points for indirect object manipulation. Interaction with objects with negative parallax on a multi-touch tabletop setup was addressed by Benko et al.'s balloon selection [5], as well as Strothoff et al.'s triangle cursor [32], which use 2D touch gestures to specify height above the surface.

Valkov et al. [36] performed a user study, in which they displayed 3D objects stereoscopically in front or behind a large vertical projection screen. They instructed users to touch the virtual 3D objects by touching *through* the objects until their finger hit the display surface and recorded user behavior. This study found that users tended to touch between the projections for the two eyes with an offset towards the projection for the dominant eye. Bruder et al. [9] further analyzed stereoscopic 2D touch interaction and identified three distinct user behaviors (see Figure 3): users consistently touched either towards the dominant eye projection, the non-dominant one, or the midpoint between the projections. While these three behaviours varied between subjects, they found little within-subjects variation.

In a different study, Valkov et al. [37] showed that users are, within some range, insensitive to small misalignments between visually perceived stereoscopic positions and the sensed haptic feedback when touching a virtual object. Moreover, users are less sensitive to discrepancies between visual and tactile feedback for objects with negative parallax. They proposed to manipulate the stereo-

scopically displayed scene so that objects are moved towards the screen when the user reaches for them [35, 37]. This only works for objects displayed close (approximately 5cm) to the surface. Yet, the problem is that objects have to be shifted in space, which leads to a disturbed perception of the virtual scene for larger manipulations.

So far, no comparative analysis exists for 2D touch and 3D mid-air interaction in stereoscopic tabletop setups. Thus, it remains unclear if 2D touch is a viable alternative to 3D mid-air selection.

2.2   Fitts' Law and Selection

Fitts' Law [15] is a well-known empirical model for user performance in selection tasks. The model predicts the movement time MT for a given target distance D and size W by $MT = a + b \times \log_2(D/W + 1)$; where a and b are empirically derived. The log term is the *index of difficulty (ID)* and indicates overall task difficulty. This implies that the smaller and farther a target, the more difficult it is to select accurately. A valuable extension supported by an international standard [20] is the use of "effective" measures. This post-experiment correction adjusts the error rate to 4% by re-sizing targets to their effective width (W_e). This enables the computation of effective throughput, a measure that incorporates both speed and accuracy, by "normalizing" the accuracy as effective scores. This *throughput* is computed as $TP = \log_2(D_e/W_e + 1)/MT$, where D_e is the effective distance (average of measured movement distances), and W_e the effective width (standard deviation of error distances multiplied by 4.1333 [24]). Previous 3D research [34] suggests that one should use the point closest to the target along the ray to compute an accurate representation of the effective width W_e, as using the actual 3D cursor position would artificially inflate the effective measure. In essence, this suggestion projects the 3D task into 2D before computing throughput for touch-based interaction techniques. Even more recent work [33] reveals that the distortion due to perspective also has an effect. This work recommends the use of the 2D projections of sizes and distances to compute a screen-projected throughput for all *remote-pointing* techniques, such as ray-pointing.

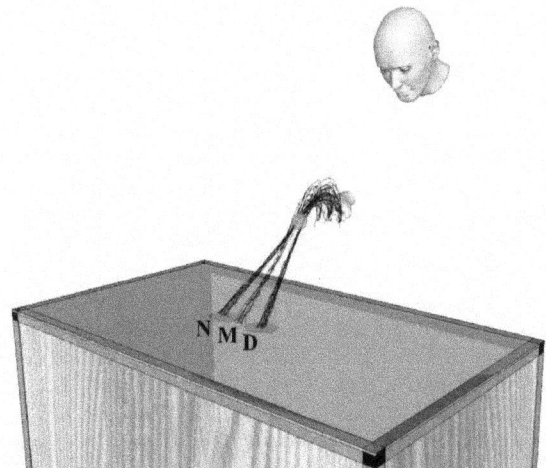

Figure 3:   Illustration of finger movement trails for user groups touching towards the dominant eye projection (D), non-dominant eye projection (N), or towards the midpoint (M) using the 2D touch technique [9]. The trails have been normalized and are displayed here for a right-eye dominant user.

3. EXPERIMENTS

Here we describe our experiments to compare the performance of 2D touch and 3D mid-air interaction. We used a Fitts' Law selection task on a tabletop setup with 3D targets displayed on the surface or at different heights above the surface, i.e., with different negative stereoscopic parallax.

3.1 Experimental Setup

For the experiment we used a 62×112cm active stereoscopic multi-touch tabletop setup. The system is shown in Figure 4. The setup uses a matte diffusing screen with a gain of 1.6. For stereoscopic back projection screen we use a 1280×800 Optoma GT720 projector at 120Hz. The active DLP-based shutter glasses are driven by the projector at 60Hz per eye. We use an optical WorldViz Precision Position Tracking X4 system with sub-millimeter precision and accuracy to track the subject's finger and head for view-dependent rendering. For this, we attached wireless markers to the shutter glasses and another diffused IR LED on the tip of the index finger of the subject's dominant hand. We tracked and logged both head and fingertip movements during the experiment. The view of the 3D scene was rendered stereoscopically using off-axis projections. We measured an end-to-end latency of approximately 55ms between physical movements and a visual response.

The visual stimulus used in the experiment is a 3D scene in a 30cm deep box, fit to the horizontal dimensions of the physical tabletop setup (see Figure 4). We matched the look of the scene to the visual stimuli used in [9, 10, 33, 34] for improved comparability. The targets in the experiment were represented by spheres, arranged in a circle (Figure 4). A circle consisted of 11 spheres rendered in white, with the active target sphere highlighted in blue. The targets highlighted in the order specified by ISO 9241-9 [20]. The center of each target sphere indicated the exact position where subjects were instructed to touch with their dominant hand in order to select a sphere. Subjects indicated target selection using a Razer Nostromo keypad with their non-dominant hand. The target spheres highlighted green when the finger of the user was within the target to provide subjects with feedback about successful selection, to minimize systematic errors in Fitts' Law experiments [23]. Head-tracked off-axis stereoscopic display was active in all conditions. The size, distance, and height of target spheres were constant within circles, but varied between circles. In other words, targets were at a constant height for each circle of targets. Target height was measured upwards from the level screen surface. All target spheres were presented with positive height, i.e., in front of the screen. The virtual environment was rendered on an Intel Core i7 computer with 3.40GHz processors, 8GB of main memory, and an Nvidia Quadro 4000 graphics card.

3.2 Methods

The experiment used a $2 \times 5 \times 2 \times 2$ within-subjects design with the method of constant stimuli. The independent variables were selection technique (2D touch vs. 3D mid-air interaction), target height (0cm to 20cm, in steps of 5cm), as well as distances between targets (16cm and 25cm) and size (2cm and 3cm). Each circle represented a different index of difficulty with combinations of 2 distances and 2 sizes. This yielded four uniformly distributed IDs ranging from approximately 2.85bps to 3.75bps, representing an ecologically valuable range of Fitts' Law task difficulties for a touch screen setup. Each circle used one of 5 different target height, between 0cm and 20cm in steps of 5cm. Distances between targets, sizes and heights were not related from one circle to the next, but presented randomly and uniformly distributed. The dependent vari-

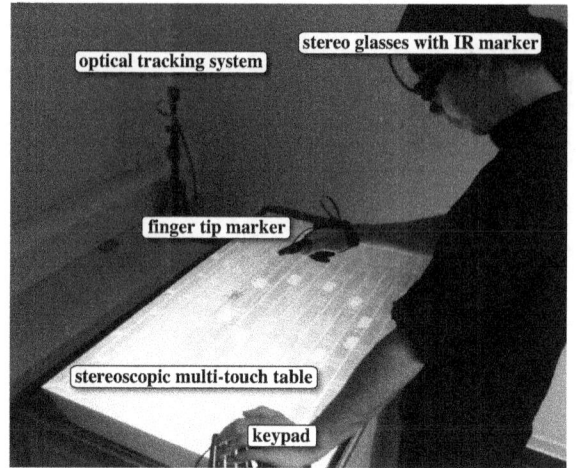

Figure 4: Experimental setup: photo of a subject during the experiment with illustrations.

ables were movement time, error distance, error rate (percentage of targets missed), and effective throughput.

The experiment trials were divided into two blocks: one for 2D touch selections and one for 3D mid-air selections. We randomized their order between subjects. At the beginning of each block, subjects were positioned standing in an upright posture in front of the tabletop surface (Figure 4). To remove a potential confound in terms of target visibility and view angle, we compensated for the different heights of subjects by adjusting the height of a floor mat below the subject's feet, resulting in an eye height of about 185cm for all subjects during the experiment. The experiment started with task descriptions, which were presented via slides on the projection surface in order to reduce potential experimenter biases. Subjects had to complete 5 to 15 training trials for both techniques to minimize later training effects. These training trials were excluded from the analysis. In order to compensate for misperceptions of the targets, we performed a calibration phase based on Bruder et al. [9]. During this calibration, subjects were instructed to touch the center of the target spheres as accurately as possible with 2D touch as well as 3D mid-air selection. Subjects had as much time as needed and they were free to place their index finger in the real world where they perceived the virtual target to be. We used the resulting calibrated positions to define the target centers in the Fitts' Law trials for each subject as described in [9, 10].

After the calibration, subjects were instructed to select the targets as quickly and accurately as possible, a common instruction in Fitts' Law experiments [33, 34]. Subjects received visual feedback when their finger was inside a target, by targets turning green. Then, subjects indicated selection by pressing a key with their non-dominant hand. If subjects pressed the key while the target sphere was not green, we recorded this as a selection error and advanced the trial state. We computed the distance of the position of the tip of the index finger to the calibrated sphere center. A valid 3D selection occurred if this distance was less than the sphere radius for 3D mid-air interactions. For 2D touch interactions, we computed the projected 3D target position and size on the 2D touch surface (see Figure 3). Then we judged a 2D touch selection to be valid if the finger position was within the projected circle (cf. [36]). There were 11 recorded target selections per circle. Circles were shown twice to each participant in randomized order for each configuration of independent variables. Thus, each participant completed a total of 80 circles, with a total of 880 recorded target selections.

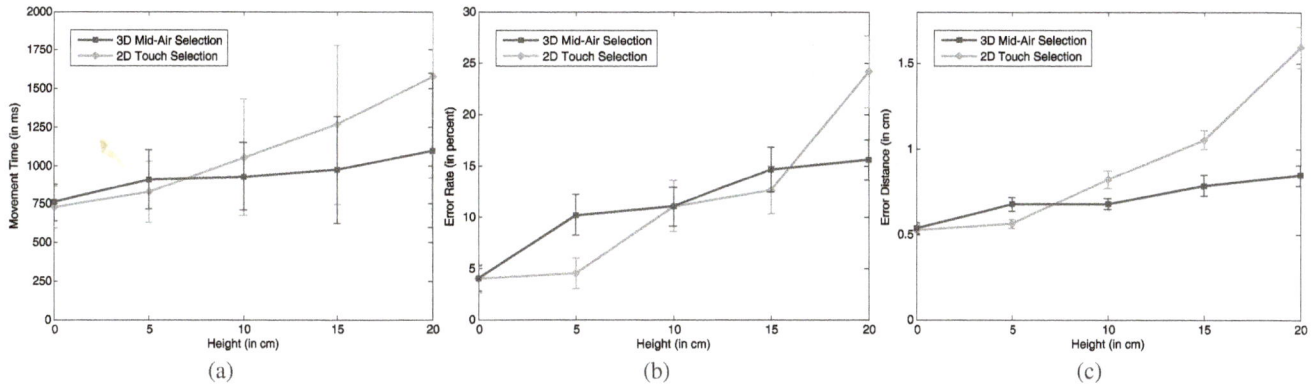

Figure 5: Results for Fitts' Law trials with target object height on the horizontal axis and pooled for (a) movement time, (b) error rate, and (c) error distance, on the vertical axis. The error bars show the standard error.

In addition to the performance data collected in the Fitts' Law trials, we also asked subjects to judge various characteristics of the techniques through subjective questionnaires. Before and after the 2D/3D interaction conditions, subjects were asked to complete a Simulator Sickness Questionnaire (SSQ). Moreover, asthenopia, visual discomfort symptoms, were measured with a questionnaire about blurred vision, ocular soreness, itching of the eyes, increased blinking, heaviness of the eyes, and double vision on 4-point scales (0=none, 1=slight, 2=moderate, 3=severe), i.e., analogous to the SSQ sickness symptoms. After each technique, subjects were asked to complete a Slater-Usoh-Steed (SUS) presence questionnaire, a NASA TLX mental workload questionnaire, as well as a general usability questionnaire, in which we asked subjects to judge the technique according to the criteria learnability, efficiency, memorability, errors, and satisfaction on 5-point Likert scales.

3.3 Participants

10 male and 5 female subjects (ages 20-35, M=27.1) participated in the experiment. Subjects were students or members of the local university. 3 subjects received class credit for participating in the experiment. All subjects were right-handed. All subjects had normal or corrected to normal vision. 1 subject wore glasses and 4 subjects wore contact lenses during the experiment. None of the subjects reported known eye disorders, such as color weaknesses, amblyopia or known stereopsis disruptions. We verified the ability for stereoscopic vision of all subjects. We measured the inter-pupillary distance (IPD) of each subject before the experiment [40], which revealed IPDs between 5.8cm and 7.0cm (M=6.4cm). We used each individual's IPD for stereoscopic display in the experiment. 14 subjects reported experience with stereoscopic 3D cinema, 14 with touch screens, and 8 had previously participated in a study involving touch surfaces. Subjects were naïve to the experimental conditions. Subjects were allowed to take a break at any time between trials to minimize effects of exhaustion or lack of concentration. The total time per subject was about 1.5 hours.

4. RESULTS

Here we summarize the results from the experiment. We had to exclude two subjects from the analysis who misunderstood the task (i.e., showed 100% incorrect selections). All other trials have been included in the analysis. As stated above, we used for each subject the calibrated target positions as valid target centers. Results were normally distributed according to a Shapiro-Wilk test at the 5% level. We analyzed the results with a repeated measure ANOVA

and Tukey multiple comparisons at the 5% significance level (with Bonferonni correction). Degrees of freedom were corrected using Greenhouse-Geisser estimates of sphericity when Mauchly's test indicated that the assumption of sphericity had been violated.

4.1 Movement Time

The results for the movement time are illustrated in Figure 5(a). We found no significant main effect of technique ($F(1, 12)$=3.870, p>.05, η_p^2=.244) on movement time. The average movement time during the experiment was M=1090ms (SD=521ms) for 2D touch, while 3D selection had M=934ms (SD=324ms).

The results show that the movement time for heights differs significantly ($F(1.272, 15.265)$=27.127, p<.001, η_p^2=.693). Post hoc tests revealed that the movement time was significantly increased when objects were displayed with heights of 15cm (p<.05) or 20cm (p<.001) in comparison to 0cm. As expected, we found a significant main effect of the ID on movement time ($F(1.220, 14.635)$=23.061, p<.001, η_p^2=.658).

We found a significant two-way interaction effect between technique and height ($F(1.360, 16.319)$=9.453, p<.01, η_p^2=.441). Post hoc tests revealed that subjects took significantly longer with 2D touch than 3D selection when objects were displayed with a height of 20cm (p<.05). We found no significant difference between the techniques for lower heights.

4.2 Error Rate

The results for error rate are illustrated in Figure 5(b). We found no significant main effect of technique ($F(1, 12)$=0.009, p>.05, η_p^2=.001) on error rate. The average error rate during the experiment was M=11.6% (SD=18.5%) for 2D touch, while 3D selection had M=11.3% (SD=14.1%).

The results show that the error rate for heights differs significantly ($F(1.848, 22.172)$=17.186, p<.001, η_p^2=.589). Post hoc tests revealed that the error rate was significantly increased when objects were displayed with a height of 20cm (p<.05) in comparison to 0cm. As expected, we found a significant main effect of the ID on error rate ($F(3, 36)$=15.359, p<.001, η_p^2=.561).

We found no significant two-way interaction effect between technique and height ($F(1.798, 21.570)$=2.685, p>.05, η_p^2=.183).

4.3 Error Distance

The results for the error distances, between the center of each sphere and the finger position during selection, are illustrated in Figure 5(c). We found a significant main effect of technique ($F(1, 12)$=5.115, p<.05, η_p^2=.299) on the error dis-

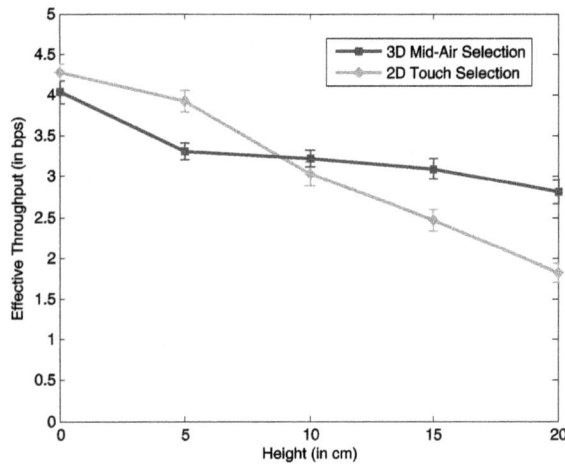

Figure 6: Effective throughput metric combining errors and movement time: The horizontal axis shows the target height, and the vertical axis shows the movement time. Higher throughput is better. The error bars show the standard error.

tance. Subjects made significantly larger errors when using 2D touch (M=0.91cm, SD=0.62cm) in comparison to 3D selection (M=0.70cm, SD=0.35cm).

The results show that the error distance for the height differs significantly ($F(1.419, 17.032)=34.99$, $p<.001$, $\eta_p^2=.745$). Post hoc tests revealed that subjects made significantly larger errors when objects were displayed with heights of 15cm ($p<.05$) or 20cm ($p<.001$) in comparison to 0cm. As expected, we found a significant main effect of the ID on error distance ($F(1.28, 15.361)=5.669$, $p<.03$, $\eta_p^2=.321$).

We found a significant two-way interaction effect between technique and height ($F(1.427, 17.120)=11.293$, $p<.002$, $\eta_p^2=.485$). Post hoc tests revealed that subjects made significantly larger errors with 2D touch than 3D selection when objects were displayed with a height of 20cm ($p<.01$). We found no significant difference between the techniques for lower heights.

4.4 Effective Throughput

The results for the effective throughput are shown in Figure 6. We found no significant main effect of technique ($F(1, 12)=1.658$, $p>.05$, $\eta_p^2=.121$) on throughput. The average throughput during the experiment was M=3.11bps (SD=1.29bps) for 2D touch, while 3D selection had M=3.30bps (SD=0.98bps).

The results show that the throughput for heights differs significantly ($F(1.696, 20.358)=71.995$, $p<.001$, $\eta_p^2=.857$). Post hoc tests revealed that throughput was significantly reduced when objects were displayed with heights of 10cm ($p<.05$), 15cm ($p<.001$) or 20cm ($p<.001$) in comparison to 0cm. As expected, we found a significant main effect of the ID on throughput ($F(3, 36)=8.083$, $p<.001$, $\eta_p^2=.402$).

We found a significant two-way interaction effect between technique and height ($F(2.408, 28.898)=23.979$, $p<.001$, $\eta_p^2=.666$). Post hoc tests revealed that throughput was significantly higher with 3D selection than 2D touch when objects were displayed with a height of 20cm ($p<.05$). In addition, we found a trend that the throughput was also higher with 3D selection for objects displayed with a height of 15cm ($p<.08$). In contrast, we found the inverse trend for objects displayed with a height of 5cm ($p<.07$). Here, throughput for 2D selection was higher. We found no significant difference between the techniques for lower heights.

4.5 Modeling

Fitts' Law can also be used as a predictive model, by regressing movement time on index of difficulty. We performed this analysis for both techniques at the five different heights. The regression lines for movement time are presented in Figure 7. The predictive quality of the model (as expressed by χ^2 values) is very high for 2D touch (for heights 0cm to 20cm $\chi^2=0.18$, 0.06, 0.006, 0.04, and 0.037) and for 3D selection (for height 0cm to 20cm $\chi^2=0.10$, 0.06, 0.08, 0.24, and 0.01).

4.6 Questionnaires

Also the results were normally distributed according to a Shapiro-Wilk test at the 5% level. Before and after each of the 2D touch and 3D selection conditions, we asked subjects to judge their level of simulator sickness and visual discomfort. Results were analyzed using paired-samples t-tests. For simulator sickness, we found a significant difference between the two conditions ($t(13)=2.86$, $p<.02$), with an average increase of mean SSQ-scores of 5.61 (SD=16.15) for the 2D touch technique, and 12.16 (SD=12.77) for 3D selections, which may be explained by missing physical support during 3D selections (cf. [8]). We found no significant difference ($t(13)=0.16$, $p>.05$) for the asthenopia questionnaire between the two techniques, but we observed a general before-after increase in visual discomfort for both 2D touch (M=0.18, SD=0.37) and 3D selection (M=0.19, SD=0.33). Again, the results do not exceed typical effects in stereoscopic display environments. For the reported sense of feeling present in the virtual scene, we did not observe a significant difference ($t(13)=0.60$, $p>.05$) for mean SUS-scores for 2D touch (M=3.92, SD=1.15) and 3D selection (M=4.08, SD=1.14). Both scores indicate a high sense of presence. We did not find a significant difference ($t(13)=0.15$, $p=.88$) between 2D touch (M=2.85, SD=0.43) and 3D selection (M=2.92, SD=0.56) on the mean five general usability criteria scores learnability, efficiency, memorability, errors, and satisfaction. Individual usability scores for 2D touch respectively 3D selection were (M=3.15 & M=3.00) for learnability, (M=3.54 & M=3.29) efficiency, (M=3.08 & M=3.43) memorability, (M=2.31 & M=2.71) errors, and (M=2.46 & M=2.00) for satisfaction. We could not find any significant differences between 2D touch and 3D mid-air selection for these metrics. We found no significant difference ($t(13)=0.46$, $p>0.05$) between 2D touch (M=10.44, SD=3.27) and 3D selection (M=9.91, SD=3.07) for the NASA TLX mental workload questionnaire scores.

At the end of the experiment, we collected additional subjective preferences in an informal debriefing session. One subject remarked here notably:

"Selecting low objects was much easier on the surface – though it seemed counterintuitive at first!"

This comment was representative for many responses regarding the 2D touch technique. All but one subject preferred touching through 3D objects for objects close to the display surface.

5. DISCUSSION

The results from the Fitts' Law experiment reveal distinct characteristics of the 2D touch and 3D mid-air selection techniques, which impact their performance and applicability for interaction with objects displayed stereoscopically at different parallaxes. For 3D objects displayed up to 10cm above the display surface, touching objects in 2D on the surface by touching "through" the stereoscopic projection outperforms 3D mid-air selection in all considered metrics. Since much research has shown that 3D mid-air selec-

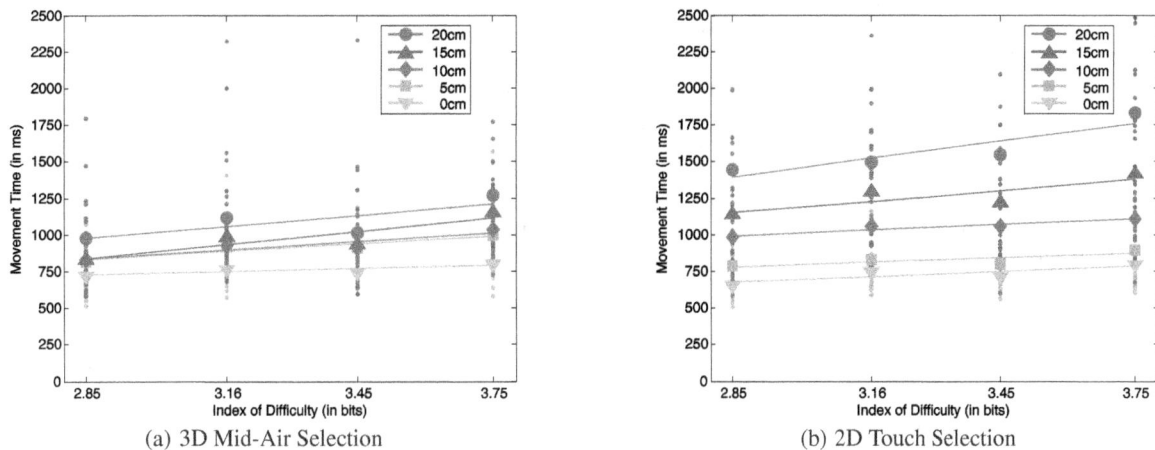

(a) 3D Mid-Air Selection	(b) 2D Touch Selection

Figure 7: Models for (a) 3D mid-air selection and (b) 2D touch selection: solid lines are regressions of the measured movement time for the five target heights.

tion of virtual objects suffers from low accuracy and precision [8], e. g., due to visual conflicts, including vergence-accommodation mismatch, diplopia, and distance misperception [11], it is a promising finding that the reduction of 3D selection tasks to 2D input with the 2D touch technique can improve performance for tabletops with stereoscopically displayed objects. However, while interactions with both techniques are equal for objects at 0cm height, the results also show that the performance for the 2D touch technique decreases drastically for large negative parallax in comparison to 3D mid-air selection. At 20cm height, 2D touch performance is less than half in terms of throughput compared to performance at the screen. 3D mid-air selection performance drops much more slowly, decreasing only by about 30% at 20cm height.

For scenarios with stereoscopic visualization on (multi-)touch surfaces, the findings are still encouraging. They suggest that interactive 3D objects do not have to be constrained at the zero-parallax level, but may deviate up to 10cm before performance with the 2D touch technique is significantly degraded. For such distances, touch input is a good choice. Overall, our results show that it is indeed possible to leverage stereoscopic distance and interposition cues over a considerable range in touch-sensitive tabletop setups for improved spatial understanding of virtual data sets.

In our experiment, we compensated for different viewer heights by raising all subjects to a consistent head level. We did this to compensate for the potential confound that a lower viewpoint has a smaller 3D view volume due to (relatively) earlier clipping by the far and near sides of the display. In future commercial systems, we expect that stereoscopic touch tables could be height adjusted to accommodate for the height of each user.

In summary we suggest the following guidelines for the realization of touch interaction in 3D stereoscopic tabletop setups: For tabletop setups using the 2D touch technique, interactive virtual objects (e. g., buttons or other elements of graphical user interfaces) should not be displayed more than 10cm above the interactive display surface. Above that, the disadvantages outperform the benefits and 3D interaction techniques should be used.

6. CONCLUSION AND FUTURE WORK

In this paper we compared interaction techniques for tabletop setups with stereoscopic display. We analyzed the differences between 3D mid-air selection and a technique based on reducing the 3D selection problem to two dimensions by touching "through" the

stereoscopic impression of 3D objects, i. e., a 2D touch on the display. The experimental results show a strong interaction effect between input technique and the stereoscopic parallax of virtual objects for all performance metrics, including movement time, errors, and effective throughput. Our main findings are:

- The 2D touch technique outperforms 3D mid-air selection for objects up to ca. 10cm height above the display surface.

- 3D mid-air selection is a better alternative for higher targets.

- Performance decreases faster for the 2D touch technique than for 3D selection with increasing height of virtual objects.

The results are encouraging for stereoscopic visualization in future touch-sensitive tabletop setups, since no additional tracking technology is needed for objects with small negative parallax. Recent sensing technologies for finger poses above display surfaces (e. g., Leap Motion [3]) will thus realize their benefits mostly only for objects at least about 10cm above the surface.

As a direction for future work, we cannot yet tell if these results hold for portable setups, where the orientation of the touch sensitive surface can change during interaction. We will pursue this topic to design more compelling user experiences as well as effective user interfaces for touch-sensitive stereoscopic display surfaces.

7. ACKNOWLEDGMENTS

This work was partly supported by grants from the Deutsche Forschungsgemeinschaft and the Natural Sciences and Engineering Research Council of Canada.

8. REFERENCES

[1] iMUTS - Interscopic Multi-Touch Surfaces. http://imuts.uni-muenster.de/, 2013.

[2] InSTInCT - Touch-based interfaces for Interaction with 3D Content. http://anr-instinct.cap-sciences.net/, 2013.

[3] Leap Motion. http://www.leapmotion.com/, 2013.

[4] Nintendo 3DS. http://www.nintendo.com/, 2013.

[5] H. Benko and S. Feiner. Balloon selection: A multi-finger technique for accurate low-fatigue 3D selection. In *Proc. of IEEE 3DUI*, pages 79–86, 2007.

[6] H. Benko, A. D. Wilson, and R. Balakrishnan. Sphere: multi-touch interactions on a spherical display. In *Proc. of ACM UIST*, pages 77–86, 2008.

[7] H. Benko, A. D. Wilson, and P. Baudisch. Precise selection techniques for multi-touch screens. In *Proc. of ACM CHI*, pages 1263–1272, 2006.

[8] F. Berard, J. Ip, M. Benovoy, D. El-Shimy, J. R. Blum, and J. R. Cooperstock. Did "minority report" get it wrong? Superiority of the mouse over 3D input devices in a 3D placement task. In *Proc. of INTERACT*, pages 400–414, 2011.

[9] G. Bruder, F. Steinicke, and W. Stuerzlinger. Touching the void revisited: Analyses of touch behavior on and above tabletop surfaces. In *Proc. of INTERACT*, 17 pages, 2013.

[10] G. Bruder, F. Steinicke, and W. Stuerzlinger. Effects of visual conflicts on 3D selection task performance in stereoscopic display environments. In *Proc. of ACM 3DUI*, pages 115–118, 2013.

[11] L.-W. Chan, H.-S. Kao, M. Y. Chen, M.-S. Lee, J. Hsu, and Y.-P. Hung. Touching the void: Direct-touch interaction for intangible displays. In *Proc. of ACM CHI*, pages 2625–2634, 2010.

[12] B. R. De Araújo, G. Casiez, J. A. Jorge, and M. Hachet. Mockup Builder: 3D modeling on and above the surface. *Computers & Graphics*, 37:165–178, 2013.

[13] J.-B. de la Rivière, C. Kervégant, E. Orvain, and N. Dittlo. Cubtile: a multi-touch cubic interface. In *Proc. of ACM VRST*, pages 69–72, 2008.

[14] A. Y. Dvorkin, R. V. Kenyon, and E. A. Keshner. Reaching within a dynamic virtual environment. *J. NeuroEng. Rehabil.*, 4(23):182–186, 2007.

[15] P. M. Fitts. The information capacity of the human motor system in controlling the amplitude of movement. *J. Exp. Psych.*, 47:381–391, 1954.

[16] L. Geniva, R. Chua, and J. T. Enns. Attention for perception and action: task interference for action planning, but not for online control. *Exp. Brain Res.*, 185(4):709–717, 2008.

[17] M. Hachet, B. Bossavit, A. Cohe, and J.-B. de la Rivière. Toucheo: multitouch and stereo combined in a seamless workspace. In *Proc. of ACM UIST*, pages 587–592, 2011.

[18] M. Hancock, S. Carpendale, and A. Cockburn. Shallow-depth 3D interaction: design and evaluation of one-, two- and three-touch techniques. In *Proc. of ACM CHI*, pages 1147–1156, 2007.

[19] O. Hilliges, S. Izadi, A. D. Wilson, S. Hodges, A. Garcia-Mendoza, and A. Butz. Interactions in the air: Adding further depth to interactive tabletops. In *Proc. of ACM UIST*, pages 139–148, 2009.

[20] International Organization for Standardization. *ISO/DIS 9241-9 Ergonomic requirements for office work with visual display terminals (VDTs) - Part 9: Requirements for non-keyboard input devices*, 2000.

[21] G. Liu, R. Chua, and J. T. Enns. Attention for perception and action: task interference for action planning, but not for online control. *Exp. Brain Res.*, 185:709–717, 2008.

[22] J. M. Loomis and J. M. Knapp. Visual perception of egocentric distance in real and virtual environments. In *Virtual and adaptive environments*, pages 21–46. 2003.

[23] C. L. MacKenzie, R. G. Marteniuka, C. Dugasa, D. Liskea, and B. Eickmeiera. Three-dimensional movement trajectories in Fitts' task: Implications for control. *Q.J. Exp. Psychology-A*, 39(4):629–647, 1987.

[24] I. S. MacKenzie and P. Isokoski. Fitts' throughput and the speed-accuracy tradeoff. In *Proc. of ACM CHI*, pages 1633–1636, 2008.

[25] A. Martinet, G. Casiez, and G. Grisoni. The design and evaluation of 3D positioning techniques for multi-touch displays. In *Proc. of IEEE 3DUI*, pages 115–118, 2010.

[26] J. P. McIntire, P. R. Havig, and E. E. Geiselman. What is 3D good for? A review of human performance on stereoscopic 3D displays. *Proc. of the SPIE, Head- and Helmet-Mounted Displays XVII*, 8383:1–13, 2012.

[27] J. Pierce, A. Forsberg, M. Conway, S. Hong, R. Zeleznik, and M. Mine. Image plane interaction techniques in 3D immersive environments. In *Proc. of ACM I3D*, pages 39–44, 1997.

[28] D. Pyryeskin, M. Hancock, and J. Hoey. Comparing elicited gestures to designer-created gestures for selection above a multitouch surface. In *Proc. of ACM ITS*, pages 1–10, 2012.

[29] J. L. Reisman, P. L. Davidson, and J. Y. Han. A screen-space formulation for 2D and 3D direct manipulation. In *Proc. of ACM UIST*, pages 69–78, 2009.

[30] J. Schöning, F. Steinicke, D. Valkov, A. Krüger, and K. H. Hinrichs. Bimanual interaction with interscopic multi-touch surfaces. In *Proc. of INTERACT*, pages 40–53, 2009.

[31] M. Slater. Place illusion and plausibility can lead to realistic behaviour in immersive virtual environments. *Phil. Trans. R. Soc. B*, 364:3549–3557, 2009.

[32] S. Strothoff, D. Valkov, and K. H. Hinrichs. Triangle cursor: Interactions with objects above the tabletop. In *Proc. of ACM ITS*, pages 111–119, 2011.

[33] R. J. Teather and W. Stuerzlinger. Pointing at 3D target projections with one-eyed and stereo cursors. In *Proc. of ACM CHI*, 10 pages, 2013.

[34] R. J. Teather and W. Stuerzlinger. Pointing at 3D targets in a stereo head-tracked virtual environment. In *Proc. of IEEE 3DUI*, pages 87–94, 2011.

[35] D. Valkov, A. Giesler, and K. H. Hinrichs. Evaluation of depth perception for touch interaction with stereoscopic rendered objects. In *Proc. of ACM ITS*, pages 21–30, 2012.

[36] D. Valkov, F. Steinicke, G. Bruder, and K. H. Hinrichs. 2D touching of 3D stereoscopic objects. In *Proc. of ACM CHI*, pages 1353–1362, 2011.

[37] D. Valkov, F. Steinicke, G. Bruder, K. H. Hinrichs, J. Schöning, F. Daiber, and A. Krüger. Touching floating objects in projection-based virtual reality environments. In *Proc. of JVRC*, pages 17–24, 2010.

[38] A. Viau, A. G. Feldman, B. J. McFadyen, and M. F. Levin. Reaching in reality and virtual reality: A comparison of movement kinematics in healthy subjects and in adults with hemiparesis. *J. NeuroEng. Rehabil.*, 1(11), 2004.

[39] D. Whitney, D. A. Westwood, and M. A. Goodale. The influence of visualmotion on fast reaching movements to a stationary object. *Letters to Nature*, 423:869–873, 2003.

[40] P. Willemsen, A. A. Gooch, W. B. Thompson, and S. H. Creem-Regehr. Effects of stereo viewing conditions on distance perception in virtual environments. *Presence-Teleop. Virt.*, 17(1):91–101, 2008.

[41] A. D. Wilson, S. Izadi, O. Hilliges, A. Garcia-Mendoza, and D. Kirk. Bringing physics to the surface. In *Proc. of ACM UIST*, pages 67–76, 2008.

Novel Metrics for 3D Remote Pointing

Steven J. Castellucci
York University
4700 Keele St.
Toronto, ON, Canada
stevenc@cse.yorku.ca

Robert J. Teather
York University
4700 Keele St.
Toronto, ON, Canada
rteather@cse.yorku.ca

Andriy Pavlovych
York University
4700 Keele St.
Toronto, ON, Canada
andriyp@cse.yorku.ca

ABSTRACT

We introduce new metrics to help explain 3D pointing device movement characteristics. We present a study to assess these by comparing two cursor control modes using a Sony *PS Move*. "Laser" mode used ray casting, while "position" mode mapped absolute device movement to cursor position. Mouse pointing was also included, and all techniques were also analyzed with existing 2D accuracy measures. Results suggest that position mode shows promise due to its accurate and smooth pointer movements. Our 3D movement metrics do not correlate well with performance, but may be beneficial in understanding how devices are used.

Categories and Subject Descriptors

H.5.2 Information interfaces and presentation (e.g., HCI): User Interfaces—evaluation/methodology.

General Terms

Measurement, Performance, Human Factors.

Keywords

3D measures, remote pointing, evaluation.

1. INTRODUCTION

Remote pointing is becoming more common, largely due to the recent availability of inexpensive multi-DOF game controllers. Many researchers are using remote pointing in both 2D user interfaces [5, 13] and in virtual reality systems [7, 16]. Thus there is interest in determining how effective these devices are for pointing. Existing measures such as throughput indicate device performance, but do not explain device movement characteristics.

We conducted a study to evaluate the pointing efficiency of the *PlayStation Move* as a representative remote pointing device. The task required controlling a 2D cursor to select targets on a large display. The study included two distinct cursor control modes using the *Move*. The first technique, "laser mode" positions the cursor where the *Move* is pointed. The second technique maps absolute device movement to cursor control. Mouse pointing was included as a known benchmark of pointing performance. The techniques were compared using the ISO 9241-9 standard [3].

We chose a simple pointing task because it is common to many interaction methods. In contrast, a 3D docking task would also

gauged participants' spatial and problem-solving skills, rather than focus on device characteristics. Further benefits of the standard are presented in the Related Work section.

We include a detailed analysis of device motion to help explain performance differences. Our analysis includes 2D measures developed by MacKenzie et al. [9]. Moreover, we propose and validate similar measures for use with 3–6DOF input devices. Our goal is to supplement existing 2D measures with tools specifically designed to investigate higher dimensional input devices.

2. RELATED WORK

Pointing interfaces are often evaluated in the context of Fitts' law [1], an empirical model of the well-known tradeoff between speed and accuracy in pointing tasks. The model is given as follows:

$$MT = a + b \cdot ID, \quad \text{where} \quad ID = \log_2(A/W + 1) \quad (1)$$

MT is movement time, A is target amplitude (distance), and W is target size, while a and b are empirically derived. The log term is the index of difficulty (ID) and indicates pointing task difficulty.

The ISO 9241-9 standard suggests using "effective" measures, a post-experiment correction to adjust the error rate to 4%. This enables the computation of throughput, a measure that incorporates both speed and accuracy by "normalizing" the accuracy. Throughput is computed as follows:

$$TP = \frac{\log_2(A_e/W_e + 1)}{MT}, \quad \text{where} \quad W_e = 4.133 \cdot SD_x \quad (2)$$

MT is the average movement time. A_e, effective distance, is the average movement distance. Effective width, W_e, is computed by projecting the cursor onto the task axis (the line between subsequent targets) and taking the standard deviation (SD_x) of these distances multiplied by 4.133. This assumes that movement endpoints are normally distributed around the target center and 4.133 (±2.066) standard deviations (i.e., 96%) of clicks hit the target [4]. W_e corrects error rate to 4%, and allows comparison between studies with differing error rates [8]. Throughput exhibits low variability for the same condition between studies [14, 18], improving comparability. For example, previous work [15] found mouse throughput was consistent across three different 3D pointing tasks. Exclusively measuring movement time can be unreliable as it varies at the expense of accuracy.

Mouse pointing throughput is typically higher than remote pointing throughput [10, 12, 15]. Still, there is interest in using remote pointing in both 2D [5, 10, 11, 13] and 3D [2, 6, 15, 17] user interface research. Our primary goal is not to re-establish the performance differences between the mouse and remote pointing. Instead, we propose and validate metrics to characterize 3D movements. This should provide better insight into *why* performance differences occur.

Metrics to evaluate 2D pointing movement characteristics were proposed by MacKenzie [9]. These measures are taken relative to the task axis and reported as per-trial averages. The first four metrics are discrete measures. *Target Re-Entry* (TRE) is the number of times the cursor re-entered the target. *Task Axis Crossing* (TAC) represents the number of times the cursor crosses the task axis. *Movement Direction Change* (MDC) quantifies the number of direction changes that occur relative to the task axis, while *Orthogonal Direction Change* (ODC) counts direction changes orthogonal to the task axis. The final three metrics are continuous measures measured in pixels. *Movement Variability* (MV) represents how parallel the traversed path is to the task axis. *Movement Error* (ME) indicates the scalar deviation from the task axis, while *Movement Offset* (MO) is the non-scalar deviation from the task axis.

These metrics provide additional insight into why performance (throughput) scores vary between 2D pointing techniques. We propose similar measures to characterize 3D movements, and then experimentally assess the value of these. In previous studies [2, 15, 17] researchers provide qualitative explanations for observed performance differences. Our metrics provide an additional quantitative tool to enrich the evaluation of 3D input devices.

3. 3D ACCURACY MEASURES

Motivated by the aforementioned 2D metrics [9], we propose three measures to help characterize 3D motions. Previous research [2, 5, 6, 15] use a motion tracked stylus or wand for 2D selection. However, none of these report how users moved the device when performing the selection task. Characterizing users' free-space 3D motions can reveal inefficiencies in movement and/or possible sources of arm or wrist fatigue. Once identified, the pointing technique can then be improved.

There are two main benefits to our 3D accuracy measures. First, high-DOF input devices can control 2D cursors; this is common in games (e.g., on Nintendo *Wii*). We use similar pointing modes in our study. While 2D metrics help explain differences in such 2D cursor techniques, they fail to capture some usage behavior. For example, one can point the device from different positions and/or orientations yielding the same cursor position (Figure 1).

Second, high-DOF devices can be used to directly select remote 3D objects via ray casting. In these cases, it is likely infeasible to use the existing 2D accuracy measures [9]. Measures that consider the higher-dimensional nature of 3D pointing are required. The following sections propose the new measures.

3.1 Depth Variability (DV)

Most trackers provide at least 3DOF of movement detection. Device depth direction may not change the 2D cursor position, but may still demonstrate some pointing inefficiency (Figure 2). *Depth variability* is the standard deviation from the average device depth during a trial. This is based on the *movement variability* measure. [9]. *DV* is computed as follows:

$$DV = \sqrt{\frac{1}{n-1} \sum (z_i - \bar{z})^2} \qquad (3)$$

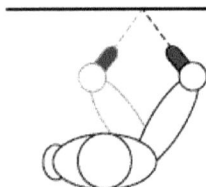

where z_i is the sample distance from $z = 0$ plane, and $\bar{z}$ is the average distance of all samples for the trial from the $z = 0$ plane. For depth-insensitive pointing techniques, *DV* should ideally be 0, as a higher number would represent unnecessary depth motion.

3.2 Rotation/Movement Ratio (RMR)

Our second measure relates to the amount of rotation vs. movement used to control a pointing technique. For example, one can select the same target by pointing at from very different positions (Figure 1), i.e., the device position "trades off" with the device orientation. It is also possible to move the device great distances, while rotating it by the same amount (Figure 3).

Rotational control seems less fatiguing than arm movement. Consequently, we propose to use the ratio between device movement and rotation as another measure of pointing efficiency. We ignore roll, as this usually will not affect selection. For pitch and yaw, we first find the difference between the maximum and minimum rotation angle for a trial. These extrema are then projected onto the display surface to find the distance between them, D_r. Next, D_m, the "movement distance" is computed as the distance between the minimum and maximum device position in the specified axis. This measure is then computed as:

$$D_r = 2 \times dist \times \tan(\Delta\Theta/2), \text{ and } D_m = \Delta x, \text{ then}$$

$$RMR_{axis} = D_r / (D_r + D_m) \qquad (4)$$

Note that *dist* is the average distance from the device to the screen and $\Delta\Theta$ is the difference between the min and max rotation angles. The difference between the min and max position is Δx. This measure indicates how much rotational control contributed to the entire pointer movement in a given trial.

3.3 Rotation Direction Change (RDC)

We measure rotation direction change frequency in each axis. For example, increasing the device pitch would reflect an increase in the cursor *y*-coordinate. An inefficient pointing technique may yield alternating increases and decreases of device pitch, i.e., rotation direction changes (Figure 4). This metric is computed as the count of such rotation direction changes, greater than a threshold, in each axis, averaged per trial. We use a 1° threshold.

4. METHOD

4.1 Participants

Twelve paid, right-handed participants (7 males, 5 females) were recruited from our university campus. Ages ranged from 20 to 31 years (mean = 23.8; SD = 3.8). Participants were frequent mouse users, but had limited experience using the *Move* controller.

4.2 Apparatus

Participants used a mouse and a Sony *PlayStation Move* to perform pointing tasks on a PC. The *Move* was connected to the PC via a *PlayStation 3* (*PS3*) gaming console using Sony's

Figure 1. Two device positions and orientations that result in the same cursor position on the screen.

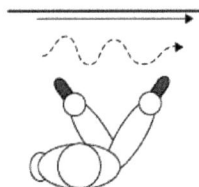

Figure 2. The solid arrow is the intended path, but the dashed arrow is the actual device movement.

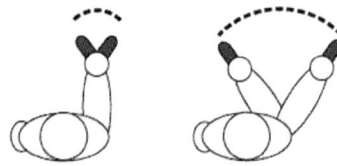

Figure 3. Wrist movement (left) and arm movement (right) traverse different rotational distances but yield the same pointer movement.

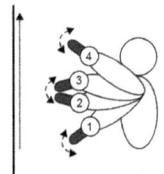

Figure 4. While moving the device to change cursor position (solid), the user often alternates rotation (dashed).

Move.Me server software, which captured buttons events and mapped *Move* position and orientation to cursor movement. *Move* latency was 78 ± 3 ms. Participants stood 2.5 m from a projected display (1.4 m diagonal at 1024×768 resolution). A height-adjustable podium provided a surface for the mouse.

4.3 Procedure

The experiment had three conditions: the mouse (baseline), and two using the *Move*. In "position mode", the *Move*'s x/y motion moved the cursor, while depth was ignored. This used absolute mapping of a small tracked rectangle to the screen. "Laser mode" placed the cursor where the *Move*'s selection ray intersected the display. Each condition was preceded by a practice session. During experimental sessions, participants were instructed to select the highlighted target "as quickly and as accurately as possible". Circular targets were arranged in a circle, with six width–distance combinations per block. Each trial concluded upon clicking (whether the target was hit or missed).

4.4 Design

The experiment used a within-subjects design with the following factors and levels:

Technique:	mouse, laser mode, position mode
Target Width:	20, 35, 60 px (22, 39, 67 mm)
Target Distance:	450, 550, 650 px (500, 611, 722 mm)

At 2 blocks of 15 selection trials each, there were 9,720 experiment trials over all 12 participants. The target width and distance combinations represent nine *ID*s (per Equation 1) ranging from 3.09 to 5.07 bits. These were presented in random order without replacement for each block and technique. The technique ordering was counterbalanced using a Latin Square. The experiment took about 30 minutes to complete.

The dependent variables were error rate and throughput. We also report motion both MacKenzie's 2D accuracy measures [9] and the our new proposed 3D measures.

5. RESULTS AND DISCUSSION

5.1 Throughput

Position and laser throughput was 43.3% and 62.6% lower than the mouse, respectively (Figure 5). Technique had a significant main effect on throughput ($F_{2,18} = 293.4$, $p < 0.0001$). A Scheffé test revealed each technique was significantly different ($p < .05$).

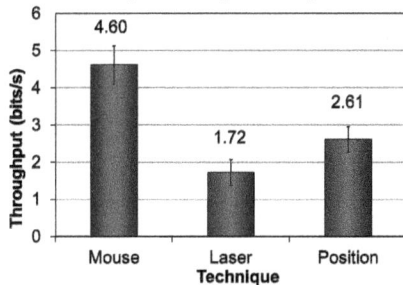

Figure 5. Throughput results, with error bars representing ±1 SD.

Jota et al. [5] report laser throughput of 3.82 bits/s, but did not use effective measures. Our results are thus better compared to Teather and Stuerzlinger's [15] "pen ray" throughput of 1.5 bits/s.

5.2 Error Rate

Error rates are summarized in Figure 6. Technique had a significant main effect on error rate ($F_{2,18} = 96.41$, $p < 0.0001$), and each technique was significantly different ($p < .05$).

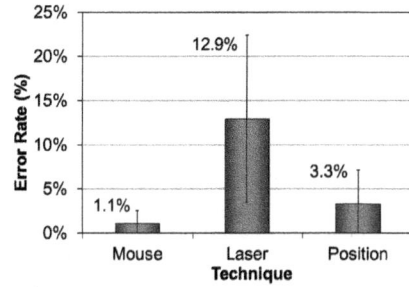

Figure 6. Error rate, with error bars representing ±1 SD.

Jota's laser mode yielded an error rate of only 3.4% [5], but used a 1D task requiring less precision. Teather's pen ray error rate of 13.6% [15] is more consistent with our results.

5.3 2D Movement Fidelity

Here, we analyze each technique according to MacKenzie's 2D accuracy measures [9]. Each of these is summarized in Table 1.

Table 1. The per-trial mean (and SD) for each metric (best result highlighted). Post hoc significance at 5% level, where non-significant groups are shown in brackets, and "<" signs indicate differences. * $p < 0.0001$. ** $p < 0.0005$. *** $p < 0.005$.

Metric	Mouse	Laser	Position	F-value	Post Hoc
TRE	0.06 (0.06)	0.51 (0.17)	0.09 (0.07)	81.68*	(M, P) < L
TAC	2.39 (0.12)	4.93 (0.61)	2.28 (0.31)	162.63*	(P, M) < L
MDC	5.38 (0.64)	12.64 (2.50)	2.91 (0.38)	137.89*	P < M < L
ODC	0.74 (0.49)	9.42 (1.74)	0.82 (0.42)	260.74	(M, P) < L
MV	16.89 (5.22)	17.92 (3.83)	13.69 (2.97)	6.89***	P < L
ME	18.41 (5.27)	15.60 (2.77)	14.15 (2.40)	6.98***	P < M
MO	3.96 (3.01)	−0.18 (2.37)	2.37 (1.83)	11.71**	L < (P, M)

Surprisingly, the *Move* modes yielded the best result in five of the metrics (Table 1). Its low TRE and ODC values signify definitive target selection and consistent cursor movement towards the target. The position mode had the best scores for most metrics. The low TAC, MDC, MV, and ME values imply straight pointer paths parallel to the task axis. The fact that position mode throughput was lower than the mouse may be because the technique required more device movement. The laser condition yielded the lowest MO, indicating pointer paths close to the task axis. The high MDC and ODC for the laser condition quantitatively illustrate the propensity for hand tremors.

5.4 3D Movement Fidelity

Our new measures (Section 3) were computed for the laser and position control modes, averaged per trial, and compared using an independent samples t-test assuming unequal variance. The laser was significantly better than position mode in several measures (Table 2). This suggests that while these measures help characterize device motion, they may not relate to performance.

Table 2. The per-trial mean (and SD) for each metric (best result highlighted). *DV* is measured in mm, all other are count/ratios without units. * $p < 0.001$. ** $p < 0.05$.

Metric	Laser	Position	t-value
Depth Variability (DV)	9.06 (3.02)	28.18 (9.85)	−13.16*
x Rotation/Movement Ratio (RMRx)	0.84 (0.04)	0.82 (0.03)	0.95
y Rotation/Movement Ratio(RMRy)	0.82 (0.04)	0.80 (0.03)	1.13
Roll Direction Change (RDC$_{roll}$)	0.29 (0.06)	0.63 (0.12)	−17.03*
Yaw Direction Change (RDC$_{yaw}$)	0.42 (0.06)	0.48 (0.12)	−3.14**
Pitch Direction Change (RDC$_{pitch}$)	0.43 (0.08)	0.49 (0.09)	−3.07**

Depth variability was significantly lower for the laser than position mode. This is likely because the z coordinate did not affect position mode, but would change the ray origin in laser mode, affecting the cursor position. Thus, in laser mode, participants scrutinized their depth motion. Depth motion in position mode was inefficient, but not necessarily detrimental. Similarly, it would not impact any of the 2D metrics where position mode performed significantly better, as depth movement would not result in cursor position changes.

Laser mode had significantly fewer rotational direction changes than position mode in all three axes, suggesting that rotational control is more important in laser mode. This makes sense, given that the ray direction controls the cursor position. In position mode, any device rotation would only affect the cursor position insofar as it changed the device position. Thus, participants were more careful with device orientation in laser mode.

There was no significant difference in RMR between modes. Both modes had relatively high ratios, suggesting that both modes were primarily controlled by wrist rotation, rather than sweeping arm motions. This makes sense, as participants would quickly find that rotating the device is easier than moving it large distances. However, it also highlights a propensity for wrist fatigue.

Ultimately, this analysis suggests the influence of rotational degrees of freedom may be stronger than positional degrees. It is well known (see e.g., [15]) that higher-DOF techniques generally perform worse. Our results suggest that the rotation-based laser mode not only performed worse, but yielded more erratic 2D cursor trails as well. Conversely, the position mode was not affected by device rotation (as reflected by our 3D measures), yet produced more efficient cursor trails, and higher performance.

6. CONCLUSION AND FUTURE WORK

We introduced three novel metrics to characterize 3D pointing and used them to characterize the PlayStation *Move* in a standardized selection task. Although there was no correlation between device movement and pointing performance, the metrics revealed and quantified how the *Move* was used during pointing. For example, the high Depth Variability of the position mode (versus laser mode) could indicate an area for improvement if movement efficiency were paramount. Alternatively, the higher DV and throughput values for position mode could illustrate a robust technique that performs well, despite user inefficiency.

The laser mode exhibited high Movement Direction Change and Orthogonal Direction Change, but also significantly better Rotational Direction Change on all three axes. Thus, one could quantitatively support using linear movement for coarse pointer control and rotational movement for fine pointer control.

For both modes, the Rotation/Movement Ratios show not all degrees of freedom are equally used – rotational motion is primarily used. This preference could forecast localized fatigue or strain after extended use. By combining our 3D metrics with existing 2D and performance metrics, designers of 3D pointing techniques can characterize and quantify device usage to show strengths and identify weaknesses in their techniques.

7. REFERENCES

[1] Fitts, P.M. 1954. The information capacity of the human motor system in controlling the amplitude of movement. *Journal of Experimental Psychology*, *47* (6). 381-391.

[2] Grossman, T. and Balakrishnan, R. 2006. The design and evaluation of selection techniques for 3D volumetric displays. In *Proc.of ACM UIST 2006*, 3-12.

[3] ISO. 2000. ISO/DIS 9241-9 Ergonomic requirements for office work with visual display terminals (VDTs) - Part 9: Requirements for non-keyboard input devices, International Standard, International Organization for Standardization.

[4] Jagacinski, R.J. and Flach, J.M. 2003. Chapter 4 - Information theory and Fitts' law. In *Control theory for humans: Quantitative approaches to modeling performance*.

[5] Jota, R., Nacenta, M.A., Jorge, J.A., Carpendale, S. and Greenberg, S. 2010. A comparison of ray pointing techniques for very large displays. In *Proc. of Graphics Interface 2010*, 269-276.

[6] Kopper, R., Bowman, D.A., Silva, M.G. and McMahan, R.P. 2010. A human motor behavior model for distal pointing tasks. *Int. J. of Human-Computer Studies*, *68* (10). 603-615.

[7] LaViola, J.J. 2008. Bringing VR and Spatial 3D Interaction to the Masses through Video Games. *IEEE Computer Graphics and Applications*, *28* (5). 10-15.

[8] MacKenzie, I.S. 1992. Fitts' law as a research and design tool in human-computer interaction. *Human-Computer Interaction*, *7*. 91-139.

[9] MacKenzie, I.S., Kauppinen, T. and Silfverberg, M. 2001. Accuracy measures for evaluating computer pointing devices. In *Proc. of ACM CHI 2001*, 9-16.

[10] McArthur, V., Castellucci, S.J. and MacKenzie, I.S. 2009. An empirical comparison of "Wiimote" gun attachments for pointing tasks. In *Proc. EICS 2009*, 203-208.

[11] Myers, B.A., Bhatnagar, R., Nichols, J., Peck, C.H., Kong, D., Miller, R. and Long, A.C. 2002. Interacting at a distance: Measuring the performance of laser pointers and other devices. In *Proc. of ACM CHI 2002*, 33-40.

[12] Natapov, D., Castellucci, S.J. and MacKenzie, I.S. 2009. ISO 9241-9 evaluation of video game controllers. In *Proc. of Graphics Interface 2009*, 223-230.

[13] Oh, J.-Y. and Stuerzlinger, W. 2002. Laser pointers as collaborative pointing devices. In *Proc. of Graphics Interface 2002*, 315-320.

[14] Soukoreff, R.W. and MacKenzie, I.S. 2004. Towards a standard for pointing device evaluation, perspectives on 27 years of Fitts' law research in HCI. *Int. J. of Human-Computer Studies*, *61* (6). 751-789.

[15] Teather, R.J. and Stuerzlinger, W. 2011. Pointing at 3D targets in a stereo head-tracked virtual environment. In *Proc. of IEEE 3DUI 2011*. IEEE Press, 87-94.

[16] Wingrave, C.A. 2010. The Wiimote and beyond: spatially convenient devices for 3D user interfaces. *IEEE Computer Graphics and Applications*, *30*. 71-85.

[17] Wingrave, C.A., Tintner, R., Walker, B.N., Bowman, D.A. and Hodges, L.F. 2005. Exploring Individual Differences in Raybased Selection; Strategies and Traits. In *Proc.of IEEE VR 2005*, 163-170.

[18] Wobbrock, J.O., Shinohara, K. and Jansen, A. 2011. The effects of task dimensionality, endpoint deviation, throughput calculation, and experiment design on pointing measures and models. In *Proc. ACM CHI 2011*, 1639-1648.

Spatial User Interface for Experiencing Mogao Caves

Leith Kin Yip Chan
Department of Industrial and
Manufacturing Systems Engineering,
The University of Hong Kong,
Hong Kong
lkychan@hku.hk

Sarah Kenderdine
Applied Laboratory of Interactive
Visualization and Embodiment,
City University of Hong Kong,
Hong Kong
skenderd@cityu.edu.hk

Jeffrey Shaw
School of Creative Media,
City University of Hong Kong,
Hong Kong
j.shaw@cityu.edu.hk

ABSTRACT
In this paper, we describe the design and implementation of the Pure Land AR, which is an installation that employs spatial user interface and allows users to virtually visit the UNESCO world heritage – Mogao Caves by using handheld devices. The installation was shown to the public at different museums and galleries. The result of the work and the user responses is discussed.

Categories and Subject Descriptors
H.5.2 [**Information Interfaces and Presentation**]: User Interfaces – *Input devices and strategies, Interaction styles.*

Keywords
Virtual Reality, Augmented Reality, Heritage Preservation.

1. INTRODUCTION
With the advance in Virtual Reality and Augmented Reality, nowadays human computer interfaces are well beyond traditional monitor, keyboard and mouse interfaces. Researchers have been actively investigating new ways of interaction and communication between man and machine. Spatial user interface, which allows users to use the third dimension to interact with the computer, shows great potential in this area. On the other hand, historical sites, such as Mogao Caves, are often difficult to access and also vulnerable to the mass tourism. By using the technology of digitization, we can capture the current state of the site in terms of 3D geometry and surface texture. By using the acquired digital data and the cutting technology of Computer Graphics, it is possible to immerse the visitors into the computer generated historical site virtually without the limitation of the physical site's accessibility. In this paper, we describe the design and implementation of Pure Land Augmented Reality Edition (Pure Land AR), which is a visualization system using tablets as the tangible user interface allowing visitors to experience and explore Mogao Caves. Feedback from users and evaluation is also presented in this paper.

2. BACKGROUND

2.1 Mogao Grottoes - UNESCO World Heritage site
Dunhuang is an ancient oasis town on the edge of the Gobi Desert in far-western China located near the meeting point of the northern and southern routes of the ancient Silk Road. It was first established as a garrison town in 111 BC and grew into a thriving trading and staging centre on the Silk Road and later as a religious centre. The Mogao Grottoes, or Caves, at Dunhuang are an amazing assemblage of separate hand excavated and decorated caves which were constructed over a millennium beginning in 366 AD. According to records, over 1000 caves were built over this period and only 492 survive today. The Mogao Caves were inscribed on the World Heritage List in 1987. Nowadays, the biggest threat to the site is tourism. The caves are very fragile, and humidity and carbon dioxide from visitors can lead to flaking and discoloration of the delicate pigment on plaster wall paintings.

In order to preserve the caves, the Dunhuang Academy[1] is pioneering an ambitious project to digitize the site. Many of the caves have been laser-scanned and texture captured [1]. By using the raw digital data, we can reconstruct 3D models of the caves (Figure 1). However, look at the 3D caves on the computer screen is nothing compared to being in the real caves. We need to have a better visualization system to fully utilize the precious data.

Figure 1. 3D model of the Mogoa Cave 220.

2.2 Visualization System and Interface
With the reduction of the cost of computer hardware and the advancement of PC based graphics processors, the Virtual Reality system is becoming more affordable and popular. Large high-

[1] Dunhuang Academy, formerly the Dunhuang Art Institute set up in 1944, is an official body established by the Chinese government to manage, preserve and promote the Mogao Caves, the Yulin Caves, and the Western Thousand Buddha Caves. The Academy has been carrying out various researches and conservation projects, of which some are done in collaboration with other local or oversea institutions.

resolution displays have been widely applied in various domains [9]. For example, a variety of different CAVE-like implementations have been designed and developed, from a simple 2-sided CAVE (front and floor screen), a full 6-sided CAVE, to a recently developed 17-sided pentagon-shaped StarCAVE [5]. All of these Virtual Reality systems give the user the immersive experience of entering a computer generated world. Augmented Reality (AR), on the other hand, rather than immersing a person into a completely synthetic world, it attempts to embed synthetic supplements into the real environment [4]. Augmented Reality (AR) further opens up a new area of user interface design since all real and tangible objects with embedded virtual entities can be treated as a tool or interface device in three-dimensional space for navigation and manipulate of objects in the virtual world. This kind of spatial interface provides a new methodology in Human-Computer Interaction. A number of studies have been done to investigate the possibility of using AR to improve the user experience of interacting with entities in a both real and virtual environment. For instance, by using outdoor tacking, mobile computing, 3D visualization and VR techniques, Archeoguide [10] allows user to have personalized tours of archaeological sites with augmented images overlaying on mobile device's live video. With the introduction of the application library ARToolKit [6], the software development of AR interface becomes more straight forward and therefore AR applications start to appear in different domains. For example, AR applications running on mobile devices help visitors to access additional multimedia information of exhibits in museums [2]. All of these new technologies help to present personalized information to the visitors in order to enrich their interest and understanding of the culture heritage [3].

3. DESIGN AND IMPLEMENTATION

To visualize the Mogao Caves, the first implementation was in a 360 degree 3D surrounding screen. In fact, the first application of the Pure Land [7] project was developed in a 360 degree projection system – AVIE [8]. While these full scale systems provide excellent immersive effect to the users, the physical size and scale of the systems often limit their mobility. It is not a trivial task for the implementation or relocation of such large scale systems. In contrast, AR systems use head mounted displays or tablet displays as the interface. The hardware for AR systems is usually lightweight and therefore making the assembly process relatively easy. This is particularly important when the installation is intended to be displayed at different locations in different parts of the world for different periods of time.

3.1 Design Concept

In this installation, the walls of the exhibition room (which share the same scale as the real cave) are covered with one-to-one scale prints of Cave 220's wireframe polygonal mesh—which provides users with visual cues as to what to explore (Figure 2). Inside the virtual world, the high-resolution photographs of the cave's paintings and sculptures are digitally rendered onto this polygonal mesh to create the composite 3D representations that are then presented to the visitors on the tablets (Figure 3) as they navigate the exhibition space. Infrared cameras track the position and orientation of the visitor tablets, while computers render the appropriate views of the digital cave, transmitted via wireless network, in real-time.

In doing so, the tablet screen shifts from being considered as an object in and of itself, to functioning as a mobile framing device for the staging of a "virtual" rendering of the real cave that relies on an intricate spatial tracking system. This is not a passive

televisual environment, but an interactive performance. Cave 220 is being exactly mapped between real space and the digital model. In this instance, Pure Land AR is activated in the twists and turns of the hand-held screen. By moving the monitor around the space, the viewer can examine three walls of the cave, and by holding the tablet aloft, he or she can also see the magnificent ceiling painting (Figure 4). Thus the tablet reveals the cave as something that is apparently located in the real space of the gallery. As the user entertains the various possibilities of moving through the space with the tablet, the changing views of the cave are fluidly and accurately shown on the screen. In this way the classic trope of a "window on the world" is virtually enacted. And given that this world is bounded by the Cave 220's walls, when the viewer brings that window into contact with the exhibition wall surface, its painting appears at exactly 1:1 scale within the frame of the tablet screen and reveal the finest detail of the mural painting. There are totally two tablets in the installation.

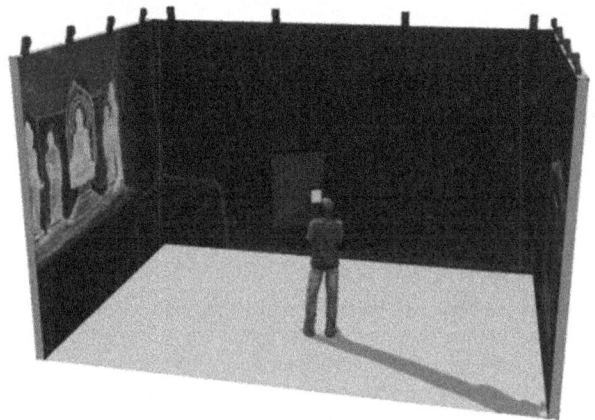

Figure 2. Setting of the Pure Land AR.

Figure 3. Handheld device with retro-reflective markers on the top.

3.2 System Implementation

There are three main components in the system: the display interface, the optical tracking system and image generators.

Two tablets are Apple iPad, which was chosen mainly because of its elegant design and long battery life. They are used as the tangible display interface devices for users to reveal the virtual world. The idea is similar to the Magic Lenses interface [1]. The tablets are installed in acrylic cases with attached retro-reflective markers. The cases protect the tablets as well as preventing the users from interfering the application running in the devices. All together they act like movable cameras and the users can use them to reveal and examine different areas of the Cave 220. The 3D model of the cave consists of around 1.3 million polygons and 1.5GB of texture. Instead of rendering the image by the tablets with limited CPU power, the images are rendered and streamed from two high performance computers via wireless network in real time. Client applications of the software Splashtop® are running on both tablets to receive the streaming video signal.

For the tracking system, we use the NaturalPoint® OptiTrack™ tracking system. This tracking system uses retro-reflective marker technology to track targets with the infrared light source that is built into individual cameras. In our setting, there are 12 infrared cameras mounted on the top edges of the wall to provide a range of coverage of about 6 meters by 3 meters. In order to track the tablets, we need to attach at least three markers on each of the target. By analyzing the images obtained by the cameras at different angles, the computer in the tracking system is able to recognize and calculate the 3D position and orientation of the tablets in real time. During the normal operation, it is very often that the user placed the tablet against the physical wall to revive the mural in one to one scale. In virtual scene, it is equivalent to placing the projection reference really closed to the cave's walls. In order to achieve satisfactory result, the ability of tracking down to millimeter movement is needed and this is the primary reason of choosing optical tracking system over other tracking technologies such as the tablet's build-in inertial orientation sensor. Since it is not practical to place head tracking markers on the heads of visitors in a gallery environment, the position of virtual camera is derived from the tablet's coordinate. The camera is set at the centre of the tablet with the perpendicular distance of 40cm, which is approximately the eye position of an average adult holding the tablet with two hands.

With the tracking system in place, the tracking information is then broadcasted to the computers (image generators) through the Ethernet using the VRPN (Virtual Reality Peripheral Network) [2] protocol. As there are two tablets, we need two computers for image generation. These computers, with 3DVIA Virtools™ as the graphics engine, are responsible for acquiring the tracking data and rendering the images to match the motion of the tablets in real-time. To achieve this, we have to build a 3D virtual scene with exactly the same setting as the physical setup in the tracker's frame of reference. Virtual cameras are attached at the approximated eye positions of the users and the images rendered from the cameras are fed to the screen of the corresponding tablets via wireless network for the presentation of the virtual world to the users. Moreover, some special effects such as appearing of restored images of seven Medicine Buddha painting will be randomly triggered in order to enhance the richness of the content. With the help of the Splashtop® Streamer, the final rendered images are continuously compressed and sent to the tablet screens.

3.3 Preliminary Result

The Pure Land AR has been exhibited both in Hong Kong International Art Fair 2012[2], NODEM 2012[3] and Shanghai

---

[2] ART HK 12 (Hong Kong International Art Fair). Hong Kong, China, 17–20 May 2012.

[3] NODEM 2012. Hong Kong, China. 2–5 December 2012. http://www.nodem.org/conferences/past/hong-kong-2012/

Biennale 2012[4], with more than 100,000 visitors. During the exhibitions, two mobile tablets allow two users and, typically, groups of three to 10 people to follow the tablets around. This method has proven to be very successful, reinforcing the social qualities of the interpretive experience. Pure Land AR thus demonstrates the dynamics of a single-user, multi-spectator interface that is important to the notion of museums as places of socialization. A group of people will always surround the user, and will follow, direct, gesture, prompt, and photograph the user's view of the world. This dynamic is integral to the interpretation, and to the performance of the work. The view that everyone should have his or her own tablet interface would deny the dynamic of this interchange and only advantage more isolated journeys of discovery [7].

The conjunction between the actual wireframe image on the exhibition walls and the life-like cave rendering seen on those walls via the tablet window operates in the borderline between the indexically real and the phantasmally virtual—between re-embodiment and dis-embodiment. Pure Land AR thus weaves a set of subtle paradoxes into its web of virtualization and actualization, and these paradoxes feed the kinesthetic excitement that is clearly evident in visitors' astonished enjoyment of this installation (Figure 4). It thus aligns with the technologies of telepresence that virtually transport the viewer between the present location and another place—in this case, from the exhibition space to Dunhuang [7].

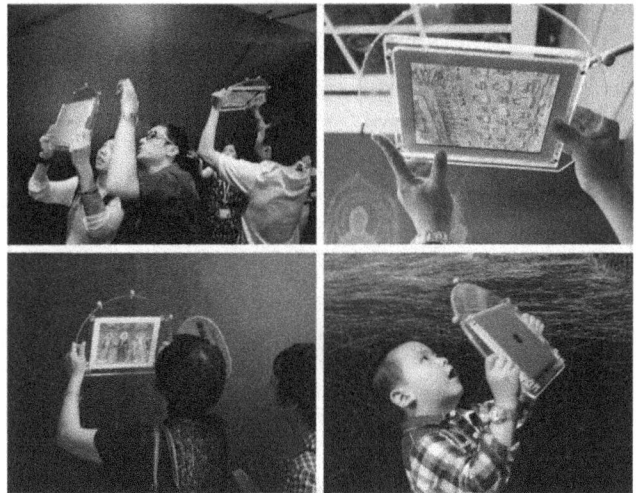

Figure 4. Visitors using the tablets to navigate the virtual model of the Cave 220.

According to the observations from docents and the interviews with selected visitors, most visitors are amazed by the ability of navigating the virtual cave with the tablets. At the beginning, visitors tend to stay at the same spot to look around with the tablets. Then they soon realize that walking around is a better way for the cave exploring. It is reported that the sense of being-there is even more prominent when they're pointing the tablets up against the wall and feeling the height and size of the mural. Visitors are also amused by the digital effect of painting restoration and animation, which in fact helps them to understand the underlying narrative meaning of the mural. The users express that the best experience is to have the tablet on hands but it is also fun to look at other people using the devices.

---

[4] 9th Shanghai Bienniale 2012. Shanghai, China. 2 October 2012– 31 March 2013. http://www.shanghaibiennale.org/en/

4. DISCUSSION AND CONCLUSION

4.1 Advantages and Limitations

Typically in the setting of museums or galleries, visitors come and go away in a matter of minutes. Simplicity is therefore the major advantage of this installation. As the interface is highly intuitive that the visitor only needs to point and watch the handheld device, the interface is suitable to almost all age groups from 2 years old kids to 80 years old elderly. The only difference in usage is just whether they can discover the randomly appearance of special effects in some areas of the mural. Another factor affecting the performance is the coverage and accuracy of the tracking system. Usually the problem of tracking failure occurs when the handheld device is being put too close to the wall, especially at the both corners. Moreover, occlusion caused by the bodies of the users or other visitors also worsens the problem. Our solution is to setup more redundant cameras looking down at different positions to increase the chance of makers capturing. Even so, there are still some extreme situations that the tracking may fail, e.g., when the user's hands covering the markers. In the case of tracking failure, the render image simply freezes and recovers automatically as soon as the tracking data is available again. In addition, as the image on the tablet is the computation result based on its movement, there is always a latency, which is the time delay, caused by the whole process of image generation. If the latency is too big, the user will find that the image is lagging behind the movement, which will greatly reduce the immersive effect. Although calculation and broadcasting of tracking data contribute to the latency, a significant portion of the latency is in fact caused by the streaming of video signal to the tablets via wireless network. Thanks to the superior performance of image streaming software and the greater tolerant to the latency with the tablet interface (as compared to the head mounted display), the image lagging problem is not obvious and we receive no complaint from the visitors about it.

4.2 Future Work

One of most wanted functionalities is the annotation capability. As the mural of the cave is highly detailed and rich in content, it will be beneficial to the visitors if the relevant information such as text, images and videos can be displayed on the tablet when the visitor is pointing to some particular interesting features on the painting. In addition, ability of taking notes and images of the virtual cave with the tablet will also strengthen visitors' involvement and make it a valuable education tool. Moreover, with the capability of the tracking system, the tablet can also be transformed into a handheld game device. For example, asking the users to find a number of specific features of the mural within some predefined time, or more dramatically, making the cave a giant puzzle game as an attraction for children. Although it will be a challenge to keep the user interface intuitive while incorporating the new functionalities, the second generation of the Pure Land AR will definitely aim at this direction.

4.3 Conclusion

Today, when the needs of heritage conservation and preservation are increasingly recognized, digital tools such as laser scanning and high-resolution photography occupy crucial roles in providing continual access for non-specialists and scholars to sites under threat. Pure Land AR employs the Spatial User Interface and makes use of this high-resolution photography and laser scanning data to provide a truly representative 1:1 scale virtual experience of the Cave 220. With the overwhelming response from the visitors, the technology of Virtual Reality and Augmented Reality is starting to unfold their true potential in the world of archaeology and cultural heritage.

5. ACKNOWLEDGMENTS

Our thanks to Dunhuang Academy for providing the digital data of the Cave 220. Copyright of the Cave 220 digital data belongs to Dunhuang Academy.

6. REFERENCES

[1] Agnew, N. *Conservation of ancient sites on the Silk Road : proceedings of the second international conference on the conservation of grotto sites, Mogao Grottoes, Dunhuang, People's Republic of China, June 28-July 3, 2004.* Getty Conservation Institute, Los Angeles, 2010.

[2] Angelopoulou, A., Economou, D., Bouki, V., Psarrou, A., Jin, L., Pritchard, C. and Kolyda, F. Mobile Augmented Reality for Cultural Heritage. In N. Venkatasubramanian, V. Getov and S. Steglich (eds.) *Mobile Wireless Middleware, Operating Systems, and Applications*, 93, (2012), 15-22.10.1007/978-3-642-30607-5_2.

[3] Ardissono, L., Kuflik, T. and Petrelli, D. Personalization in cultural heritage: the road travelled and the one ahead. *User Modeling and User-Adapted Interaction*, 22, 1-2 (2012), 73-99.10.1007/s11257-011-9104-x.

[4] Bimber, O. and Raskar, R. Modern approaches to augmented reality. In *Proc. ACM SIGGRAPH 2005 Courses*, ACM (2005), 1.http://doi.acm.org/10.1145/1198555.1198711.

[5] DeFanti, T. A., Dawe, G., Sandin, D. J., Schulze, J. P., Otto, P., Girado, J., Kuester, F., Smarr, L. and Rao, R. The StarCAVE, a third-generation CAVE and virtual reality OptIPortal. *Future Gener. Comput. Syst.*, 25, 2 (2009), 169-178.http://dx.doi.org/10.1016/j.future.2008.07.015.

[6] Kato, H. and Billinghurst, M. Marker Tracking and HMD Calibration for a Video-Based Augmented Reality Conferencing System. In *Proc. 2nd IEEE and ACM International Workshop on Augmented Reality*, IEEE Computer Society (1999), 85.

[7] Kenderdine, S. Pure Land: Inhabiting the Mogao Caves at Dunhuang. *Curator: The Museums Journal*, 2, 52 (2013), 199-218.

[8] McGinity, M., Shaw, J., Kuchelmeister, V., Hardjono, A. and Favero, D. D. AVIE: a versatile multi-user stereo 360 interactive VR theatre. In *Proc. Proceedings of the 2007 workshop on Emerging displays technologies: images and beyond: the future of displays and interacton*, ACM (2007), 2.

[9] Ni, T., Schmidt, G. S., Staadt, O. G., Livingston, M. A., Ball, R. and May, R. A Survey of Large High-Resolution Display Technologies, Techniques, and Applications. In *Proc. IEEE conference on Virtual Reality*, IEEE Computer Society (2006), 223-236.http://dx.doi.org/10.1109/VR.2006.20.

[10] Vlahakis, V., Ioannidis, N., Karigiannis, J., Tsotros, M., Gounaris, M., Stricker, D., Gleue, T., Daehne, P. and Almeida, L. Archeoguide: an augmented reality guide for archaeological sites. *Computer Graphics and Applications, IEEE*, 22, 5 (2002), 52-60.10.1109/MCG.2002.1028726.

Seamless Interaction using a Portable Projector in Perspective Corrected Multi Display Environments

Jorge H. dos S. Chernicharo
cherni@riec.tohoku.ac.jp

Kazuki Takashima
takashima @riec.tohoku.ac.jp

Yoshifumi Kitamura
kitamura @riec.tohoku.ac.jp

Research Institute of Electrical Communication, Tohoku University
2-1-1 Katahira, Aoba, Sendai, Miyagi
980-8577, Japan

ABSTRACT

In this work, we study ways to use a portable projector to extend the workspace in a perspective corrected multi display environment (MDE). This system uses the relative position between the user and displays in order to show the content perpendicularly to the user's point of view in a deformation-free fashion. We introduce the image created by the portable projector as a new, temporary and movable image in the perspective corrected MDE, creating a more flexible workspace to the user. In our study, we combined two ways of using the projector (handheld or head-mounted) with two ways of moving the cursor on the screens (using a mouse or a laser-pointing based strategy), proposing four techniques to be tried by the users. Also, two exploratory evaluation experiments were performed in order to evaluate our system. The first experiment (5 participants) aimed to evaluate how using a movable screen in order to fill the gaps between displays affects the performance of the user in a cross-display pointing task; while the second (6 participants) aimed to evaluate how using the projector to extend the workspace impacts the task completion time in an off-screen content recognition task. Our results showed that while no significant improvement of the performance of the users could be seen on the pointing task, the users were significantly faster when recognizing off-screen content. Also, the introduction of the portable projector reduced the overall task load on both tasks.

Categories

H5.2 [User Interfaces]: Interaction styles. I.3.6 [Methodology and Techniques]: Interaction techniques.

General Terms

Design, Human Factors

Keywords

Interaction techniques, 3D user interface, extended workspace

1. INTRODUCTION

In the modern world, where multitasking is a necessity, multi-display environments are becoming very popular. Especially in companies and research institutes, where effectiveness and

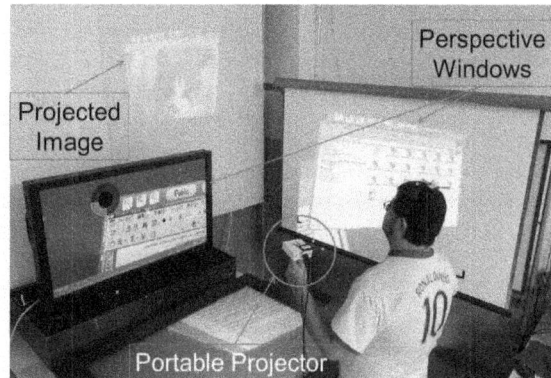

Figure 1: Overview of the proposed system

productivity are very important, more and more people are using multiple screens in order to reasonably get a larger workspace. Indeed, many studies [18, 19] suggest that the task efficiency of the users improves if they are able to access more than one screen of information at a time, without the need of toggling back and forth between multiple windows. However, a weak point of traditional MDE systems is that, once the setup is established, it is not easily modifiable. Yet, the optimal display positioning usually depends on what task the user is performing at the moment. For example, a left-right duo display setup can be efficient when working on spreadsheets, but not for browsing code lines. However, because the users are not able to modify the workspace, they tend to adapt their tasks to the available environment, which can potentially hinder their performance. While systems using traditional MDE setups have been exhaustively researched by innumerous groups [e.g. 2, 16], not many studies have focused on this issue.

Furthermore, ordinary display devices usually assume that the user is looking to the screen from a perpendicular point of view. This causes the content to look distorted from the users' perspective, resulting in decreased visibility and usability [21]. Nacenta et al. developed E-Conic, a perspective aware MDE system [14] that automatically corrects the point of view distortion. This system also allows the users to easily create a seamlessly connected workspace by gathering multiple different displays and three dimensionally arranging them at various angles and positions. Nevertheless, although it does offer more flexibility to the user than a traditional MDE, there is still room for improvement. For example, while a perspective aware system allows the user to work in a seamlessly connected 3D workspace, there are still "holes" (the space between the displays themselves) where the user cannot see the workspace, and there is still space outside the limits of the displays where work could be done (e.g., the walls behind the displays, ceiling, floor or other available surfaces). In this sense, we believe we could further improve the usability of the system if we allowed the users to freely modify the workspace, by changing the position of the displays or even adding new displays to the environment.

In this study, we propose using a portable projector in order to create a temporary, movable new image within the perspective corrected MDE. This allows the user to seamlessly extend the main workspace and adapt it to the current task in real time, creating an even more flexible environment. In our system the users can employ the projector to fill in any gaps between the displays, allowing for a true seamless multi display experience, which can be very useful if they are browsing contents that spread over multiple screens (like a spreadsheet, or a graph) that are physically distant. Also, the projector can be used to extend in real time the available workspace, greatly increasing users' productivity. For example, when browsing a map, the users can easily point the projector over the top of a desktop display to project the image on a wall, revealing a new region of the map, without the need of scrolling down the contents and potentially losing sight of important areas. The perspective-corrected aspect of the system allows us to correctly present the content on the movable screen even when it is projected on a very oblique angle.

In this work, we explore different ways to use the mobile projector (handheld or attached to the head of the user) and different pointing techniques (mouse, laser pointing), and evaluate our system through a series of point-and-click and pattern-recognition tasks. The results of this study will allow us to better understand how to use the portable projector within a perspective corrected MDE, giving us a better base for future development.

The main contributions of this work are: the introduction of a portable projector as a tool to create a new temporary and movable image within a perspective corrected MDE; application scenarios that illustrate how using a portable projector to seamlessly extend the workspace of a MDE can make the system more comfortable to the user; and empirical evidence, compatible with previous results by other groups, that the introduction of the projected image is advantageous to the overall environment.

2. RELATED WORK
2.1 Multi Display Environments
Research on multi display environments has been active for decades now. Earlier work in this field focused on using smaller personal displays (desktop monitors) to single user experience, and using larger displays (tabletops and large vertical displays) to multi-user interaction[10]. More recent works investigate systems composed of combinations of both small and large displays [3, 16], and also systems using tablets and portable computers [11, 17]. However, most of the previous works on MDEs are based on the assumption that the user's line of view is perpendicular to the screen. The objects displayed on the screen are, therefore, rendered under this assumption. However, depending on the relative position between the user and the screen, they may appear distorted from the user's point of view (because of different relative distances, rectangles become trapezoids, circles become ellipsoids and so on). Because of this, tasks like reading texts, clicking on an icon or resizing a window can become harder for the user.

E-conic [14] was proposed as one solution for this problem. It features a perspective aware interface where the content is always

shown perpendicularly to the user's point of view. This system allows the user to seamlessly see and manipulate the contents across various screens disposed at different angles and positions. In their study, Nacenta et al. evaluated the system through 5 tasks that compared the performance of the users when using a perspective corrected MDE and when using a traditional MDE. The results showed that the users performed from 8% to 60% better when using a perspective corrected environment. This shows that having tridimensional information about the objects in a MDE offer great benefits to the user.

2.2 Portable Projectors
Projector devices are becoming increasingly smaller, lighter and powerful. From small and pocket sized projectors, to cell phone accessories and even built-in devices, popularity of portable devices in the market has grown steadily over the last years. Their low weight and small size allows the user to easily carry them around, and the relatively big size of the projected screen makes them suitable for co-located multi-user information sharing.

Many groups have studied the possibilities of using portable projectors for interaction. Cauchard et al. [5] suggested various designs and interaction techniques for mobile and embedded pico-projectors. Beardsley et al. [1] discussed the issue of interacting with the projected image itself, focusing in the problem of moving a cursor across the projection. Hosoi et al. [8] designed a game where users navigate a robot using projected images from their handheld devices. Cauchard et al. [6] showed a technique to dynamically offset the angle of a projection from a handheld device in order to allow users to choose where to display the information. Rapp et al. [15] explored the "Flashlight Metaphor" for handheld projectors, where the users interact as if they were working in a very large workspace, in which only the region illuminated by the projection becomes visible.

Most of the cited works only used one projector and focused on single user experiences. However, the portable nature of handheld projectors allows each user to have their own device, thus opening up many opportunities for interaction. Cao et al. [4] explored a multi-device multi-user scenario using the flashlight metaphor, where the users can share the same workspace while still having individual control over parts of the overall virtual display. Willis et al. [22] designed a handheld projector that allows users to dynamically interact with each other in shared interactive spaces without the need of any external apparatus (like sensors of fixed cameras). Finally, Molyneaux et al. [12] explored two scenarios using handheld projectors combined with depth cameras, achieving a system with great spatial and geometry awareness.

3. SYSTEM OVERVIEW
3.1 Perspective Corrected MDE
E-conic [14] uses two basic functions, perspective windows and perspective cursor, to achieve a seamlessly connected MDE. Both functions utilize the relative positions between the displays and the user. The position of the displays is previously measured and stored in the system (or can be dynamically retrieved by using positional sensors), while the position of the user is tracked in real-time by a 3D position tracking system. These functions allow the system to dynamically change, according to the point of view of the user, the way the contents are shown on the displays.

3.2 Perspective Windows
Perspective windows are able to show the exact same contents as traditional windows (such as pictures, web browsers and so on),

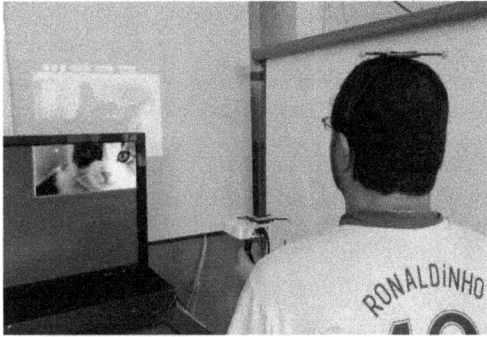

Figure 2: The projected image seamlessly connects with the image from the fixed display (handheld setup)

but also have the ability to change the way the information is presented. Using the relative positional information between the displays and the user, the system can change the appearance of the windows in a way that they appear as if they were perpendicular to the user's line of sight, and are seamlessly seen even if they are spread over several displays. By using perspective windows, the user is able to comfortably observe the content on the displays from any position. As will be detailed later, the perspective windows play a very important role in the rendering of the projected image. Perspective windows can be seen on Figure 1.

3.3 Perspective Cursor

The system also uses the positional information in order to map the Perspective Cursor [13]. By using the perspective cursor, all the screens become connected in a large continuous 3D workspace defined according to the connectivity observed from the point of view of the user. This allows the user to seamlessly move the cursor around and between all the displays even if they are disposed at different planes and angles. The Perspective Cursor is an important technique in our system, because it allows the user to naturally move the cursor between the fixed displays and the projected image, even if the latter is displaced to a new position.

4. PROPOSED SYSTEM

Both in a conventional MDE, and in E-conic, the user cannot easily modify the workspace once the system is set up. In this way, we propose using a portable projector to allow the user to dynamically create a new movable image in the perspective corrected MDE. This new screen allows the user to temporarily expand and efficiently use the workspace.

We use a modified version of E-conic, with a portable projector included. Our system takes into account not only the position of the fixed displays and the user, but the position of the projector and of the projection surfaces as well. The hardware setup used on this study is shown on Figure 1. The static display set consisted of a 50" tabletop display, a 45" vertical plasma display and a 65" vertical projector screen, set at a resolution of 1280x1024. Our system is able to change the image size and the C-D gain on each screen according to its size and resolution, allowing for a smooth and seamless inter-display interaction.

4.1 Image Created using the Portable Projector

In E-conic, the position of the displays is necessary in order to render the seamless workspace. In our system, we include the image created by the portable projector as an additional movable

display in the system. For this reason, it is important to define the position of the projected image in order to use the features of the perspective corrected MDE. It is defined through the position of the portable projector and the position of the projection surfaces. Two LED manual-focus projectors were used as our prototypes during this study: a Dell M110 Ultra-Portable Projector (Res: 800x600, weight: 360g, max. luminosity: 300 ANSI Lumens) and a Sanwa 400-PRJ014 (Res: 800x600, weight: 220g, max. luminosity: 85 ANSI Lumens).

4.1.1 Projection Surfaces

The system allows the user to project the image from the portable projector on any available surface around the fixed displays (like the walls or the ceiling). In our implementation, the system recognizes the projected image as being a *physical* display floating on the projection surface. In this way, from the perspective of the system, there is no difference between projecting an image on a certain point in space and setting a physical display on that position. This allows the content on the projected image to benefit from the same properties (namely, the perspective windows and perspective cursor) of the contents on the fixed displays.

Since the position and orientation of the projection surface is a necessary parameter for calculating the position of the projected image, it should be known beforehand or dynamically measured by adequate 3D sensors. For simplicity, in our specific implementation scenario the projection surfaces were defined as the walls behind the fixed displays. However, as E-conic allows all the displays in the system to be disposed in any position and angle, there is no special limitation constraining their position.

4.1.2 Position of the Center of the Image

The position of the center of the projected image is calculated as the intersection of the direction the projector is facing (which is acquired in real time using the 3D position tracking system) and the projection surface. The projected image is then rendered based on the position of its center relatively to the fixed displays, and a previously defined size and resolution. Although simple mathematical manipulations could be used to change on the fly the size and resolution of the projected screen, in our specific implementation scenario the users do not move relatively to the projection surface (since their movement is constrained by the tabletop display shown on Figure 1), making it unnecessary. This also allows us to use fixed focus on our projectors (nevertheless auto focus laser projectors could also be used).

4.1.3 Contents in the Projected Image

The system allows the user to project the new image on any surface around the fixed displays, and dynamically move it to any desired position. Also, by using the positional information of the displays, the system is able to seamlessly connect the projected image with the fixed screens, as can be seen on Figure 2. (Please note that the user does not see the portion of the image that is being projected on the plasma display, since it is a non-reflexive surface. In order to maintain the seamless aspect of our system, we render the same content of the projector on an adequate position on the plasma display)

In the proposed system, it can be assumed that the users will have a fixed display in front of them most of the time. In this way, the image from the projector will often be projected in a direction that is not perpendicular to the projection surface. As such, the projected image itself will appear distorted, as well as the content. However, if the projection angle is narrow enough (i.e., if the

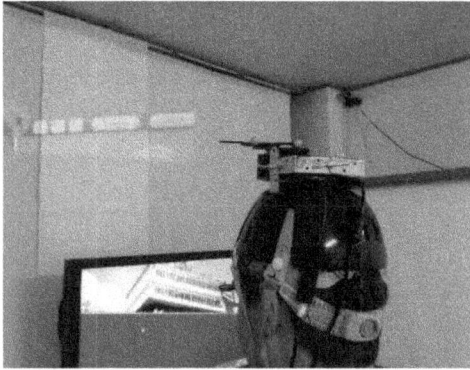

Figure 3: Using the projector head-mounted

image is projected near the fixed display), the distortion will not be too noticeable. Furthermore, the perspective window effect can be used to reduce the distortion of the projected contents.

4.2 Interaction Techniques

We propose two ways to move the projector: using one hand or attached to the head of the user (Figure 3) and two ways of moving the perspective cursor on the screen: using a mouse or using a laser-pointing technique. Then we combine each strategy to move the projector with each strategy to move the cursor, resulting in 4 techniques to be used.

We feel that the head-mounted technique was a reasonable choice for our scenario, since it allows the users to easily keep the projected screen always in front of their eyes, which helps to ease the effects of visual separation cited on previous studies (e.g. [20] and [7]). Moreover, as it is hands-free, the users are able to simultaneously perform other tasks with their hands. Although it can seem to be an unrealistic approach at the first sight, we believe that the increasingly fast advances on miniaturization technology will soon allow projectors to become so small and light that they could be easily attached to a hat or glasses. In this way, our approach could be easily deployed on real-world scenarios.

Other possible alternative choices, as a shoulder mounted projector or a fixed steerable projector were not considered in this study since we feel that the former would be very awkward for the users (especially when moving the projector up and down), while the latter would not fit the basic idea of our study, which is using a portable projector as an ad-hoc extension of a static MDE.

The laser pointer was chosen because it is the most common and familiar way to move a cursor when using large and distant displays, as the ones used in our study. Our pointing device consisted of a 3D marker (whose direction was calculated and used to move the pointer on the screens), with an attached clickable button.

The four combinations presented in this study, handheld + mouse (HandMouse), handheld + laser (HandLaser), head-mounted + mouse (HeadMouse) and head-mounted + laser (HeadLaser), all have their unique features. combine the two most typical ways to move the devices, HandMouse taking advantage of being the way the users are more accustomed to; HandLaser introduces a direct and fast way to move the cursor around the displays; HeadMouse introduces an easy way to keep the projected screen always in front of user's eyes; and HeadLaser allows the user to constantly look to the screens, without any need to look down to reach the mouse.

4.3 Limitations and Tradeoffs

4.3.1 Shadow

In our system, since we are interacting in a workspace composed of physical displays, a bezel is created by the shadow of the display on the projection when projecting between the displays and the dedicated projection space. While it does possess a limitation of our system, since E-Conic (in which our system is based) connects the images on the displays as they are seen from the point of view of the user, the closer the projector is to the line of sight of the user, the smaller will be the occluded portion of the image. When using a portable projector, the users mostly hold it close to their body, which makes the shadow not too noticeable from their point of view. Especially when using the projector head-mounted (in which the projector is placed very close to the users' point of view) the effects of the shadow become almost negligible, which is another positive point towards the use of this technique.

4.3.2 Size and Weight of the Projector

When using portable projectors, it is necessary to consider the tradeoff between maximum luminosity and size/weight of the projector. Although there are various pico-projectors in the market that are far smaller and lighter than the ones used on our study, they are usually not bright enough to project on distant surfaces. In this way, we chose not so light yet bright enough projectors to be used in our study. The projectors are small enough to be easily carried with one hand and light enough so they can be attached to the body of the user (the head, for example) without excessive burden, while still giving a reasonably bright image in a mild illuminated room.

5. INTERACTION SCENARIO

The addition of a movable projected image to the MDE system allows the user to expand, in any direction, the workspace defined by the fixed displays. This opens many possibilities for new interaction techniques which would not be possible on traditional or existing MDEs. In this work we highlight two simple interaction techniques.

5.1 Extending the Visible Workspace

Sometimes, the user needs to see contents that extend over the limits of the fixed displays. For example, if the user is browsing through a map and wants to see a region that is being shown outside the display; or if the user is working on a spreadsheet and wants to see the data in a column that is over the limits of the display. In a usual environment, the user should drag the contents so the desired area become visible on the screen, or should make them smaller so the whole information fits on the display. However, by dragging the content the user loses sight of part of the contents that were previously shown on the screen; and by making them smaller, the overall visibility of the data is reduced. Also, both operations (point-and-click and point-and-drag tasks) are potentially time consuming.

We propose using the portable projector to expand the main workspace in a way the users can easily access the otherwise "hidden" information. The user can simply point the projector to the desired area, and the information is shown in the projected image, as if the fixed display was expanded on that direction. Also, the perspective corrected system allows this expansion to be completely seamless. This interaction allows the user to take a quick look on the information outside the displays before deciding if this information needs to be brought to the main workspace. If

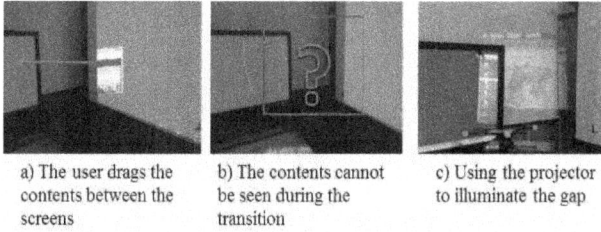

a) The user drags the contents between the screens

b) The contents cannot be seen during the transition

c) Using the projector to illuminate the gap

Figure 4: Cross-display interaction in a perspective-corrected MDE

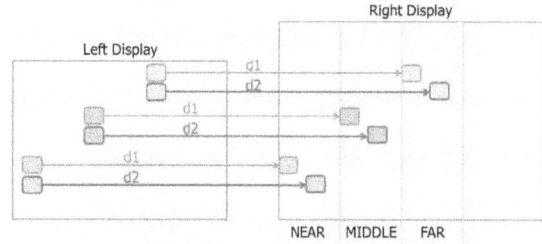

Figure 5: Position and distance between the targets on the point-and-click task

the information is not necessary, the user simply moves the projector away. On the other hand, if it is necessary, the user can drag it (possibly using the projector itself) to the main workspace.

The proposed method is expected to be substantially easier and faster than the previous interaction techniques (point, click and drag the contents). Also, it should be more comfortable for the users since they are able to have a quick look of the information without actually moving (or resizing) it, thus improving the effectiveness of the system.

5.2 Improving the Seamlessness of the System

When using a MDE system composed of displays of different sizes disposed on various angles, it is probable that there will be gaps between the screens. While the perspective MDE used in this study minimizes this problem by allowing the user to work in a seamlessly connected workspace, the usability of the system is still constrained by the physical position of the displays. This happens because in order to keep the visual consistency of the seamlessly connected workspace (and also to correctly map the Perspective Cursor), a virtual gap between the displays is necessary when they are physically separated (as can be seen on Figure 4). In this way, although the workspace itself is seamless, the user is only able to interact in the visible portion of it. An example of this issue can be seen on Figure 4b.

We propose using the handheld projector to illuminate the gaps between the displays during the interaction. The projected image creates a connected visible workspace, improving the seamlessness of the system. It is expected that this interaction will make the system easier and more intuitive to use.

5.3 Exploratory User Experience

5.3.1 Method

In order to better understand the behavior of our system, we performed a preliminary user study, where five participants (all male, ages between 23 and 31 years old, right handed) were invited to test and give their opinions about the proposed system.

We designed two simple tasks based on the interaction techniques presented in section 5.1 and 5.2. On Task 1, in order to investigate the intuitiveness of the proposed interaction, we asked the participants to discover the content of a window positioned partially outside one of the fixed displays. They could use the cursor to drag the window to a position where the contents could be seen in full, or they could position the portable projector in a way the hidden part of the window become visible. On Task 2, in order to investigate the seamlessness of the proposed system, we asked the participants to move a window between two displays with a gap between them (as shown on Figure 4). In the first scenario, the participants should move the window without using the projector to illuminate the gap. In the second, they should illuminate the gap with the projector while moving the window.

The study was conducted on 4 sessions (one for each technique presented on section 4.2). On each session, the user was asked to try the system freely for 5 minutes and then to perform the two tasks described on the paper. After each session, the users were given two questionnaires, one containing 7 questions about the usability of the system (easiness, simplicity, intuitiveness, quickness, seamlessness, enjoyableness, satisfaction), graduated on a 7-point scale; and one containing questions about the task load (using the NASA Task Load Index). Finally, the users answered a questionnaire about their overall experience, which also asked for free comments about the system.

5.3.2 Results

According to the results about the usability of the interaction techniques, HeadMouse performed overall better than the other techniques. In particular it was considered more intuitive (average scores: HandMouse: 5.0, HandLaser: 5.2, HeadMouse: 5.6, HeadLaser: 5.4) and simpler (HandMouse: 5.4, HandLaser: 4.8, HeadMouse: 5.6, HeadLaser: 5.6) to use. The users also felt that the system seemed to be more seamless when using this technique (HandMouse: 5.6, HandLaser: 5.4, HeadMouse: 5.8, HeadLaser: 5.2). Nonetheless, all the four techniques received relatively high scores. In addition, the total average scores for NASA TLX (HandMouse: 3.68, HandLaser: 4.53, HeadMouse: 4.19, HeadLaser: 4.31) showed that none of the techniques was excessively demanding to the users. These results were further verified according to the free comments from the users.

6. QUANTITATIVE USER STUDY

While the previous study gave us better insights about the usability of the proposed system, a more throughout examination is necessary in order to evaluate how the introduction of the portable projector impacts the system as a whole. In this way, two controlled user studies were performed. 6 subjects (ages between 21 and 24 years old, 5 right-handed and 1 left-handed, 4 male and 2 female) were asked to perform the two tasks explained below. On both tasks, the projector was kept on all the time, and put away when not necessary. In these studies, although the previous results indicated that HeadMouse performs better in this kind of scenario, we chose to use HandMouse, since it seemed to be more familiar to the users (thus minimizing any learning effects). HandnMouse also performed relatively well on the previous study, making it suitable for the qualitative user study. In this way, the subjects moved the mouse with their dominant hand, and used their other hand to move the projector, except when the task asked them to use only the projector (in this case, the subjects moved the projector with their dominant hand). After each task, the users were asked to answer a NASA-TLX test.

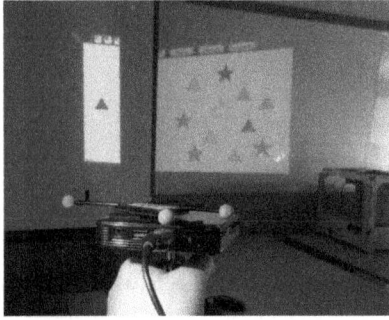

Figure 6: User performing the pattern-recognition task

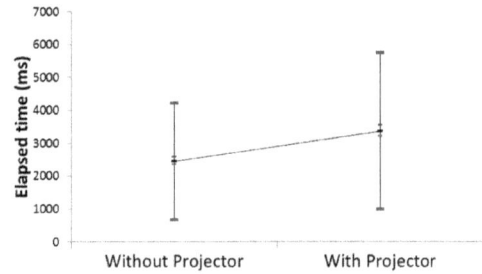

Figure 7: Average task completion time
(Pointing Task)

6.1 Pointing Task

We designed a task based on Fitts' experiment, in order to investigate how the introduction of a projected image impacts user performance on pointing tasks across a gap between multiple displays.

6.1.1 Experimental Design

We used a simple 4-factor design, interaction technique x target distance x target location x direction. A repeated measurement within subject design included 2 interaction techniques (with/without projector), 2 possible target distances (710 mm and 760 mm), 3 possible target positions (near, middle distance and far from the gap) and 2 possible directions (forwards and backwards movement). The position of the target was chosen as a factor since it is expected that the closer the target is to the gap, the larger the number of overshoots (when the user moves the cursor farther than necessary) will be.

We used an all crossed design that resulted on 24 combinations with 3 repetitions, in a total of 72 trials per participant. A counter balanced order of techniques was set among participants to reduce order effects. The task design can be seen on Figure 5.

6.1.2 Task

The task consisted in clicking back and forth between two targets positioned on different displays separated by a physical gap between them, similar to the previous experiment (Figure 4a). For each cycle (click on START, click on FINISH, click back on START), it was measured the time between each click, the number of miss-clicks (clicks outside the targets) and if the user overshot the target or not (move the cursor farther than necessary), for both the forward and the backwards movements. Although it would be possible to make the target to appear *in* the gap, we chose to use a separated task (Pattern-recognition) to highlight interactions with content outside the displays.

The users should perform the task once without the projector, and once using the projector to illuminate the gap. When using the projector, the participants were asked to position the projected screen just in front of their eyes, click the start target, move the projector to illuminate the gap, and then move the cursor. We chose to design the task in that way in order to highlight the mobility of the portable projector (otherwise, the user could continuously illuminate the gap with the projector during the task, which could influence the results).

6.2 Pattern-recognition Task

We also designed a pattern-recognition task in order to evaluate if using the projector is a faster technique than using a mouse to discover the contents of a window partially off-screen.

6.2.1 Experimental Design

We used a 2-factor design, interaction technique x number of patterns. A repeated task within the subjects included interaction technique (with/without projector) and 3 possible numbers of patterns (4, 5 or 6 patterns). The all-crossed design resulted on 6 possible combinations with 3 repetitions, in a total of 18 trials per participant.

6.2.2 Task

Similarly to the task explained on section 5.1, the participants were presented with a window positioned partially outside the screen. In order to discover the hidden contents, they can drag the window to a position where the contents can be seen in full, or they can use the projector to illuminate the outside area. The window is positioned in a way that the content to the right of a vertical line appear off-screen. The task is to find the number of shapes similar to the one shown to the left of the vertical line (in this example, the task is to find the total number of triangles on the right image, and the answer is 6). The task is performed using the projector and also without it (in this case, the user drags the window using a mouse), and repeated for various different images (with different shapes and number of figures) presented in a random order. An example of using the projector to discover off-screen content can be seen on Figure 6. We measured the task completing time, and checked the number of errors. It is expected that the task completing time will be much shorter using the projector than using the mouse to drag the window.

This task evaluates the seamless aspect of our system, by asking the participants to compare parts of the same window shown in different displays (in this case, the projection screen on the left and the projection from the portable projector on the right on Figure 6). Also, it evaluates the validity of using a movable projected screen as an ad-hoc extension to the workspace defined by the fixed displays.

6.3 Results and Discussion

6.3.1 Pointing Task

Completion Time: A four-way ANOVA by technique, distance, area and direction was carried out on the task completion time. We found a main effect of technique (F (1, 408) = 20.47, p < .001), and no effects of the other parameters. A Tukey HSD test showed that the introduction of the portable projector brought a significant (albeit small) increase in the overall task completion time (as can be seen on Figure 7). This result is within our expectations, since our interaction adds one more step to the pointing task, because the users need to actively position the projector in order to illuminate the gap before moving the cursor. We believe that this increased time could be minimized by using the head-mounted strategy for moving the projector, since our

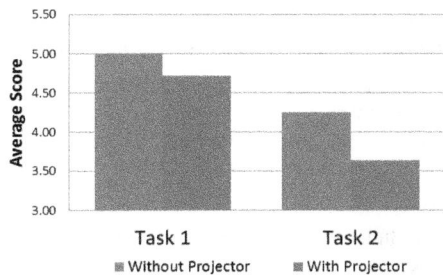

Figure 8: Averaged score of NASA TLX test

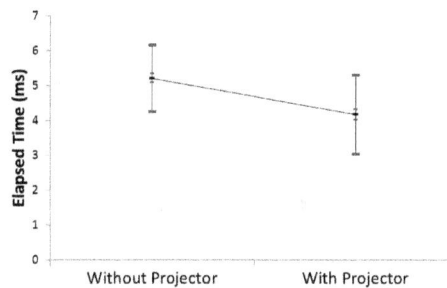

Figure 9: Average task completion time (Pattern Recognition Task)

previous study showed it to be faster and easier for the users. Also, it allows the user to iluminate the gap naturaly just by looking at it, which does not effectively add a new step to the task (compared with not using the projector at all). This technique will be studied in further details in a next work.

Number of overshots/missclicks: A four-way ANOVA by technique, distance, area and direction was carried out on the number of overshoots and number of miss-clicks. Although previous studies have shown that a physical gap between displays does hinder users' performance on cross-display tasks [9], and thus filling this gap with the projected image should be beneficial to the overall system, no significant difference was found between using or not the projector. We believe that, although the visual feedback itself (provided by the projector) is a beneficial effect to the overall performance of the users, the bimanual nature of the proposed interaction hinders their performance. Moreover, the proposed task showed to be excessively easy to the users, generating a small number of overshoots and miss-clicks on both techniques. Time restraints prevented a more throughout study at this point, but better design choices, as tasks involving cross-displays dragging (instead of pointing) and context-based tasks, as well as more difficult settings (e.g. smaller cursor, wider gaps and so on), together with body-mounted techniques for moving the projector will be considered on future studies.

NASA TLX: The averaged result of a NASA TLX test for all the users showed a small yet significant (5.6%) decrease in the task load between using the projector and not using it (Figure 8, left). Although our proposed interaction, by being a bimanual task, increases the physical and mental demands of the users, the test result showed that their levels of frustration and effort decrease. This result shows that, even though the performance of the users wasn't optimum, they did enjoy using our proposed system.

6.3.2 Pattern Recognition Task

Task completion time: A two-way ANOVA by technique and number of objects was carried out on the task completion time. We found a main effect on both technique (F (1, 102) = 28.84, p < .001) and number of objects (F (2, 102) = 7.32, p < .001). A Tuckey HSD test on technique showed that using the projector was significantly faster than using the mouse (Figure 9). This is within our expectations, since the users only need to point out the projector to find the hidden contents, while they need to point out and drag the window with the mouse (which is potentially time consuming) in order to complete the task. The perspective correction also played an important role, allowing the participants to correctly see the content even if the projection is oblique to the surface, creating a true seamless extension of the workspace.

NASA TLX: The averaged score of the NASA TLX test showed a reduction of 14.6% the task load on the subjects when using the projector (Figure 8, right). This confirms the results of the preliminary user experience, which suggested that using the portable projector to expand the workspace makes the system easier and faster to the users.

6.3.3 Discussion

The overall result opens up for ideas for interactions exploring the features shown on both the Pointing and Pattern-recognition tasks. On the pointing task, the overall task completion time was slightly longer when using the projector, while it was shorter on the pattern recognition task. Nevertheless, NASA TLX showed a reduction of the task load on both tasks. In this way, it can be interesting to explore the performance of the users in tasks that combine cross-displays interactions with off-screen content recognition.

However, due to time restraints we weren't able to gather a sufficient number of participants. Although we did get some interesting results, we understand that they should be taken only as a grain of salt, as more participants are needed in order to get more elusive data.

7. CONCLUSION AND FUTURE WORK

We proposed multiple ways to use a portable projector within a perspective corrected multi display environment. Our method allies the stability of a static MDE with the dynamicity of a portable projector, in order to design new interactive ways to use such system. We proposed two ways to use the projector (head-mounted and handheld) and two ways to move the cursor on the screens (mouse and laser pointer), combined in 4 possible techniques. Two interaction scenarios were proposed in order to evaluate these techniques, aiming to fill the physical gaps between displays, and to seamlessly extend the interaction workspace. The results of an exploratory user study showed that all the four techniques make the system more seamless and intuitive, without excessively demanding to the users.

Also, a quantitative user study was performed in order to further evaluate our proposed system. The results showed that while our system didn't show any significant improvement on user performance in a cross-display task, it did significantly reduce the user task load. Also, to use the projector to recognize off-screen content showed to be significantly faster than using a mouse. However, we understand that the reduced number of participants (6 participants) could have an effect on our results, and thus more throughout examination should be necessary. We intend to perform the described tasks again with more participants in the near future, as well as developing newer evaluation techniques.

In this work we separately explored the impact of the projector on the seamlessness and usability of the system. Next work will focus on merging the features of both pointing and pattern-recognition tasks in order to explore how the projector contributes to the overall system, as well as developing more throughout evaluation techniques.

Subsequent works will also explore body-mounted strategies to moving the projector, in order to avoid bimanual task operations. Also, we plan to explore possibilities for multi user support as well, using multiple portable projectors. In order to make the system even more flexible, real-time measurement of the position of the projection surfaces will also be necessary. For this purpose, we intend to explore combinational use of a set of cameras and a structured light subliminally thrown by the portable projector, as well as other position measurement techniques.

ACKNOWLEDGEMENTS

This work was supported in part by JSPS KAKENHI Grant Number 24650034. The authors would also like to thank all the involved in this project, for their cooperation and insightful opinions and suggestions.

REFERENCES

[1] Beardsley, P., Baar, J. V., Raskar, R., and Forlines, C. "Interaction using a handheld projector," IEEE Computer Graphics and Applications, pp. 39-43, 2005.

[2] Bi, X. and Balakrishnan, R. "Comparing usage of a large high-resolution display to single or dual desktop displays for daily work," In Proc. of Conference on Human Factors in Computing Systems, pp. 1005-1014, 2009.

[3] Biehl, J. T. and Bailey, B. P. "ARIS: an interface for application relocation in an interactive space," In Proc. of Graphics Interface, pp. 107-116, 2004.

[4] Cao, X., Forlines, C. and Balakrishnan, R., "Multi-user interaction using handheld projectors," In Proc. of Symposium on User Interface Software and Technology, pp. 43-52, 2007.

[5] Cauchard, J., Fraser, M. and Subramanian, S., "Mobile multi-display environments," In Adjunct Proc. of Symposium on User Interface Software and Technology, pp. 39-42, 2011.

[6] Cauchard, J., R., Fraser, M., Alexander, J. and Subramanian, S. "Offsetting displays on mobile projector phones," In Proc. of UbiProjection 2010.

[7] Cauchard, J., R., Löchtefeld, M., Irani, P., Schoening, J., Krüger, A., Fraser, M. and Subramanian, S. "Visual separation in mobile multi-display environments," In Proc. of Symposium on User Interface Software and Technology, pp. 451-460, 2011.

[8] Hosoi, K., Dao, V.N., Mori, A. and Sugimoto, M. "CoGAME: Manipulation using a handheld projector," In Proc. of Conference and Exhibition on Computer Graphics and Interactive Techniques Emerging Technologies, article No. 2, 2007.

[9] Hutchings, D., "An investigation of Fitts' law in a multiple-display environment," In Proc. of Conference on Human Factors in Computing Systems, pp. 3181-3184, 2012.

[10] Kraemer, K., L. and King, J., L. "Computer-based systems for cooperative work and group decision making," ACM Computing Surveys 20, pp. 115-146, 1988.

[11] Lyons, K., Pering, T., Rosario, B., Sud, S. and Want, R. "Multi-display composition: supporting display sharing for collocated mobile devices," In Proc. of Conference on Human-Computer Interaction, pp. 758-771, 2009.

[12] Molyneaux, D., Izadi, S., Kim, D., Hilliges, O., Hodges, S., Cao, X., Butler, A. and Gellersen, H. "Interactive environment-aware handheld projectors for pervasive computing spaces," In Proc. of International Conference on Pervasive Computing, pp. 197-215, 2012.

[13] Nacenta, M., A, Sallam, S., Champoux, B., Subramanian, S. and Gutwin, C. "Perspective Cursor: perspective-based interaction for multi-display environments," In Proc. of Conference on Human Factors in Computing Systems, pp. 289-298, 2006.

[14] Nacenta, M., A., Sakurai, S., Yamaguchi, T., Miki Y., Itoh Y., Kitamura Y., Subramanian S. and Gutwin, C., "E-conic a perspective-aware interface for multi-display environments," In Proc. of Symposium on User Interface Software and Technology, pp. 279-288, 2007.

[15] Rapp, S., Michelitsch, G., Osen, M., Williams, J., Barbisch, M., Bohan, R., Valsan, Z. and Emele M. "Spotlight Navigation: Interaction with a handheld projection device," In proc. of International Conference on Pervasive Computing, pp 397-400, 2004.

[16] Rekimoto, J., "A multiple device approach for supporting whiteboard based interactions," In Proc. of Conference on Human Factors in Computing Systems, pp. 344-351, 1998.

[17] Rekimoto, J. and Saitoh, M., "Augmented surfaces: a spatially continuous work space for hybrid computing environments," In Proc. of Conference on Human Factors in Computing Systems, pp. 378-385, 1999.

[18] Richtel., M., "In data deluge, multitaskers go to multiscreens," The New York Times February 2012. http://www.nytimes.com/2012/02/08/technology/for-multitaskers-multiplemonitors-improve-office-efficiency.html (accessed in February 10, 2012).

[19] Ross, S. "Two screens are better than one," Microsoft Research 2003. http://research.microsoft.com/en-us/news/features/vibe.aspx (accessed in February 10, 2012).

[20] Tan, D., S. and Czerwinski, M., "Effects of visual separation and physical discontinuities when distributing information across multiple displays," In Proc. of Conference on Human-Computer Interaction, pp. 252-255, 2003.

[21] Wigdor, D., Shen, C., Forlines, C. and Balakrishnan, R. "Effects of display position and control space orientation on user preference and performance," In Proc. of Conference on Human Factors in Computing Systems, pp. 309-318, 2006.

[22] Willis, K., D., D., Poupyrev, I., Hudson, S., E. and Mahler, M., "SideBySide: ad-hoc multi-user interaction with handheld projectors," In Proc. of Symposium on User Interface Software and Technology, pp. 431-440, 2011.

Free-Hands Interaction in Augmented Reality

Dragoş Datcu   Stephan Lukosch
Faculty of Technology, Policy and Management
Delft University of Technology
Jaffalaan 5, 2628BX
Delft, The Netherlands
{d.datcu; s.g.lukosch}@tudelft.nl

ABSTRACT

The ability to use free-hand gestures is extremely important for mobile augmented reality applications. This paper proposes a computer vision-driven model for natural free-hands interaction in augmented reality. The novelty of the research is the use of robust hand modeling by combining Viola&Jones and Active Appearance Models. A usability study evaluates the hands free interaction model in with a focus on the accuracy of hand based pointing for menu navigation and menu item selection. The results indicate high accuracy of pointing and high usability of the free-hands interaction in augmented reality. The research is part of a joint project of TU Delft and the Netherlands Forensic Institute in The Hague, aiming at the development of novel technologies for crime scene investigations.

Categories and Subject Descriptors

H.1.2 [**User/Machine Systems**]: Human factors
H.5.2 [**User Interfaces**]: Interaction styles

General Terms

Algorithms, Measurement, Performance.

Keywords

Free-Hands Interaction, Augmented Reality, Crime Scene Investigation.

1. INTRODUCTION

Augmented reality technology already proved to offer viable solutions for hand motion and gesture interaction in assembly design [35], real-time hand gesture interface for surgeons for controlling and navigating medical images from MRIs, CTs [1] and X-rays [34], teleconferencing [2], entertainment [31] and conceptual design and prototyping [32].

Within a joint project of TU Delft and The Netherlands Forensic Institute – NFI in The Hague [43], novel tools to help the personnel involved in crime scene investigation (CSI) have been developed to more efficiently investigate a crime scene. Figure 1 illustrates a CSI investigator wearing the augmented reality equipment and performing free-hand gesture interaction with the system. Such tools provide support at the crime scene for collecting and processing forensic data, and for the collaboration between local

investigators and experts giving assistance from remote locations [8][25].

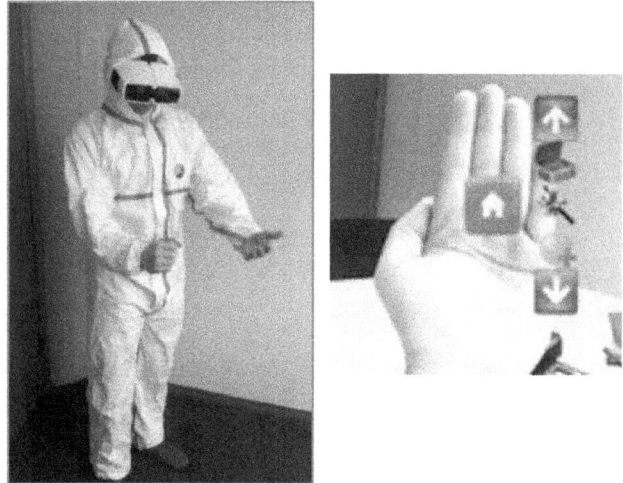

Figure 1. Crime scene investigator accessing the augmented reality interface by free-hand gestures.

In line with requirements elicited in open discussions with five international CSI experts at the early stage of the project (see Table 1), Poelman et al. previously realized a system prototype [25] based on augmented reality that includes a computer vision based free-hand gesture interface.

Table 1. Requirements for the CSI system [25]

R1	Contactless augmentation alignment (no markers on the crime scene) to keep the crime scene as uncontaminated as possible.
R2	Lightweight head-mounted display (HMD).
R3	Connection with experts working remotely.
R4	Bare hands gestures for user interface operation to have free-hands to physically interact with the crime scene.

According to these requirements, the CSI application scenario has to rely on free-hands interaction in augmented reality. The augmented reality headset is the only hardware equipment allowed (according to requirement **R2**). Voice recognition is not applicable because of the potentially noisy environment. Wearing special gloves with additional sensors or makers is not possible as those need to be easily exchanged. Using active devices such as GestureWrist [46] or wrist-worn 3D hand tracker [45] are not to be considered as possibilities as the head mounted device already adds enough technology in the view of crime scene investigators. Also, no other physical buttons, mouse devices, mobile devices are allowed (according to requirement **R1**). Given these constrains, this paper focuses on novel free-hands pointing methods for menu navigation and menu item selection.

During test sessions run at the NFI field lab, several issues linked to the human computer interface that make the free-hands interaction still a challenging task were noticed [21]. More specifically, free-hands selection and pointing operations (requirement R4) cannot be successfully performed in all environments and by all users due to the limited robustness of the computer vision models previously developed for detecting and processing the hand. According to Billinghurst and Thomas [3], however, it is essential to allow users to easily point to or select small details like menu items in the augmented view.

Motivated by the need to develop more precise free-hand interaction, this paper novel approach for tracking free-hands for user interface interaction in augmented reality and evaluates the usability and accuracy. The presented approach combines algorithms of Viola&Jones hand detection [33], tracking using optical flow with AGAST visual features [22] and Active Appearance Models [6] for hand contour extraction for free-hand interaction in augmented reality for the CSI domain. Thereby, it addresses the following requirements:

- Selection of the menu items using free-hand gestures.
- Robust and precise hand detection and tracking in conditions of varying illumination and limited occlusions.
- Hand as a 3D pointing device.

The rest of the paper has the following structure: the next section presents related work on hand interaction for augmented reality. The following section presents the details on the hand based interaction design and the system architecture to support free-hand interaction. The following section reports on the achieved pointing accuracy. Then, the setup and results of the usability study are described. Finally, conclusions are presented and future work is discussed.

2. RELATED WORK

Local systems like the ones described in [2][9][16][18][32][34][26][31][13] are physically located in a fixed environment, generally allow for high precision sensors mounted as part of that environment, have a relatively small set of events to handle, and benefit from controlled view and lighting conditions. Therefore they generally present better performance. Compared to a user in a desktop scenario for which there is barely any limitation when choosing between various sensing devices, the mobile systems [4][11][44] require users to have as few and as lightweight as possible physical devices to carry.

Sensors tracking body, hand and finger movements such as Microsoft Kinect [40], Asus WAVI Xtion or Leap Motion [41] have already opened and continue to expand the horizon of possibilities for human computer interaction [23]. The work of Radkowski and Stritzke [26] presents a Kinect based system for augmented reality that allows users to use both hands to select, manipulate and assemble 3D models of mechanical systems. Hackenberg et al. [13] propose a method based on a fast light-independent gesture and hand tracking algorithm using a time-of-flight camera for 6-DOF barehanded 3D multi-touch interaction. Reifinger et al. [28] propose an automatic hand-gesture recognition system for augmented reality applications that makes use of distance classifiers to process static gestures like pointing and grasping and of statistical model classifiers for dynamic gestures such as drawing letters in the air. The user wears two light weighted infrared tracking targets at his thumb and index finger. The above approaches all rely on location information from additional sensors. Unfortunately, additional sensors are not applicable in the CSI scenario.

Hand detection and tracking for free-hand interaction is done by skin color segmentation [4] [5] [12] [16][18][36][37][30][34][47], markers [17], colored markers attached to user's fingertips [32], depth camera information [2][7][24][26], or by whole hand patterns described in terms of Haar-like features [1][9][10][44]. The systems that allow for interaction by using two hands simultaneously [11][9][7][32] [30][17] present the advantage of handling more complex operations in shorter time. Depending on the complexity of the gestures to be recognized, some systems employ detection and tracking at the finger level [4][32][30][35][9]. Skin color hand segmentation is generally not robust to dynamic contexts and varying lighting illumination therefore not appropriate to be used in the CSI scenario.

Song et al. [31] use a stereo camera and background subtraction technique to track the user's hands and fingers in 3D space for mixed reality games with physics simulation. Fang et al. [9] use Adaboost classifier for hand detection and optical flow on flock of hand color features to obtain stable hand tracking. After segmenting the hand area using HSV color space, multi-scale features are detected across the binary image to properly recognize six categories of gestures. Yao et al. [36] describe a hand gesture classifier that is learned through online principal component analysis with a subspace updating mechanism that can be adjusted adaptively to different situations. The CamShift algorithm is used to compute the position of the hand center and the Kalman filter to accurately track the hand even in situations when the hand is covered by other objects. Liu and Lovell [19] advance an active statistical model for hand gesture extraction and recognition. After applying skin color based segmentation on HSV color space, the Camshift algorithm and the Kalman filter algorithm track the hand in the video sequence and Active Shape Model is used to determine the contour of the hand. Hu et al. [15] present a novel hand pointing estimation system using two regular cameras, including hand region detection and hand finger estimation. The authors use Active Appearance Models to extract and track 14 key points along the hand contour from a top view and a side view. The 3D pointing direction estimation is then obtained by combining the results from the two views. Active Appearance Models are used by Gross et al [11] to track the hand and to extract features for identification in a biometric and identification setup.

The discussed approaches for free-hand interaction offer solutions that are limited to their initial application domains. However, the applicability of such hand interaction models to the CSI scenario is not feasible due to the restrictions imposed by requirements R1-R4 (Table 1). No external hardware sensors at the crime scene or attached to the investigator's body are allowed. Computer vision methods are to be used for the solution. Hand detection based on color or foreground segmentation algorithms are not robust enough for light-changing, dynamic environment. Hand detectors that model hand shape and texture are to be investigated.

3. DESIGN

Free-hand gesture interaction has to be user adaptive, user friendly and gesture independent [27]. The presented approach provides user-adaptive interaction by using novel method to robustly process hands in dynamic environments like in CSI domain. User-friendliness and gesture independence is addressed by defining four intuitive hand postures for menu navigation and selection (see Figure 2). The designed free-hands interaction requires the user to use both hands simultaneously. Navigation and selection tasks are supported by automatic detection of hand objects and extraction of hand shapes. Time-based touch-less triggers in augmented reality are activated by holding the cursor for certain time over the sensitive areas of menu items. This mechanism supports the control of the cursor for menu navigation and menu items selection with the dominant hand. The non-dominant hand controls the location of menu in AR view. The menu automatically disappears after few seconds from the moment non-dominant hand is detected or after some time period without interaction by dominant hand.

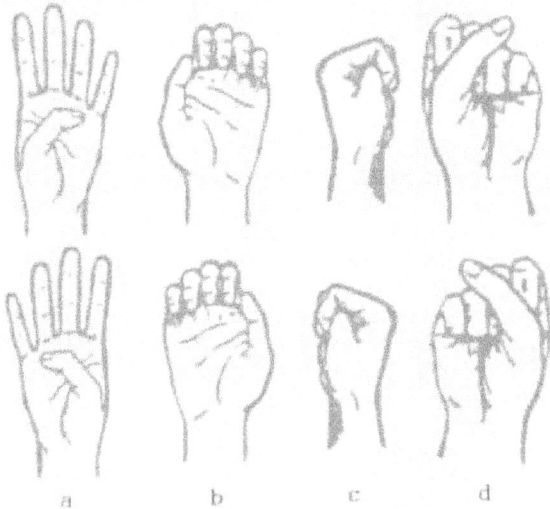

Figure 2. Left (top) and right (down) hand postures considered for 2D detection.

In the current approach the detection of dominant and non-dominant hands is done using robust hand detection by adapted Viola&Jones object detectors [33]. These detectors compute 2D rectangular regions of hands, for different hand postures.

The rectangular region of non-dominant hand is used to position the menu in AR. To improve the menu positioning, 2D hand contours are computed by Active Appearance Models [6]. Based on location of specific key points on the contour of non-dominant hand, 3D spatial orientation of the menu is determined using a pose estimation algorithm for planar targets viewed by a perspective camera [29].

Similarly, pointing with the dominant hand is roughly approximated relative to the boundaries of rectangular region determined by Viola&Jones detector. Active Appearance Models are used to further refine the pointing location for different hand postures. The tracking of hands is done using Lukas-Kanade optical flow [20] running on AGAST visual features [22].

3.1 Hand Detection

Viola&Jones method has been initially proposed as a fast technique to perform object detection [33]. This method uses discrete Adaboost, a supervised method that performs binary classification. During training, a so-called strong classifier is iteratively generated by adding several so-called weak classifiers that perform just better than random guessing. Each weak classifier is trained on a data set generated by applying resampling or re-weighting on the instances of the original hand data set.

In the context of hand detection, this method uses four types of simple features derived from pixel intensities over adjacent regions on the surface of the hand.

Table 2 shows the true positive rate, the precision and the speed (in frames per second) indicators of the fist posture classifier (1433 images) and of the palm posture classifier (755 images) on a processor Intel Core i7-2720QM@2.20Ghz running Windows 7 operating system. All the hand image samples used for testing were not part of the data set used for training. The speed of the classifiers is computed given a resolution of 320 pixels width and 240 pixels height.

Table 2. Classification performance

Detector	True positive rate	Precision	Fps
Fist	81.72%	99.57%	18
Palm	74.93%	86.18%	20

3.2 Active Appearance Hand Model

Active appearance model (AAM) [6] is a statistical method that handles shape and texture variations of photo-realistic appearance. Seen as a top-down approach, AAM makes use of prior knowledge on the grey-level appearance, shape structures as well as their relationships, in order to build generative models for the global analysis of a specific class of objects.

In the current approach, several hand-oriented AAMs are used to retrieve the 2D shapes of palm and fist posture in AR, following a series of local analyses, all starting from locations within or around the Viola&Jones rectangular hand area. A local analysis consists of an iterative process taking the average hand appearance at the beginning and gradually decreasing the fitting error by adjusting the model parameters. The fitting error E is the error for iteratively matching the model hand to the image hand.

Running several AAM analyses with different values of the translation, rotation and scaling parameters overcomes the limited performance of a single AAM and increases the chance to correctly extract the shape of the image hand. The hand AAM model with the lowest fitting error provides the key points and contours identifying the shape of the hand in the image.

A small set of key points of the hand shape is further considered to improve the positioning of the menu by non-dominant hand and to estimate the location of the tip of the pointer finger by the dominant hand.

The extraction of shape and texture of the hand from an image is equivalent to an optimization problem that involves the criterion of minimizing the difference between the real hand image and the one generated by the appearance model. The distance measure can be written as follows: $r(p) = g_{im} + g_m$, where g_{im} is the vector of grey level values of the hand patch in the input image and g_m is the vector of grey level values for the hand image as it is estimated by the current model parameters p.

The matching implies finding the optimal appearance model parameters which would lead to the minimization of a scalar measure on the image difference, such as the sum of squares of elements $E(p) = r^T r$.

Building a hand appearance model implies a prior acquisition of a hand data set for each hand posture. Each hand sample is consistently annotated with a set of landmark points. Each sample of hand shape is described using n 2D key points forming a shape vector: $x = (x_1, ..., x_n, y_1, ..., y_n)^T$, where $n = 62$. The 2D points in shape vector define separate contours of convex regions for each finger and palm base (see examples in Figure 3). Extreme deformations of the hand shape are not intended for being modeled by AAM. Further statistical analysis is applied so as to obtain shape data samples represented in the same coordinate system.

The appearance model parameters c and shape transformation parameters t identify the position of the model points in the image. For matching, pixels are sampled around the image region g_{im} and then the texture model is computed $g_s = T_u^{-1}(g_{im})$. The model texture can be written as: $g_m = \overline{g} + Q_g c$ and so the difference between the model and the image may be written as follows: $r(p) = g_s + g_m$ and $p^T = (c^T, t^T, u^T)$. The hand texture is collected by a customized rasterisation technique that samples pixels on the surface of the hand from individual closed contours of AAM shape. The appearance model may be written as: $x = \overline{x} + P_s W_s^{-1} P_{cs} c$ and $g = \overline{g} + P_g P_{cg} c$, where P_{cs} and P_{cg} are matrices describing the modes of variation and W_s is introduced as the weight that compensates for the units of distance and units of pixel intensity.

The model hand is fit to the image hand during an iterative procedure that alters the model parameters c, pose t and texture transformation u until the error $E(p)$ gets into an acceptable range. For a specific current residual, a p is chosen so that the value of $|r(p + \delta p)|^2$ is minimum. The choice has the form: $\delta p = -R r(p)$, where: $R = \left(\frac{\partial r^T}{\partial p} \frac{\partial r}{\partial p} \right)^{-1} \frac{\partial r^T}{\partial p}$. The term $\frac{\partial r}{\partial p}$ is computed once, during training, by altering the elements of p with some amount (typically up to 0.5 standard deviation) and by computing the residuals for the hand images in the training data set.

4. POINTING ACCURACY

This section presents an analysis of the pointing accuracy for menu navigation and menu item selection in AR when using a Viola&Jones palm detector to estimate the location of the tip of pointer finger, relative to the boundaries of detected rectangular hand area and when using Active Appearance Models to enable finger-based pointing. The experimental setup implies pointing with the tip of pointer finger from the dominant hand to control the location of the cursor.

4.1 Technical Setup

In the AR system, the models for detection, recognition and tracking are implemented using C++ programming language, Boost::Thread library [42] for parallel computing and the open computer vision library OpenCV [38]. Hand detection and tracking run simultaneously on video streams from both left and right video cameras attached to the augmented reality glasses. The graphical interface is implemented using C++ programming language and Ogre library for 3D rendering [39].

4.2 Experimental Setup

In order to test the hand detection for pointing, one user performed menu navigation and menu item selection in AR. The user wore a colored marker at the fingertip. The video data from the cameras of the AR glasses are stored for later offline processing. For testing the accuracy of pointing, Viola&Jones and Active Appearance Model algorithms are applied on 200 frames randomly selected from the video sequence.

As a first step, an automatic color detector determines and tracks the location of the color marker in each frame. This information serves as the ground truth for the actual test. All results are manually checked to ensure the color marker is detected correctly in all test frames.

Secondly, Viola&Jones hand detection algorithm is run automatically for all frames. The result consists of rectangular areas identi-

fying hand regions (red rectangles in Figure 3). Given a rectangular area, the location of the fingertip is approximated at a relative location within the hand rectangle (yellow circles in Figure 3).

Thirdly, the location of the tip of the finger by the hand Active Appearance Model is computed as the average location of three key points at the tip of the pointer finger of the dominant hand (blue circles in Figure 3). The same figure depicts with green line segments the AAM shapes and key points along each hand contour.

4.3 Results

Figure 3 shows both errors for estimating the location of fingertip by Viola&Jones approximation (blue line segment) and by AMM (orange line segment). Figure 3(a) shows an example for which both Viola&Jones and AAM provide results close to the ground truth of the pointer finger tip of the dominant hand. Viola&Jones pointing errors are small (up to 20 pixels) when the hand is not angled and the detected rectangular area matches the real dimensions of the hand. As illustrated in Figure 3 (b, c, d), rotated hands generally lead to high approximation errors and wrong pointing results with Viola&Jones only. In turn, deformable models like Active Appearance Models can accurately extract the contour of the palm, even in conditions of rotation, scaling and translation, relative to the initialization step set by Viola&Jones. Depending on the initialization, generalization in modeling palm appearance and strategy of updating model parameters, some cases are still difficult to handle even with AAM. An example of wrong hand shape extraction by AAN is showed in Figure 3 (c).

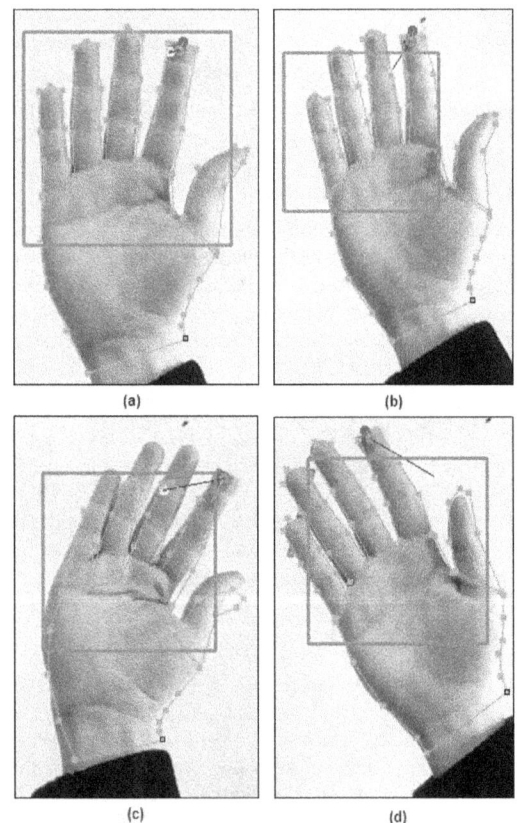

(a) (b) (c) (d)

Figure 3. Examples of palm detection and shape extraction.

As shown in the box plots from Figure 4, the median error by Active Appearance Models is 7.76 pixels. This level of error is acceptable for handling free-hands pointing in AR by only computer vision methods. The median error of Viola Jones is 33.02 pixels, more than 4 times bigger than in case of using Active Appearance Models. This result clearly indicates the superiority of AAM over Viola&Jones palm detector for pointing estimation. The results indicate that computer vision-driven hand models are robust for free-hand pointing in CSI domain.

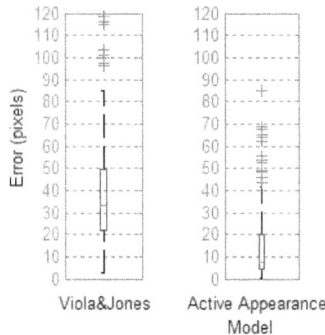

Figure 4. Box plots showing finger pointing errors using Viola&Jones (left) and Active Appearance Models (right).

5. USABILITY STUDY

To investigate the appropriateness of free-hand interaction in AR, a usability study is conducted using two methods. First, an experiment tests the user performance in selecting specific menu items by measuring the task accomplish times and by checking the mistakes made. Second, the quality of interaction is measured based on user's appreciation in written questionnaires based on NASA Task Load Index (TLX) method [14]. This method assesses task load on six different scales as follows: mental demand, physical demand, temporal demand, performance, effort and frustration (Table 3). Each scale has seven points with low, medium and high increments.

Table 3. NASA Task Load Index (TLX) questions

Q1	**Mental Demand**: How mentally demanding was the task?
Q2	**Physically Demand**: How physically demanding was the task?
Q3	**Temporal Demand**: How hurried or rushed was the pace of the task?
Q4	**Performance**: How successful were you in accomplishing what you were asked to do?
Q5	**Effort**: How hard did you have to work to accomplish your level of performance?
Q6	**Frustration**: How insecure, discouraged, irritated, stressed and annoyed were you?

5.1 Experimental Setup

A group of 25 users participated in the study. Each user was assigned an experiment with several parts in which the user had to conduct different selection tasks. Participants are between 24 and 55 years old. The percentage of female participants in the experiments is 35%. About 68.42% of the subjects had no experience related to user interfaces in augmented reality while 21.05% had some experience and only 5.26% were advanced augmented reality users. In order to get used to the equipment, the participants could interact with the augmented reality system before experiments and perform various menu item selections. The experiment setup implies a laptop and Vuzix Wrap 920AR augmented reality glasses.

The palm detector is assigned to the non-dominant hand and the fist posture detector is assigned to the dominant hand. The dominant hand controls the location of the cursor in the AR interface. Figure 5 illustrates a snapshot of the free-hand interaction with the menu interface of the augmented reality based CSI system prototype.

During the experiment, each participant is assigned a set of menu item selections related to common procedures in CSI domain, such as blood spat analysis, bullet trajectories, distance measurements, taking pictures, recording videos or labeling and annotation of evidence.

Accomplishing one task assumes activating the menu interface, navigating to the specific option in the hierarchy of menu items and selecting the indicated menu item. The participants are notified about the current task in a screen-projected box showing information about shortest path to the target menu item. By this, real life situations are simulated, when users already know the menu structure. The AR menu consists of 21 different items, each having assigned an icon. The menu does not exceed four levels in depth. During experiments, interaction events with regard to hand gestures, cursor movements, menu activation and deactivation, menu navigation and menu item selection are logged.

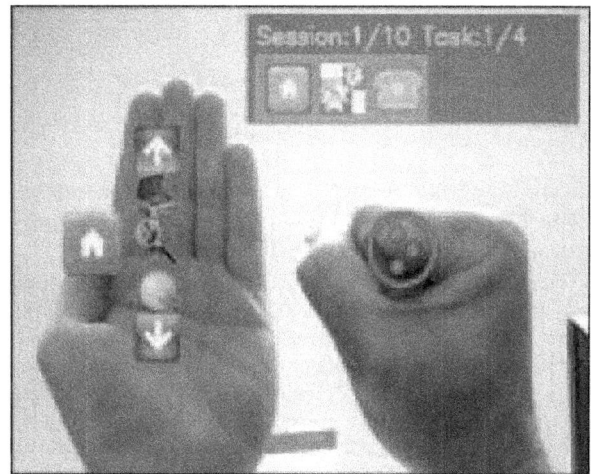

Figure 5. AR interface for free-hands interaction.

5.2 Results

The experiments are evaluated by considering three sources of information. First, the data collected during the experiments is analyzed for objective indications of with regard to interaction performance. Second, the questionnaires filled in by the subjects and the additional comments are analyzed to obtain subjective assessment for the quality of the augmented reality interaction.

5.2.1 Quantitative Interaction Analysis

Data logged during interaction experiments are used to evaluate the times needed to complete selections and to track menu and cursor position on the screen. Figure 6 illustrates an example of tracking the free-hands user interaction in AR.

Red disks on the graphic indicate menu item selections. Based on data collected during experiments, it is possible to compute the learning rate of the users with respect to the task completing time. Figure 7 shows the learning curve of a subject completing a sequence of tasks during test session.

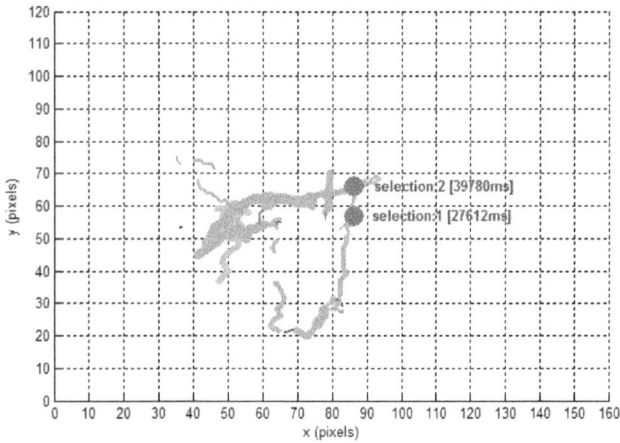

Figure 6. Example of tracking menu movement (cyan), cursor movement (green) and menu item selections (red) during a task. Bigger width of green line suggests the user keeps the cursor in the area for longer time.

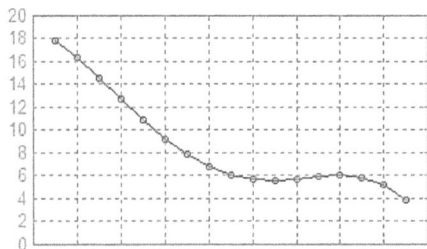

Figure 7. Example of interaction learning curve during test session by task completion time (in seconds), in case of one participant.

The vertical axis shows menu selection times in seconds for consecutive tasks depicted along the horizontal axis. The learning curve indicates that the participant is able to adapt to the free-hand interaction in AR. The left side of Figure 8 (a) shows the average task fulfillment time during training and testing. On average, the participants need less than 30 seconds per task to navigate to randomly assigned menu items. This time is approximately 10 seconds shorter compared to average task fulfillment time during testing. Again, the result supports the learning curve indicator (Figure 7) of users being able to adapt to the interaction by free-hand gestures.

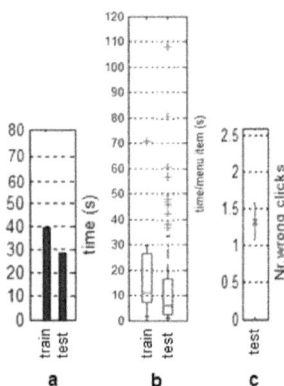

Figure 8. Task fulfillment time (in seconds) per task (during training and testing)(a), time per depth level of menu item (b) and number of erroneous menu selections during testing (c).

To remove the bias of the path length to task menu items, Figure 8 shows the full range of data, outliers and standard deviation of selection times corrected with the depth level of each menu item. The corrected time is the time necessary for participants to select a randomly assigned menu item, divided by the depth level of that menu item. The median time for navigating to a menu item during testing is approximately 5 seconds, almost half the median time necessary for completing a task during training.

The red dots shown in Figure 8b represent outliers. As showed in the box plot, test outliers vary more than train outliers.

Learning sessions at the beginning of experiments are short (about 5 to 10 minutes). If all participants at the experiment have roughly the same bad performance at the beginning and during learning session, they have different learning rates for getting accustomed with the interaction capabilities of the system. While many users adapt quickly to the free-hands interaction in AR, some others such as older people and the ones with no previous experience with AR, get used to the system slower or have difficulty to adapt. During testing, some users are still learning to interact while others' learning curve converged already.

As indicated by the number of erroneous menu item selections per task during testing (Figure 8c), the average participant made at least one error before completing a menu item selection task.

5.2.2 NASA Task Load Index (TLX) Questionnaires

Figure 9 illustrates the histograms of answers given by subjects in NASA TLX questionnaire. Only 11.76% of the testers indicate that the pace of free-hand interaction in augmented reality was hurried or rushed (Q3). The percent of testers saying that they had very low performance in accomplishing their tasks is 30%, while more than half (55%) of participants indicate that they were very successful in finishing tasks (Q4). In the same time, only 20% of testers mention they did feel insecure, discouraged, irritated, stressed and annoyed while fulfilling the experiment tasks (Q6). This result is positive in relation to the result of question Q4 on performance, leading to the conclusion that spatial interaction is appropriate for AR. Only 35% of the participants at the experiment indicate that tasks were very mentally demanding (Q1). Regarding to Q2, a proportion of about 50% of testers indicate that free-hands interaction is physically demanding while 40% of them mention they had to work hard to accomplish the requested level of performance (Q5). These two results will be investigated in a separate research study, in order to identify the reasons and to further adapt the free-hand design for easier interaction. Subjective responses of the participants show that the experiment is organized properly, the software prototype used is adequate for testing and that free-hands interaction in augmented reality is feasible in the context of accessing the CSI mobile system.

5.2.3 Discussion

The evaluation indicates that navigation and selection in AR are doable by computer-vision driven free-hand gestures. Quantitative feedback from the participants shows that users adapt quickly to free-hands interaction style while accessing the AR system. The hand postures modeled are appropriate for interacting with the menu interface. So far, four natural hand postures have been considered but the interaction can be extended to support more hand postures and complex hand gestures.

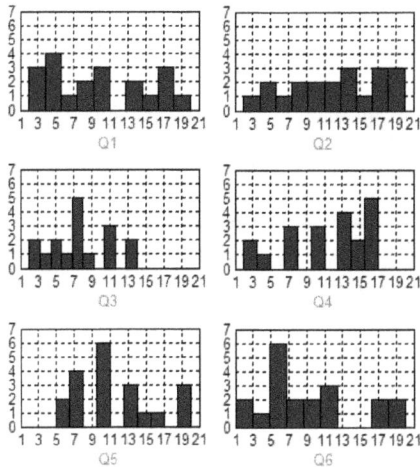

Figure 9. The NASA TLX user test histograms on seven steps Likert scale with low, medium and high increments.

6. CONCLUSIONS AND FUTURE WORK

This paper described a method to reliably detect hands using Adaboost classifier with Viola&Jones features, to track hands using optical flow with AGAST visual features and to compute the hand contour using Active Appearance Models, in the context of free-hand interaction in augmented reality for the CSI domain. In order to determine the performance of the running prototype system, an experimental setup was made to determine the accuracy of the pointing for menu navigation and menu item selection in AR by two algorithms. Results show that image processing algorithms offer accurate estimation for pointing by finger and that using Active Appearance Models improves the accuracy, as compared to Viola&Jones.

Eventually, the described augmented reality system will be ready to be used in real scenarios and be deployed for the crime scene investigation personnel of the Netherlands Forensic Institute for their daily operations. Future work will address a 3D active appearance hand model. This step involves the collection and annotation of a database of 3D hand samples. In addition, the use of more complex hand gestures which implies also the modeling of the dynamics at the finger level will be investigated.

7. REFERENCES

[1] Achacon Jr., D., L., M., Carlos, D., M., Puyaoan, M., K., Clarin, C., T., and Naval Jr., P., C., 2009. REALISM : Real-time hand gesture interface for surgeons and medical experts.

[2] Benko, H., Jota, R. and Wilson, A. 2012. MirageTable: free-hand interaction on a projected augmented reality tabletop. In: *Proceedings of the SIGCHI Conference on Human Factors in Computing Systems*, ISBN: 978-1-4503-1015-4, 199-208.

[3] Billinghurst, M., and Thomas, B., H. 2011. Mobile Collaborative Augmented Reality, Springer, Recent Trends of Mobile Collaborative Augmented Reality Systems, ISBN: 978-1441998446, Editors: L. Alem and W. Huang, 1-19.

[4] Chen, Q., Georganas, N., D., and Petriu, E., M., 2007. Real-time Vision-based Hand Gesture Recognition Using Haar-like Features, In *Proceeding IEEE Conference Instrumentation and Measurement Technology* – IMTC'07, ISBN: 1-4244-0588-2, 1-6.

[5] Choi, J., Park, H., Park, J., and Park, J.-Il, 2011. Bare-Hand-Based Augmented Reality Interface on Mobile Phone, *10th*

IEEE International Symposium on Mixed and Augmented Reality - ISMAR'11, 275-276.

[6] Edwards, G., J., Taylor, C., J., Cootes, T., F., 1998. Interpreting face images using active appearance models. In *Proceedings Third IEEE International Conference on Automatic Face and Gesture Recognition*. 300.

[7] Corbett-Davies, S., Green, R., and Clark, A., 2012. Physically interactive tabletop augmented reality using the Kinect, In *Proceedings of the 27th Conference on Image and Vision Computing* - IVCNZ'12, ISBN: 978-1-4503-1473-2, New Zealand, ACM New York, 210-215.

[8] Datcu, D., Swart, T., Lukosch, S., and Rusak, Z., 2012. Multimodal Collaboration for Crime Scene Investigation in Mediated Reality. 14th ACM International Conference on Multimodal Interaction - ICMI, Santa Monica, California, USA, October 22-26.

[9] Fang, Y., Wang, K., Cheng, J., and Lu, H., 2007. A real-time hand gesture recognition method. *IEEE International Conference on Multimedia and Expo*, ISBN: 1-4244-1016-9, 995-998.

[10] Fernandes, B., and Fernández, J., 2010. Using Haar-like Feature Classifiers for Hand Tracking in Tabletop Augmented Reality, *XII Symposium on Virtual and Augmented Reality*, Brazil, 6-13.

[11] Gross, R., Li, Y., Sweeney, L., Jiang, X., Xu, W., and Yurovsky, D., 2007. Robust Hand Geometry Measurements for Person Identification using Active Appearance Models, *First IEEE International Conference on Biometrics: Theory, Applications, and Systems* - BTAS 2007, ISBN: 978-1-4244-1597-7, 1-6.

[12] Ha, T., and Woo, W., 2006. Bare Hand Interface for Interaction in the Video See-Through HMD Based Wearable AR Environment, In *Proceedings of the 5th international conference on Entertainment Computing* - ICEC'06, ISBN: 978-3-540-45259-1, 354-357.

[13] Hackenberg, G., McCall, R., and Broll, W., 2011. Lightweight Palm and Finger Tracking for Real-Time 3D Gesture Control, *IEEE Virtual Reality Conference 2011*, ISBN: 978-1-4577-0039-2, 19-26.

[14] Hart, S., 2006. Nasa-Task Load Index (Nasa-TLX); 20 Years Later. Human Factors and Ergonomics Society Annual Meeting Proceedings, 50, 904-908.

[15] Hu, K., Canavan, S. and Yin, L. 2010. Hand Pointing Estimation for Human Computer Interaction Based on Two Orthogonal-Views, 2010 International Conference on Pattern Recognition, 3760-3763.

[16] Lee, T., and Hollerer, T. 2008. Hybrid Feature Tracking and User Interaction for Markerless Augmented Reality. *Virtual Reality Conference* - VR '08. IEEE, ISBN: 978-1-4244-1971-5, 145-152.

[17] Lee, J., Y., Rhee, G., W., Seo, D.,W., 2010. Hand gesture-based tangible interactions for manipulating virtual objects in a mixed reality environment. *Int Journal Adv Manuf Technology*, 51:1069–1082.

[18] Li, Y., Sun, C., Pan, Z., Zhang, M., Guo, K., and Tang, X., 2010. Robust features extraction for barehand desktop HCI, ACM CHI 2010 Workshop on Whole-Body Interaction.

[19] Liu, N., and Lovell, B., C., 2005. Hand Gesture Extraction by Active Shape Models, In *Proceedings of the IEEE Digital Imaging Computing: Techniques and Applications* – DICTA'05, ISBN: 0-7695-2467-2.

[20] Lucas, B. D. and Kanade, T. 1981. An iterative image registration technique with an application to stereo vision. In: Proceedings of Imaging Understanding Workshop, 121-130.

[21] Lukosch, S., Poelman, R., Akman, O., and Jonker, P., 2012. A Novel Gesture-based Interface for Crime Scene Investigation in Mediated Reality, In *Proceedings of the CSCW workshop on Exploring collaboration in challenging Environments.*

[22] Mair, E., Hager, G., D., Burschka, D., Suppa, M. and Hirzinger, G. 2010. Adaptive and Generic Corner Detection Based on the Accelerated Segment Test. *Computer Vision – ECCV'10*, Lecture Notes in Computer Science, Volume 6312, 183-196.

[23] bin Mohd Sidik, M., K., bin Sunar, M., S., Bin Ismail, I., bin Mokhtar, M., K., Jusoh, N., B., M., 2011. A Study on Natural Interaction for Human Body Motion Using Depth Image Data. *Workshop on Digital Media and Digital Content Management* - DMDCM, 97-102.

[24] Piumsomboon, T., Clark, A., Billinghurst, M., 2011. Physically-based Interaction for Tabletop Augmented Reality Using a Depth-sensing Camera for Environment Mapping. In *Proceedings Image and Vision Computing New Zealand* - IVCNZ'11, 161-166.

[25] Poelman, R., Akman, O., Lukosch, S., and Jonker, P. 2012. As if being there: mediated reality for crime scene investigation. In *Proceedings of the ACM 2012 Conference on Computer Supported Cooperative Work*. CSCW'12. ACM, New York, NY, 1267-1276.

[26] Radkowski, R., Stritzke, C. 2012. Interactive Hand Gesture-based Assembly for Augmented Reality Applications. In *The Fifth International Conference on Advances in Computer-Human Interactions* - ACHI'12, ISBN: 978-1-61208-177-9, 303-308.

[27] Rautaray, S., S., Agrawal, A., 2012. Vision based hand gesture recognition for human computer interaction: a survey, *Artificial Intelligence Review.*

[28] Reifinger, S., Wallhoff, F., Ablassmeier, M. Poitschke, T., and Rigoll, G., 2007. Static and Dynamic Hand-Gesture Recognition for Augmented Reality Applications. In *Proceedings of the 12th international conference on Human-computer interaction: intelligent multimodal interaction environments*, ISBN: 978-3-540-73108-5, Springer-Verlag.

[29] Schweighofer, G., and Pinz, A., 2006. Robust Pose Estimation from a Planar Target algorithm, *IEEE Transactions on Pattern Analysis and Machine Intelligence*, Volume 28, 2024-2030.

[30] Shi, J. and Zhang, M., and Pan, Z., 2011. A real-time bimanual 3D interaction method based on bare-hand tracking. In *Proceedings of the 19th ACM international conference on Multimedia* – MM'11, ISBN: 978-1-4503-0616-4, New York, NY, USA, 1073-1076.

[31] Song , P., Yu, H., and Winkler, S., 2009. Vision-based 3D finger interactions for mixed reality games with physics simulation. *International Journal of Virtual Reality.* 8(2), 1-6.

[32] VanWaardhuizen, M., Oliver, J., and Gimeno, J. 2011. Tabletop augmented reality system for conceptual design and prototyping. *In Proceedings of the ASME 2011 World Conference on Innovative Virtual Reality* - WINVR2011, ISBN: 978-0-7918-4432-8, Milan, Italy, 395-405.

[33] Viola, P. and Jones, P. 2002. Robust Real-time Object Detection. *International Journal of Computer Vision*, Number 2, Volume 57, 137-154.

[34] Wachs, J., P., Stern, H., I., Edan, Y., Gillam, M., Handler, J., Feied, C., Smith, M., 2008. A Gesture-based Tool for Sterile Browsing of Radiology Images, *Journal of the American Medical Informatics Association*, Volume 15, Number 3, 321-323.

[35] Wang, Z., B., Shen, Y., Ong, S., K., and Nee, A., Y., C., 2009. Assembly Design and Evaluation based on Bare-Hand Interaction in an Augmented Reality Environment, *International Conference on CyberWorlds* - CW '09, ISBN: 978-1-4244-4864-7, 21-28.

[36] Yao, M., Qu, X., Gu, Q., Ruan, T., and Lou, Z., 2010. Online PCA with adaptive subspace method for real-time hand gesture learning and recognition. *Journal WSEAS Transactions on Computers*, Volume 9 Issue 6, 583-592.

[37] Yoon, J.-H., Park, J.-S., and Sung, M. Y., 2006. Vision-Based bare-hand gesture interface for interactive augmented reality applications, In *Proceedings of the 5th international conference on Entertainment Computing* - ICEC'06, 386-389.

[38] OpenCV computer vision library, http://opencv.willowgarage.com/wiki/.

[39] Ogre3D graphics rendering engine library, http://www.ogre3d.org/.

[40] http://en.wikipedia.org/wiki/Kinect.

[41] http://en.wikipedia.org/wiki/Leap_Motion.

[42] Boost::Thread, http://www.boost.org/doc/libs/1_52_0/doc/html/thread.html.

[43] CSI The Hague, the Netherlands Forensic Institute, http://www.csithehague.com/.

[44] Kölsch, M., Turk, M., Hollerer, T., Chainey, J. 2004. Vision-Based Hand-Gesture Applications, Intl. Conference on Mobile and Ubiquitous Systems - MobiQuitous.

[45] Kim, D., Hilliges, O., Izadi, S., Butler, A. D., Chen, J., Oikonomidis, I., Olivier, P. 2012. Freehand 3D interactions anywhere using a wrist-worn gloveless sensor, Proceedings of the 25th annual ACM symposium on User interface software and technology - UIST '12, 167-176.

[46] Rekimoto, J. , 2001. GestureWrist and GesturePad. Unobtrusive Wearable Interaction Devices, Proceedings of the 5th IEEE International Symposium on Wearable Computers - ISWC '01, ISBN: 0-7695-1318-2, 12.

[47] Lee, M., Green, R., Billinghurst, M., 2008. 3D Natural Hand Interaction for AR Applications, 3D Natural Hand Interaction for AR Applications. Lincoln, New Zealand: 23rd International Conference Image and Vision Computing, New Zealand, 1-6.

Performance Effects of Multi-sensory Displays in Virtual Teleoperation Environments

Paulo G. de Barros
Worcester Polytechnic Institute
100 Institute Road
Worcester, MA, USA, 01609
+1 508-831-6617
pgb@wpi.edu

Robert W. Lindeman
Worcester Polytechnic Institute
100 Institute Road
Worcester, MA, USA, 01609
+1 508-831-6712
gogo@wpi.edu

ABSTRACT

Multi-sensory displays provide information to users through multiple senses, not only through visuals. They can be designed for the purpose of creating a more-natural interface for users or reducing the cognitive load of a visual-only display. However, because multi-sensory displays are often application-specific, the general advantages of multi-sensory displays over visual-only displays are not yet well understood. Moreover, the optimal amount of information that can be perceived through multi-sensory displays without making them more cognitively demanding than visual-only displays is also not yet clear. Last, the effects of using redundant feedback across senses on multi-sensory displays have not been fully explored. To shed some light on these issues, this study evaluates the effects of increasing the amount of multi-sensory feedback on an interface, specifically in a virtual teleoperation context. While objective data showed that increasing the number of senses in the interface from two to three led to an improvement in performance, subjective feedback indicated that multi-sensory interfaces with redundant feedback may impose an extra cognitive burden on users.

Categories and Subject Descriptors

H.5.2 [**User Interfaces**]: Auditory (non-speech) feedback, Graphical user interfaces, Haptic I/O, Evaluation/methodology, H.5.1 [**Multimedia Information Systems**]: Artificial, augmented, and virtual realities, I.2.9 [**Robotics**]: Operator interfaces.

General Terms

Design, Performance, Measurement, Human Factors.

Keywords

Multi-sensory interfaces; robot teleoperation; virtual environment; urban search-and-rescue; visual, audio and vibro-tactile feedback.

1. INTRODUCTION

Since the creation of *Sensorama* [15] in 1962, all human senses have been used by the entertainment industry, as well as researchers in the area of Virtual Reality, as sources of information display for virtual environments (VEs). They have

been evaluated in terms of their impact on user presence [35], and performance [3]. Despite that effort, few researchers have looked into integrating all senses into a single display or measuring the effect of such integration on user perception, or user efficiency and effectiveness [16]. This work evaluates the impact on user performance and cognition of multi-sensory feedback (vision, hearing and touch) in a virtual robot teleoperation search task.

Results show that a well-designed, tri-sensory display can increase user performance and reduce workload compared to a bi-sensory display. Results also show that redundant feedback is only useful if it helps user awareness of unnoticed parts of the displayed data.

The remainder of this paper is organized as follows. Section 2 reports related work. Section 3 summarizes our interface. The experiment hypotheses are detailed in Section 4, followed by a description of our study in Section 5. Section 6 summarizes the results, which are analyzed in Section 7. Last, Section 8 draws conclusions about the results and describes future areas of work.

2. RELATED WORK

Multi-sensory interface research encompasses a large variety of research areas. In the context of this work, focus will be given to Virtual Reality (VR) and Human-Robot Interaction (HRI).

Research on the integration of multiple senses in perception has shown that sense prioritization is dependent on the reliability of sensory channels [10]. Although systems providing multi-sensory stimulation have been used for some time now, studying the effects the conjunctive use of multiple senses to interact with real and virtual worlds has seldom been undertaken [4][16][19][37]. Moreover, the results obtained by individual researchers are difficult to generalize due to their task-specific nature [33].

Of all the senses, vision is by far the one that has been the most studied, with stereoscopic head mounted displays, CAVEs and powerful GPUs. Hearing has been explored for adding realism to scenes, but also to help in performing specific tasks, such as search and localization [12]. Stereoscopic, surround and bone-conduction [23] sound systems have been experimented with as audio displays with and without the use of HRTFs [11]. For touch and proprioception [27], vibro-tactile [2] and force feedback [16] have been used to signal actions [36], support interactions with virtual objects and display geo-spatial data using specialized [5][21] or mobile devices [30][31]. Multi-modal displays have also been reported to reduce user workload [3]. Contact feedback classifications for vibro-tactile devices have been proposed [22] and have even been used to guide the blind [5].

In the area of HRI, specifically urban search-and-rescue (USAR) teleoperation, interface design and implementation guidelines have yet to be standardized, although some progress has been made [8][25][34]. Interfaces for real USAR teleoperation often simply consist of keyboard, mouse, gamepads [38], and touchscreens [26] or visual displays [28].

Although current USAR teleoperation interfaces aim to improve Situation Awareness (SA) [9] and efficiency [12][28][38], little effort has been put on validating reductions in the operator cognitive load. Adding multisensory cues has been partially explored [5][6][7][32][38], and although novel visual interfaces have been evaluated [18][28], research in this field still lacks an extensive evaluation of the benefits of multi-sensorial interfaces.

Previous studies in USAR virtual robot teleoperation, vehicle driving [37] and pedestrian navigation [29] have shown that adding properly designed vibro-tactile displays to visual ones can improve navigation performance [6]. It has also been found that redundant feedback in such displays led to higher levels of SA, and increased navigation performance variability among operators [7]. Nonetheless, the reason behind such an effect is not yet well understood and could be the result of interface design issues affecting the reliability of the display multi-sensory channels [10].

With the exception of a few user studies comparing the use of audio or vibration with visual-only interfaces [11][12][16], to our knowledge, little has been done in evaluating the impact of individual components of USAR multi-sensory robot interfaces.

The current work builds on these previous results, and evaluates the effect of adding audio feedback to a bi-sensory interface (vision and touch), and the effect of redundant data presentation in multi-sensory displays. Notice that the focus of this work is on the output to the user, not the input from the user.

3. ROBOT INTERFACE

Results from previous studies suggest that vibro-tactile feedback by itself is not an optimal navigation interface. Instead, it should be used as a supplement to other interfaces [29]. In this work, three multi-sensory interfaces with increasing complexity were created by supplementing a vibro-tactile one with extra feedback.

Interface 1, the control case interface that was used as a starting point for the two other interfaces evaluated here, was designed following USAR interface guidelines and is based on the work of Nielsen [28] and de Barros & Lindeman [6]. It is composed of a visual interface (Figure 1) with a vibro-tactile belt display (Figure 2a). The visual interface fuses information as close as possible to the operator's point of focus, around the parafoveal area [19].

The visual part of Interface 1 contains a third-person view of the robot (dimensions: 0.51m × 0.46m × 0.25m), which sits on a blueprint map of the remote environment and has the video from the robot camera (60° FOV, rotating range: ±100° horiz. and ±45° vert.) presented on a rotatable panel. The blue dots on the map appear as nearby surfaces detected by robot sensors. The camera panel orientation matches the camera orientation relative to the robot. Furthermore, the robot avatar position on the map matches the remote robot position in the real-world VE. A timer with the elapsed time is shown in the top-right corner of the screen.

The vibro-tactile feedback belt (Figure 2a) is an adjustable neoprene belt with eight tactors (ruggedized eccentric DC mass motors [24]) positioned at the cardinal and intermediate compass points (forward = north). Tactor locations were adjusted for subject waist. The tactors provide the user with collision

proximity feedback (CPF). The closer the robot is to colliding in the direction the tactor points, the more intense a tactor in the belt continuously vibrates, similar to the work of Cassineli [5]. The vibro-tactile feedback is only activated when the robot is within a distance $d \leq 1.25m$ from an object. If an actual collision occurs in a certain direction, the tactor pointing in that direction vibrates continuously at the maximum calibrated intensity. The intensity and range values were identified as optimal in a pilot study.

Interface 2 builds upon Interface 1 and adds audio feedback. The first type of sound feedback is a stereoscopic bump sound when collisions between the virtual robot and the VE occur. The second type of sound feedback is an engine sound that increases its pitch as speed increases to give feedback about robot moving speed.

Interface 3 builds upon Interface 2 but adds extra visual feedback to the interface. A ring of eight dots is displayed on the top of the robot and mimics the current state of the vibro-tactile belt. It is an improvement over previous work on redundant displays [7]. The positioning on the belt of each tactor is associated with one of the dots in the ring and their locations match. The more intensely a tactor vibrates, the more red the dot associated with that tactor becomes (as opposed to its original color black). The second added visual feature is a speedometer positioned on the back of the robot as a redundant display for the engine sound. Table 1 summarizes the interface features that each interface contains.

For all three interfaces, the user controlled the virtual robot using a Sony PlayStation2 Dual-shock® gamepad (Figure 2b).

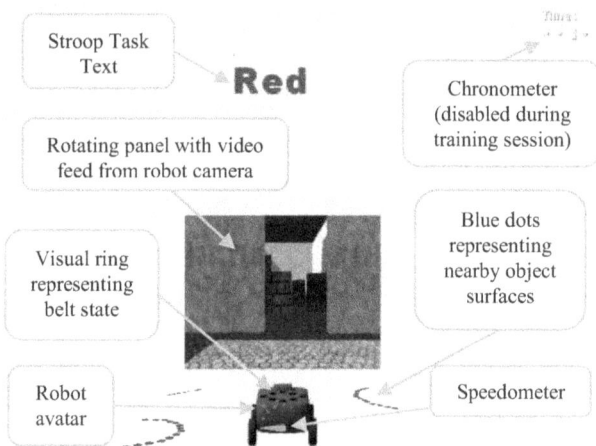

Figure 1. Visual components for all three interfaces. The visual ring and speedometer are only part of Interface 3.

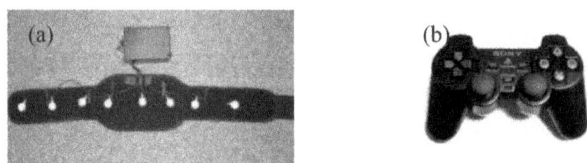

Figure 2. (a) Vibro-tactile belt; (b) PlayStation® 2 controller.

Table 1: Display features for interfaces treatments.

Interface Number	Standard Visual Interface	Vibro-tactile feedback	Audio feedback	Visual ring and speedometer
1	X	X		
2	X	X	X	
3	X	X	X	X

The right thumbstick controlled robot movement using differential drive. The left thumbstick controlled camera pan-tilt [7]. The controller allowed subjects to take pictures with the robot camera.

Sound feedback was displayed through an Ion iHP03 headset. The headset was worn for all treatments. An ASUS G50V laptop was used in the study. It was positioned on top of an office table at 0.5m from the subject's eyes. The environment was run in a window with resolution of 1024×768 at a refresh rate of 17 fps.

4. HYPOTHESES

The use of vibro-tactile and enhanced interfaces has been shown to improve user performance [2][4][16][18]. Results from other previous work [6] have shown that vibro-tactile feedback can improve performance if used with a visual interface as a complementary source of collision proximity feedback (CPF) in a simple virtual teleoperation task. What is not a consensus yet among these and other studies [37], however, is whether the use of redundant feedback actually brings overall benefits.

Additionally, in another study using redundant feedback as a graphical ring [9], the results were inconclusive due to interface occlusion problems. This motivated us to improve on this interface and create a similar ring structure, but now sitting on top of the robot avatar to resolve the reported occlusion problem. With this new ring layout, it is possible that the redundant visual display benefits outweigh any potential disadvantages.

Our current study evaluates the impact on cognitive load and performance of adding redundant and complementary audio-visual displays to a control interface with vibration and visual feedback. Based on the insights collected from other previous work, our previous studies and with the interface enhancements proposed, the following two results are hypothesized:

H1. Adding redundant and complementary sound feedback to the control interface should improve performance in the search task;

H2. Adding redundant visual feedback should lead to even further improvements in performance in the search task.

5. USER STUDY

The current study was designed to confirm whether the enhancement of a visual-tactile interface with extra audio and visual information would lead to a reduction or increase in operator cognitive load and performance. We opted for a fielded interface experiment [7]. Our interface attempts to approximate what is used by researchers and experts to perform a real robot teleoperation task. This approach increases the chances of detecting the effects of multi-sensory feedback in a reasonably realistic virtual robot teleoperation context, as opposed to a lab-oriented approach, where low-complexity interfaces are tested.

5.1 Methodology

To evaluate the validity of the proposed interfaces, a search task was designed to best reproduce what happens in real USAR teleoperation situations, but in a slightly simpler manner. Subjects had to search for twelve red spheres (radius: 0.25m) in a debris-filled environment. Subjects were unaware of the total number of spheres. They were asked to find as many spheres as possible in as little time as possible and also avoid robot collisions. When the experiment was over, subjects drew sketchmaps of the VE showing the locations of the spheres found.

The experiment consisted of a within-subjects design where the search task was performed by each subject for all interface types (Table 1). The *independent variable* (*I.V.*) was the type of interface, with three possible treatments: Interface 1 (control), Interface 2 (audio-enhanced) and Interface 3 (visually-enhanced). Interface and virtual world presentation order for each subject was balanced using Latin Square to compensate for any effects within trials. The virtual worlds were built with the same size (8m x 10m), number of objects, walls and hidden spheres. They had similar complexity in terms of optimal traversal paths, traversal time, number of obstacles, and sphere levels of occlusion. The pictures taken with the robot camera (800×640) were displayed on a web page during sketchmap drawing when the search was over.

While performing the main search task, each subject also performed a secondary task, a visual Stroop task [13]. Users had to indicate whether the color of a word matched its meaning. For example, in Figure 1, the word "red" does not match its color. The words were presented periodically (every 20±~5s) for 7.5±~2.5s, disappearing after that. Users were asked to answer the Stroop task as soon as they noticed the word on screen using the gamepad. The purpose of this task was to measure user cognitive load variations due to exposure to interfaces with different levels of multi-sensory complexity. The NASA-TLX test [14] was taken after each of the interface treatments to measure user workload.

The objective *dependent variables* (*D.V.*) were the following: the time taken to complete the search task, average robot speed, the number of collisions, the number of spheres found, the number of collisions per minute, the ratio between number of collisions and path length, the number of spheres found per minute, the ratio between number of spheres found and path length, and the quality of the sketchmaps. These variables were normalized on a per-subject basis. Here is an example that explains this normalization process: if subject *A*, for a *D.V. X*, had the following results (*Interface 1*, *Interface 2*, *Interface 3*) = (10, 20, 30), these values would be converted to (10/60, 20/60, 30/60) ~ (0.17, 0.33, 0.5). The reason behind such normalization is presented in Section 6.1.

In addition to these variables, cognitive load was compared using the Stroop task results. The Stroop task objective *D.V.*s were: the percentage of incorrect responses, response time, and percentage of unanswered questions. The first two variables were analysed for three data subsets: responses to questions where color and text matched, responses to questions where color and text did not match, and all responses. These variables were also normalized. For subjective *D.V.*s, the treatment and final questionnaires compared subjects' impressions of each interface. The former was completed three times for each interface. The latter was completed once and comparatively rated all three interfaces. Subjective workload was measured using the NASA-TLX questionnaire.

The study took approximately 1.5±0.5 hours per subject. The experiment procedure steps are listed in Table 2. For each trial, the time and location of collisions were recorded. Subject gender and age, how often they used computers, played video games, used robots, used remote-controlled ground/aerial/aquatic vehicles (RCVs) and used gamepads was collected in the demographics questionnaire. For all but the first two questions, a Likert scale with four values ("daily" (1), "weekly" (2), "seldom" (3) or "never" (4)) was used. The spatial aptitude test had nine questions about associating sides of an open cube with its closed version and questions about map orientation. Subjects had strictly five minutes to complete the spatial test. The instructions page explained the experiment procedure, the task and the interface.

The training sessions used environments similar in complexity to the ones used in the real task. During training sessions (~4 min.), subjects had to find one red sphere and take a picture of it. The idea was to make subjects comfortable with the robot controls and output displays. The treatment questionnaire is summarized in Table 3. Subjective questions (3-8) were adapted from the SUS [35] and SSQ [20] questionnaires and followed a Likert scale (1-7). The final questionnaire is summarized in Table 4 and its questions 1-5 were also given on a Likert scale (1-7).

The sketchmaps were evaluated using the approach proposed by Billinghurst & Weghorst [1], but on a 1 to 5 scale. Maps were scored twice by two evaluators. The definition used for scoring map goodness is similar to the ones used in [1] and [6], that is, how well the sketched map helps in guiding one through the VE.

Table 2: Experimental procedure for one subject.

Step	Description
1	Institutional Review Board approved consent forms;
2	Demographics questionnaire;
3	Spatial aptitude test;
4	Study instructions and Q&A session;
5	User wears belt and headset. Robot interface explained;
6	Task review;
7	Training explanation and Q&A followed by training task;
8	Study task review and Q&A followed by study task;
9	During task, video and objective data is recorded;
10	Trial is over: treatment questionnaire with sketch map;
11	NASA-TLX questionnaire;
12	Five-minute break before next trial;
13	Steps 7-12 repeated for the other two interface treatments;
14	Three treatments are over: final questionnaire.

Table 3: Treatment questionnaire summary.

#	Question description
1	Report the number of spheres found;
2	Draw on a blank paper a map of the house and objects and indicate location of spheres found;
3	How difficult it was to perform the task compared to actually performing it yourself (if the remote environment was real);
4	Sense of being there in the computer generated world;
5	To what extent there were times during the experience when the computer generated world became the "reality" for you, and you almost forgot about the "real world" outside;
6	Whether the subject experienced the computer generated world more as something he saw, or somewhere he visited;
7	When navigating in the environment whether the subject felt more like driving or walking;
8	How nauseated the subject felt;
9	How dizzy the subject felt.

Table 4: Final questionnaire summary.

#	Question description
1	How difficult it was to learn;
2	How confusing it was to understand the information presented;
3	How distracting the feedback provided was;
4	How comfortable its use was;
5	How it impacted the understanding of the environment;
6	General comments about experiment.

5.2 Virtual Environment

The virtual worlds and robot interface (Figure 1) were built on the C4 game engine (www.terathon.com). According to the AAAI Rescue Robotics Competition classification, the experiment VE has difficulty level yellow. It is a single level with debris on the floor [17].

6. RESULTS

This section presents the significant results obtained in this study. Therefore, if a variable is not discussed in detail in this section, its results led to no statistically significant difference (SSD).

In order to generate the results presented here, data was processed in two ways. Continuous values were processed using a single-factor ANOVA with confidence level of $\alpha = 0.05$. This analysis was done before and after the normalization process described in 5.1. Trends had a confidence level of $\alpha = 0.1$. When a SSD among groups was found, a Tukey test (HSD, 95% confidence level) was performed to reveal the groups that differed from each other. In order to reveal such differences in more detail, data was further analyzed with ANOVA ($\alpha = 0.05$) in a pair-wise fashion.

Owing to their categorical nature, the Likert scale data obtained from the treatment and final questionnaires were processed using the Friedman test for group comparisons and the Wilcoxon Exact Signed-Rank test for pair-wise comparisons.

6.1 Demographics

A total of 18 university students participated in the experiment. Their average age was 25 years ($\sigma = 3.18$). In terms of experience levels among groups exposed to interfaces in different orders, SSDs were found for computer and RCV levels. Group 123 had more computer experience than Group 312. On the other hand, Group 312 had more RCV experience than Group 123. These differences were the main motivator for applying the data normalization explained in Section 5.1.

6.2 Subjective Measures

For the treatment questionnaires, a SSD was found for *Being there* for Interface 1 and Interface 2 (Figure 3a). The latter led to higher being there levels compared to the former ($\chi^2 = 6.28$, $p = 0.04$, $d.o.f. = 2$). Moreover, a SSD was also found for *Walking* results between Interface 2 and Interface 3 (Figure 3b). When exposed to Interface 3, moving around the computer-generated world seemed to subjects to be more like walking than when exposed to Interface 2 ($\chi^2 = 7.82$, $p = 0.02$, $d.o.f. = 2$). These results seem to support H1, but go against the claim in H2.

The final questionnaire showed interesting results, especially for Interface 2. On the one hand, a pair-wise Wilcoxon test showed Interface 2 was more difficult to use than Interface 1 ($w = 18.5$, $z = -1.75$, $p = 0.09$, $r = -0.29$, Figure 4a). On the other hand, Interface 2 was more comfortable to use than Interface 1 ($\chi^2 = 5.51$, $p = 0.06$, $d.o.f. = 2$, Figure 4b). It also more positively impacted the comprehension of the environment compared again to Interface 1 ($\chi^2 = 10.98$, $p < 0.01$, $d.o.f. = 2$, Figure 4c).

Interface understanding levels also differed (Figure 4d). Using Interface 2 and Interface 3 made it more straightforward to understand the information presented than using Interface 1 ($\chi^2 = 5.52$, $p = 0.06$, $d.o.f. = 2$). A pair-wise Wilcoxon test showed that Interface 2 had a statistically significant increase compared to Interface 1 ($w = 10.0$, $z = -2.15$, $p = 0.04$, $r = -0.36$). The same pair-wise comparison for Interface 3 and Interface 1 only showed a trend however ($w = 15.0$, $z = -1.89$, $p = 0.07$, $r = -0.31$). These results from the final questionnaire seem to support H1, but do not present any evidence in support of H2.

For the NASA-TLX questionnaire, a trend indicated that Interface 2 had a higher temporal workload score than Interface 1 ($w = 37.0$, $z = -1.87$, $p = 0.06$, $r = -0.31$, Figure 5a). This measure indicates how hurried or rushed subjects felt during the task. Subjects felt more in a rush when exposed to Interface 2. Because no difference in task time was detected among interface groups, the only other factor that could have affected subjects' rush levels would have to be related to the visual timer on screen and subjects' behavior towards it. A plausible explanation would be that subjects were able to check the timer more often to see how efficiently they were doing. This behavioral change would only be possible if the rest of the interface was less cognitively demanding. Hence, an increase in timer look-ups could have been due to a decrease in cognitive demand from the rest of the interface. If this claim is true, such a decrease would support H1. For the NASA-TLX performance measure, a trend has indicated a lower rating for Interface 3 compared to Interface 1 ($w = 103.0$, $z = 1.80$, $p = 0.08$, $r = 0.30$, Figure 5b). This measure indicates how successful subjects felt in accomplishing the task. In other words, Interface 3 made subjects feel as if they performed worse than with Interface 1. This result goes against what was claimed in H2.

6.3 Objective Measures

For the objective measures, two variables led to relevant results. For the normalized number of collisions per minute (Figure 6a), trends were found between pairs of interfaces (1, 2) ($F [2, 15] = 3.70$, $p = 0.06$) and (1, 3) ($F [2, 15] = 3.65$, $p = 0.06$). For the normalized number of collisions per path length SSDs were found for the same pairs of interfaces (1, 2) ($F [2, 15] = 4.32$, $p = 0.04$) and (1, 3) ($F [2, 15] = 4.16$, $p = 0.05$). These results support H1.

No SSDs were obtained by the analysis of the Stroop task data, although there was a slight decrease in response time for Interface 2 and Interface 3, as can be seen in Figure 7a.

The mean, S.D. and median for the number of collisions, number of spheres found, task time, average robot speed (m/s) and map quality are shown in Table 5, but no SSD was found for these.

Table 5: The triplets (mean μ, S.D. σ, median η) for the dependent variables' non-normalized data.

D.V.	Interface 1	Interface 2	Interface 3
Cols.	(17.1, 9.9,16)	(12.8, 8.6, 11)	(14.7, 11.6, 9)
Sphs.	(8.1, 2.6, 9.0)	(7.7, 2.5, 8)	(8.2, 2.7, 8.5)
Time	(275, 112, 232)	(291, 109, 265)	(272, 93, 269)
Speed	(.56, .06, .56)	(.54, .05, .54)	(.54, .06, .54)
Map	(3.1, 1.0, 3.1)	(3.0, 1.2, 3.0)	(3.0, 1.0, 3.2)

6.4 Subject Comments

Subject comments were collected on the treatment and final questionnaires. The comments were categorized according to interface features (touch, audio, extra GUI, map, etc.) or experimental features (Stroop task, learning effects). For each category, the comments were divided into positive and negative ones. One score point was added for each comment for a feature.

There was a prevalence of positive comments directed to the audio interface. One subject stated: "Adding the audio feedback made it feel much less like a simulation and more like a real task. Hearing collisions and the motor made it feel like I was actually driving a robot." Another said, "The sound made it much easier to figure out what the robot was doing. It was clear when there was a collision." Most comments praised the collision sound, but not so much the motor sound.

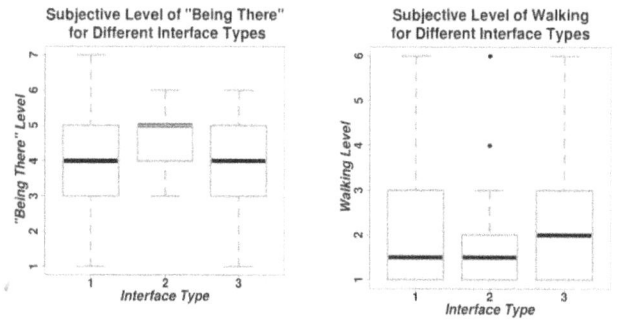

Figure 3: (a) Interface 2 increased user sense of being in the VE; (b) Interface 3 made users feel more like walking rather than driving.

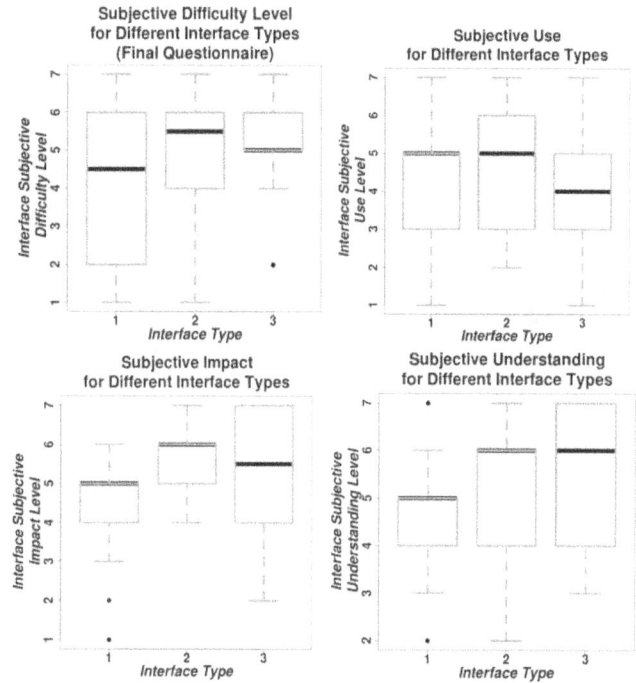

Figure 4: (a) Interface 2 was deemed more difficult to use than Interface 1, but it was also (b) more comfortable and (c) better impacted comprehension than Interface 1; (d) both Interfaces 2 and 3 helped better understand the environment than Interface 1.

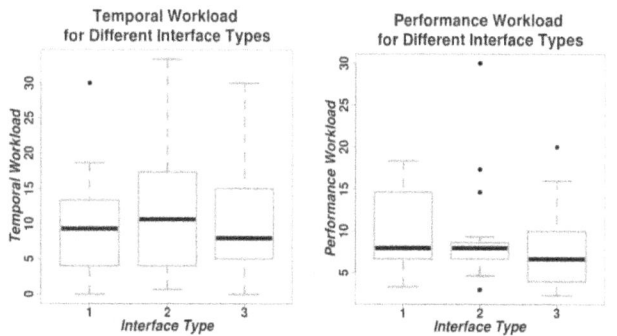

Figure 5: (a) Subjects felt significantly more rushed when using Interface 2 than with Interface 1; (b) Interface 3 caused subjects to feel as if they performed worse than Interface 1.

For the belt, it seemed that having it on all the time, even when it was evident no collision was imminent, annoyed subjects. A few subjects admitted that the belt was useful for navigation however. Many subjects seemed to ignore the belt feedback for the vast majority of the time and only used it when either a collision had already occurred or when passing through narrower places. These comments comply with the ones obtained in other studies [6].

For redundant feedback, it seemed to have distracted more than helped. One subject mentioned: "The visual speed feedback was not very useful at all, since the auditory speed feedback conveyed the idea much more effectively, so the visual speedometer became a distraction." The comments support the slight worsening in results for Interface 3 detected in Figures 3b and 7a.

Subjects' comments confirm the results obtained from subjective and objective measures supporting H1, but rejecting H2.

7. DISCUSSION

The main goal of this work was to search for answers to the question of how much one can make use of multi-sensorial displays to improve user experience and performance before an overwhelming amount of multi-sensorial information counter-balances the benefits of having such an interface. As a second goal, this work aimed at assessing the potential benefits, if any, of having redundant feedback in multi-sensory displays.

In other previous work [6], it was shown that, in the context of virtual robot teleoperation, adding touch-feedback to a visual-only interface as an aid to collision avoidance significantly improved user performance. In addition, other work [7] showed that adding redundant visual feedback for representing the same information as touch feedback could lead to a performance decrease, although the reason for that was assumed to be occlusion problems and not the fact that display of information was redundant.

Based on the interface and experiment results of these and other previous studies, our current study explored enhancing a visual-tactile interface with audio and redundant visual displays. Our enhancements over previously proposed interfaces allowed us to more accurately measure not only the impact of adding feedback to an extra human sense, but also to measure the effects of different types of redundant feedback in multi-sensory displays.

Unlike the belt feedback, which provided collision proximity feedback as the robot approached the surface of a nearby object, the collision audio display provided feedback only after a collision had occurred. This difference in feedback behavior led to an interesting result. Even though the audio feedback provided was an after-the-fact type of feedback, it led to further reductions in the number of collisions with the environment. But the audio display could not have helped reduce collisions in the same way as the touch display because of this difference in time of feedback. And the speed with which subjects moved the robot was not significantly affected by the engine sound feedback. Hence, two possible explanations for such reductions are:

1. The sound feedback made the remote VE feel more real and helped subjects become more immersed and focused on the task, leading them to perform the task with fewer collisions,
2. The sound feedback allowed subjects to better understand the relative distances between the robot and the remote VE. By experimenting with collisions a few times, subjects used sound feedback to learn what visual distance to maintain from walls to better avoid collisions from a robot camera perspective.

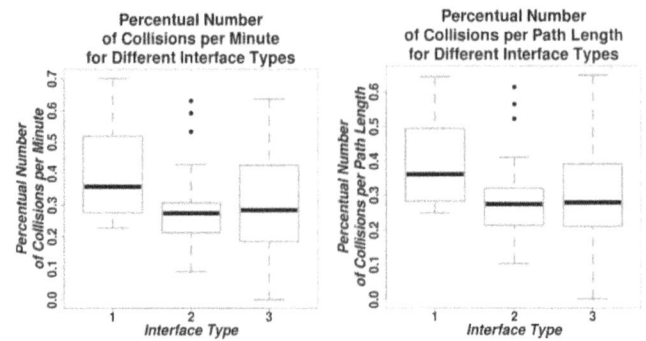

Figure 6: Both Interface 2 and Interface 3 caused a decrease in number of collisions: (a) per minute; (b) per path length.

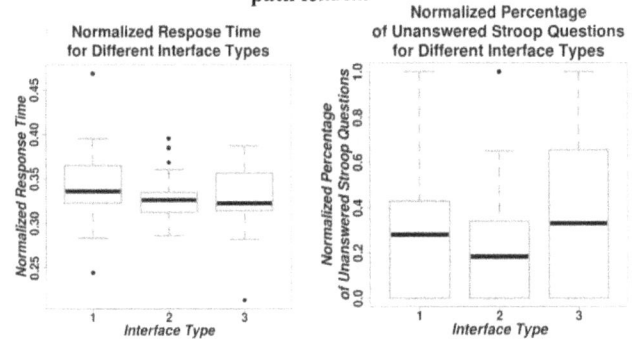

Figure 7: Stroop task results for (a) normalized response time and (b) normalized percentage of unanswered questions.

Even though both explanations matched subject feedback on the topic, we believe that the latter is a more plausible one. The distance estimation between the robot and the remote VE was not as easy to do using only the vibro-tactile feedback from the belt due to the continuous nature of the cues it provided.

Subjective feedback and objective data indicated that the engine sound did not have a major role in improving understanding of the relationship between robot and environment. Nevertheless, it was reported that this sound did improve their presence levels. Hence, the addition of the sense of hearing to the multi-sensory display improved performance and Hypothesis 1 (H1) was confirmed.

Hypothesis 2 (H2), on the other hand, was rejected. As mentioned earlier, results from similar studies on redundant feedback were inconsistent [6][37]. This work showed that redundant feedback may not always improve performance. In fact, its effect may vary depending on how the multi-sensory interface is integrated.

One explanation for the degradation in results for Interface 3 is considered here. It seems that the addition of new visual features created a new point on screen users needed to focus on. The basic visual interface (used in Interface 1 and Interface 2) already demanded a great deal of the user's attention with points of focus for: the timer on the top-right corner, the Stroop task text field, the robot camera panel and the map blueprint. Hence, adding more focus points in Interface 3 might have reduced user performance more than the amount of performance improvement that the addition of such interface features could have added.

However, would the same results be obtained if the extra visual information added was novel instead of redundant? In the case of this study, because the information displayed by the enhanced visual display was already being presented in other forms, no information was gained for most subjects, who already effectively read that same information through the vibro-tactile belt. For these subjects, the visual enhancements were either ignored or caused distraction, the latter to the detriment of their performance. Nonetheless, it would be interesting to compare the improvement results of individually using an audio-visual only interface or a visual-only interface with the speedometer and visual ring added to the current audio-visual-tactile interface.

Last, the use of the touch and audio feedback as opposed to the visual feedback for collision detection and proximity might be an indication that, when offered the same information through different multi-sensory displays, users may try to balance load among multiple senses as an attempt to reduce their overall cognitive load. Interesting though this claim may seem, the results obtained here are unable to support this notion. The verification of such a claim and the search for an answer to the question stated in the previous paragraph is the subject of future studies.

8. CONCLUSION

The main goal of this work was to give one more step towards understanding the effects on users of multi-sensory interfaces. We have explored the effects of adding audio to an existing visual-tactile interface. The context in which this exploration took place was in a virtual robot teleoperation search task in a 3D VE.

The study has shown that adding audio as the third sense to the bi-sensorial interface (visuals, touch) resulted in improvements in performance. This meant the user had not yet been cognitively overwhelmed by the control case display and could still process further multi-sensory data without detriment on performance.

This study also presented evidence indicating that displaying more data to a certain sense (vision) when it is already in high cognitive demand is detrimental to performance if the added data does not improve the user's SA of the system and environment. It remains to be seen how much of an effect the information relevance of the newly added visual data has on counter-balancing such detriment in performance. In order to measure such an effect, a new study needs to be carried out to compare the impact of a multi-sensory interface by adding more visual data that is not yet conveyed through other senses (novel data) versus adding visual data that is already conveyed through another sense (redundant data).

Redundancy could be beneficial to mitigate the fact that vision is uni-directional. A visual display could become at least partially omni- or multi-directional by adding redundant feedback through senses such as hearing and touch. The larger the number of focus points on screen, and the larger their relative distance, the higher the chances are that the user will miss some information or event. Having data redundancy spread across a multi-sensory display in a balanced, fused, non-distracting and non-obtrusive manner could reduce event misses and increase SA and comprehension.

Following the same thread of reasoning, it would be interesting to explore the validity of the following more general statement:

Redundant information over multiple senses brings no benefit to the user of a multi-sensorial display that already maximizes the user's omni-directional perception of relevant data.

In other words, the more omni-directional a display is, the more data can be perceived by the user simultaneously, the smaller the chances are that changes in the data displayed are missed, and hence, the smaller the need is for providing redundant data displays.

Admittedly, the study presented here barely scratches the surface of such a topic. Similar studies exploring the optimization of multi-sensorial omni-directionality must be performed and their results cross-validated for this statement be considered as plausible. Such studies should aim at complementing not only visual displays using other senses, but also complementing displays for other senses such as touch, with which it is only possible to feel as many surfaces as one's body pose can touch.

This work has provided a glimpse into the potential performance increase that multi-sensory displays can provide to 3D spatial user interaction. It has shown that multi-sensory displays can not only lead to more natural forms of information presentation but also display more information with reduced cognitive cost.

Nevertheless, the question of how complex multi-sensory displays can get is still not completely answered. Using three senses in an interface proved to be better than using only two, but what if more senses are considered? Is it possible to display data to olfactory and gustatory senses to improve displays for practical applications? Our research group aims at improving the current answers we have for these questions in future studies.

9. ACKNOWLEDGMENTS

The authors appreciate the research funding support from the Worcester Polytechnic Institute Computer Science Department.

10. REFERENCES

[1] Billinghurst, M. and Weghorst, S. 1995. The use of sketch maps to measure cognitive maps of virtual environments. *Virtual Reality Annual International Symposium*, 40-47.

[2] Blom, K.J. and Beckhaus, S. 2010. Virtual collision notification. In *Proceedings of IEEE Symposium on 3D User Interfaces*, 35-38.

[3] Bowman, D., Kruijff, E., LaViola Jr., J., Poupyrev, I. 2005. *3D User Interfaces: Theory and Practice*, parts 2 and 3, 27-310, Addison-Wesley, Boston, MA. 2005.

[4] Burke, J.L., Prewett, M.S., Gray, A.A., Yang, L. Stilson, F.R.B., Coovert, M.D., Elliot, L.R., and Redden, E. 2006. Comparing the effects of visual-auditory and visual-tactile feedback on user performance: a meta-analysis. In *Proceedings of the 8th International Conference on Multimodal Interfaces*. ACM, New York, NY, 108–117.

[5] Cassinelli, A., Reynolds, C., and Ishikawa, M. 2006. Augmenting spatial awareness with haptic radar. *Tenth International Symposium on Wearable Computers*. (Montreux, Switzerland, October 2006). ISWC'06, 61-64.

[6] de Barros, P.G., Lindeman, R.W. 2012. Poster: Comparing Vibro-tactile Feedback Modes for Collision Proximity Feedback in USAR Virtual Robot Teleoperation. *Proc. of IEEE 2012 Symposium on 3D User Interfaces*. 3DUI'12, 137-138. 2012.

[7] de Barros, P.G., Lindeman, R.W., Ward, M.O. 2011. Enhancing robot teleoperator situation awareness and performance using vibro-tactile and graphical feedback. *Proceedings of IEEE 2011 Symposium on 3D User Interfaces*. 3DUI'11, 47-54.

[8] Drury, J.L., Hestand, D., Yanco, H.A., and Scholtz, J. 2004. Design guidelines for improved human-robot interaction.

Extended Abstracts on Human Factors in Computing Systems. CHI '04, 1540.

[9] Endsley, M.R., and Garland, D.G. 2000. Theoretical underpinning of situation awareness: a critical review. *Situation Awareness Analysis and Measurement*, Lawrence Erlbaum, Mahwah, NJ.

[10] Ernst, M.O. and Bülthoff, H.H. 2004. Merging the senses into a robust percept. Trends in cognitive sciences. 8, 4 (Apr. 2004), 162–9.

[11] Gonot, A. et al. 2007. The Roles of Spatial Auditory Perception and Cognition in the Accessibility of a Game Map with a First Person View. *International Journal of Intelligent Games & Simulation.* 4, 2 (2007), 23–39.

[12] Grohn, M. et al. 2005. Comparison of Auditory, Visual, and Audiovisual Navigation in a 3D Space. *Transactions on Applied Perception.* 2, 4 (2005), 564–570.

[13] Gwizdka, J. 2010. Using Stroop Task to Assess Cognitive Load. *ECCE.* (2010), 219-222.

[14] Hart, S.G. 2006. NASA-Task Load Index (NASA-TLX): 20 Years Later. *Proc. of the Human Factors and Ergonomics Society 50th Ann. Meeting*, HFES '06, 904-908.

[15] Heilig, M. L., *Sensorama Simulator*, U. S. Patent 3,050,870, 1962.

[16] Herbst, I. and Stark, J. 2005. Comparing force magnitudes by means of vibro-tactile, auditory and visual feedback. *IEEE International Workshop on Haptic Audio Visual Environments and their Applications.* HAVE'05, 67–71.

[17] Jacoff, A., Messina, E., Weiss, B.A., Tadokoro, S., and Nakagawa, Y. 2003. Test arenas and performance metrics for urban search and rescue. In *Proceedings of IEEE/RSJ International Conference on Intelligent Robots and Systems.* IROS'03. 3, 3396-3403.

[18] Johnson, C.A., Adams, J.A., Kawamura, K. 2003. Evaluation of an enhanced human-robot interface. In *Proceedings of the IEEE International Conference on Systems, Man, and Cybernetics.* SMC'03. 900-905.

[19] Kaber, D.B., Wright, M.C., Sheik-Nainar, M.A. 2006. Investigation of multi-modal interface features for adaptive automation of a human–robot system. In *International Journal of Human-Computer Studies*, 64, 6 (Jun. 2006), 527-540.

[20] Kennedy, R.S., and Land, N.E., 1993. Simulator sickness questionnaire: an enhanced method for quantifying simulator sickness. *The International J. of Aviation Psychology*, 3, 3, 203-220.

[21] Koslover, R.L. et al. 2012. Mobile Navigation Using Haptic, Audio, and Visual Direction Cues with a Handheld Test Platform. *IEEE Transactions on Haptics.* 5, 1 (Jan. 2012), 33–38.

[22] Lindeman, R.W. 2003. Virtual contact: the continuum from purely visual to purely physical. In *Proceedings of the 47th Annual Meeting of the Human Factors and Ergonomics Society.* HFES'03, 2103-2107.

[23] Lindeman, R.W., Noma, H., and de Barros, P.G. 2007. Hear-Through and Mic-Through Augmented Reality: Using Bone Conduction to Display Spatialized Audio. *IEEE Int'l Symp. on Mixed and Augmented Reality*, 1-4.

[24] Lindeman, R.W. and Cutler, J.R. 2003. Controller design for a wearable, near-field haptic display. In *Proceedings of the 11th Symposium on Haptic Interfaces for Virtual Environment and Teleoperator Systems*, 397-403.

[25] McFarlane, D.C. and Latorella, K.A. 2002. The scope and importance of human interruption in human-computer interaction design. *Human*-Computer *Interaction*, 17, 1-61.

[26] Micire, M. et al. 2011. Hand and finger registration for multi-touch joysticks on software-based operator control units. 2011 IEEE Conference on Technologies for Practical Robot Applications (Apr. 2011), 88-93.

[27] Mine, N., Brooks Jr., F.P., Sequin, C. 1997. Moving Objects in Space: Exploiting Proprioception in Virtual-Environment Interaction, *Proc. of SIGGRAPH*, Los Angeles, CA, 19-26.

[28] Nielsen, C.W., Goodrich, M.A., and Ricks, B. 2007. Ecological interfaces for improving mobile robot teleoperation. *IEEE Transactions on Robotics*, 23, 5, 927-941.

[29] Pielot, M. and Boll, S. 2010. Tactile Wayfinder: Comparison of Tactile Waypoint Navigation with Commercial Pedestrian Navigation Systems. (2010), 76–93.

[30] Pielot, M. and Poppinga, B. 2012. PocketNavigator: Studying Tactile Navigation Systems. (2012), 3131–3139.

[31] Raisamo, R. et al. 2012. Orientation Inquiry: A New Haptic Interaction Technique for Non-visual Pedestrian Navigation. EuroHaptics Conference (2012), 139–144.

[32] Sibert, J., Cooper, J., Covington, C., Stefanovski, A., Thompson, D., and Lindeman, R.W. 2006. Vibrotactile feedback for enhanced control of urban search and rescue robots. *Proc. of the IEEE* Symposium *on Safety, Security and Rescue Robots,* Gaithersburg, MD, Aug. 2006.

[33] Sigrist, R. et al. 2013. Augmented visual, auditory, haptic, and multimodal feedback in motor learning: A review. Psychonomic bulletin & review. 20, 1 (Feb. 2013), 21–53.

[34] Steinfeld, A., Fong, T., Kaber, D., Lewis, M., Scholtz, J., Schultz, A., and Goodrich, M. 2006. Common metrics for human-robot interaction. In *Proceedings of the 1st ACM SIGCHI/SIGART Conference on Human-Robot Interaction*, 33-40.

[35] Usoh, M., Catena, E., Arman, S., and Slater, M. 2000. Using presence questionnaires in reality. *Presence-Teleoperators and Virtual Environments*, 9, 5, 497-503.

[36] Thullier, F. et al. 2012. Vibrotactile Pattern Recognition: A Portable Compact Tactile Matrix. IEEE Transactions on Biomedical Engineering. 59, 2 (Feb. 2012), 525–530.

[37] Van Erp, J.B.F. and Van Veen, H.A.H.C. 2004. Vibrotactile in-vehicle navigation system. Transportation Research. F, 7 (2004), 247–256.

[38] Yanco, H.A., Baker, M., Casey, R., Keyes, B. Thoren, P., Drury, J.L., Few, D., Nielsen, C., and Bruemmer, D. 2006. Analysis of human-robot interaction for urban search and rescue. In *Proceedings* of *the IEEE Symposium on Safety, Security and Rescue Robots.*

Spatial Setups: A Study of Mobile Configurations in Remote Collaborative Task

Leonardo Giusti[1]
lgiusti@mit.edu

Kotval Xerxes[2]
xerxes.kotval@alcatel-lucent.com

Amelia Schladow[1]
schladow@mit.edu

Nicholas Wallen[1]
nwallen@mit.ed

Francis Zane[2]
francis.zane@alcatel-lucent.com

Federico Casalegno[1]
casalegno@mit.edu

[1] MIT – Mobile Experience Lab,
20 Ames street, Cambridge, 02142 MA
[2] Alcatel-Lucent Bell Labs
600 Mountain Avenue, New Providence, 07974 NJ

ABSTRACT

This paper presents the results of a qualitative investigation on the use of mobile devices for remote, video-mediated assistance on physical tasks. In particular, we studied how a user and remote expert spatially configure mobile devices in two different tasks, each characterized by a different workspace scale: (1) repairing a Lego model, (2) replacing a punctured bike tube. The main result of this small-scale pilot study was the identification of specific device configurations that satisfy varying collaborative needs in different workspace scales. These results inform the future development of advanced services for remote collaboration.

Categories and Subject Descriptors

H.5.m [**Information Interfaces and Presentations**]: Miscellaneous

Keywords

Remote Collaboration, Mobile Technologies, Spatial User Interaction.

1. INTRODUCTION

This paper explores how existing mobile technologies can enhance services for remote assistance, particularly during physical tasks where two or more individuals work together manipulating three-dimensional objects in the real world: e.g. a remote expert might guide a user through emergency repairs to a car or help a remote user to assemble furniture.

Current applications for remote collaboration do not fully consider the complexity of using devices while working. Most video-conferencing software is suited to face-to-face collaboration, but struggles to support collaboration on physical tasks, where users share a space and volumetric items. For the user and remote expert to comprehend the situation and thereby

ground the collaboration, the interface should support spatial considerations.

Mobile devices often have two cameras able to stream high-quality videos. Increasing computational power and disposable bandwidth provide opportunities unexploited by current video-conferencing software (e.g. Skype, Google Talk). This small pilot study aims to advance video-based remote collaboration by analyzing behaviors and device setups adopted during collaboration on physical tasks.

The presented pilot study analyses how a user and a remote expert set-up and use devices in the physical space during two different tasks, each characterized by different scales. One task asks participants to repair a lego model in a smaller, desk-based scenario, and the other task has participants collaborating to replace a punctured bicycle tire in a larger, more active, room-based scenario. These two scales were chosen to provoke reference to the spatial environment and to explore how people adapt the device configurations to the different scale of the context.

Our study seeks to extend video-mediated collaboration research by engaging the physical space and looking to the future with both single and multiple device scenarios.

2. RELATED WORK

In their influential study, Gaver et al. [4] challenge the assumption that a face-to-face view is critical to remote collaboration. They suggest that a setup with multiple cameras helps participants to better collaborate by establishing a task-centered point of view. A challenge of their study was to "... establish a mutual frame of reference towards objects of interest" [4]. "Grounding" is a fundamental process in the establishment of such a mutual frame of reference [2]. A fundamental pillar of this grounding process is "joint attention", typically defined as two individuals coordinating visual attention toward an object of mutual interest. Joint attention means more than just two individuals attending to the same thing; "it is two people experiencing the same thing at the same time and knowing together that they are doing this: they need to be aware (in some sense) that they are sharing attention" [7]. Kirk, Rodden, and Fraser [5] explored grounding in their study on remote gestures in collaborative physical tasks. They highlight the influence of gesture in assisting language to ground a collaboration; however, their study examines user behaviors in a fixed setup, where the user has no influence over camera management. Additionally, the study focuses on physical tasks at a small, table-based scale, where it is important to gain common ground knowledge of mutual referents, but not necessarily of the entire space and setup [5]. It is essential to maintain task awareness and mutual understanding throughout the collaboration, but depending on the physical space and manual demands of the task, awareness and understanding require different mediation dynamics [6]. Most current systems for group activities do not support references to the external space [3]. Research shows that actions and comprehension are closely linked to context.

This paper focuses on mobile devices for remote collaboration. Mobile devices provide a communication channel for collaboration that can be integrated into the space; as indicated by Cole & Stanton [3], remote collaboration in a physical environment can make use of diverse devices without limiting activities to the screen.

In our pilot study, we observed how people configure mobile devices and setup a stage for remote collaboration by arranging devices. In particular, we studied strategies adopted to establish joint attention with respect to different workspace scales and external references. We use our study of setup methods, references, and general dynamics to identify a set of device configurations and suggest design factors for task awareness and mutual understanding.

3. PRELIMINARY STUDY
3.1 Observational Plan
We conducted a small pilot study with single and multiple device setups in two physical tasks: repairing a Lego model and replacing a punctured bicycle tube.

Eight subjects (5 females, 3 males) between the ages of 22 and 27 participated to the study. Four groups (A, B, C, D) of two subjects completed the tasks in two device configurations, as described in table 1.

For each task, one subject acted as an expert (remote expert) and instructed the other (user). In each group, roles have been switched after the first task. Before starting, the remote expert was familiarized with the task and materials (a researcher instructed the subject showing how to perform the task), while the user had no prior knowledge.

Table 1. Observation plan

	Repairing a Lego model	Replacing a punctured bike tube
Single device	Group A, B	Group C, D
Multiple devices	Group C, D	Group A, B

3.1.1 Subjects
A pre-questionnaire was administered to understand the subjects' background in using mobile devices and video-conferencing services. All the involved subjects use video-conference tools (e.g. Skype, Google Talk) regularly to talk with friends in other locations or for work (e.g. contact clients, discussions with an advisor). Seven of the eight subjects mentioned that they liked being connected despite the physical distance and that it is more interactive and natural than a phone call; however, some

mentioned frustration at not feeling co-located, namely due to current systems' inability to share items and capture the remote user's space.

3.1.2 Task Descriptions
In repairing a Lego model, the user had to rebuild a partially disassembled Lego model with the help of a remote expert. This task required a collaborative diagnosis of the situation, specifically, understanding how the model was broken and how it could be reconstructed with the given toolset. The task entailed: the remote expert and the user understanding the workspace and collaboratively identifying the specific Lego elements available; the remote expert formulating a plan to restore the model and the user in turn following instructions from the remote expert; and completing a shared assessment of intermediate operations and of the final output. For available resources, the expert had the model's instruction booklet, paper, and a pen.

To repair the punctured bicycle tube, the user had to remove the tube and replace it with a new one. Specifically, this task required: identifying individual bike parts and assessing the user's available tools; the user following instructions from the remote expert, who in turn had to monitor the completion of task sub-goals; and finally, both the user and remote expert mutually assessing the final output. For resources, the user had a set of bicycle repair tools and the expert had paper and a pen.

With the aim well-defined from the onset, the bike task focused less on diagnosis and more on referencing, instructing, and assessing. Furthermore, this task implied a different workspace scale; the Lego assembly task took place on a tabletop, whereas in the bike repair task, the user operates on the floor, moving around and shifting attention.

3.1.3 Setup
In the initial configuration of the single device trials, the remote experts and users were connected through a Skype call: the remote expert had a desktop computer and the user had a mobile phone. The remote user could choose to use the front or the back camera of the mobile phone. In the initial configuration of the multiple device trials, the remote expert had a desktop computer and a tablet reciprocally connected with the mobile phone and the tablet of the user. Here, the user could choose between the front and the back cameras of both the mobile phone and the tablet while the remote expert could switch between the front and back cameras of the tablet.

3.1.4 Data Collection and Analysis
Both the remote expert and the user were video recorded. Three researchers observed the studies, independently analyzed the video, and took notes for later discussion.

4. RESULTS
In each task the remote expert and user rearranged the setup as needed. In general, initial interactions were mediated by face-to-face conversations: user and remote expert had a front camera chat. Then, based on the different task and technological setup, they adjusted for an apt configuration. The following describes the stable configurations and technological setups for each task with some variations.

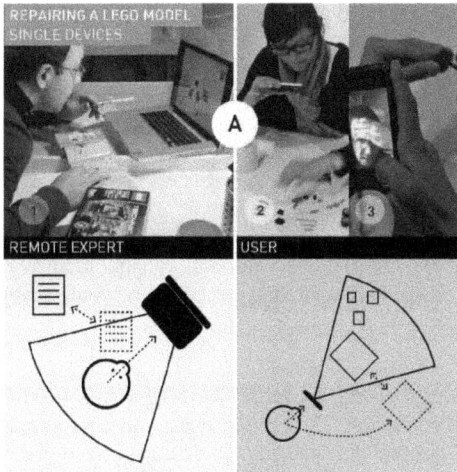

Figure 1. Repairing a Lego Model, Single Device Condition.

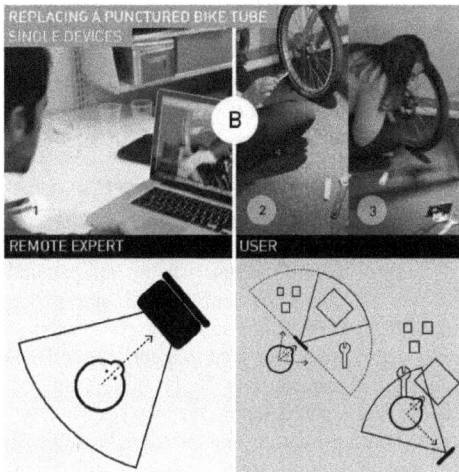

Figure 2. Replacing a punctured bike tube, Single Device Condition.

4.1 Single Device - Repairing a Lego model

The user configured her area to broadcast her workspace, while the remote expert received this broadcast on the computer (see figure 1, A). The user's area featured the mobile phone capturing her active workspace, while other Lego parts were off-camera and only displayed upon request from the remote expert (see figure 1, A2). The user mainly used the rear camera; the main stream on her mobile phone screen showed the remote expert's face while the picture-in-picture window served as a local monitor of her activity (see figure 1, A3). The remote expert viewed the stream of the user's workspace and requested closer views of specific elements when needed. The remote expert consulted the instructions and made drawings in his private space to hold up and share with the user (see figure 1, A1).

4.2 Single Device - Replacing a punctured bike tube

Similar to the previous task, the user configured the stage so that the phone broadcasted her workspace (see figure 2, B2) and could be used to zoom into specific elements (e.g. tools, bicycle). However, to have her hands free and still provide the expert with a constant understanding of activity, the user often switched to a

"third-person point of view" by setting down the phone to capture a workspace overview (see Figure 2, B3). The remote expert displayed only his face (see Figure 2, B1), so the user continuously turned to the mobile phone for assurance.

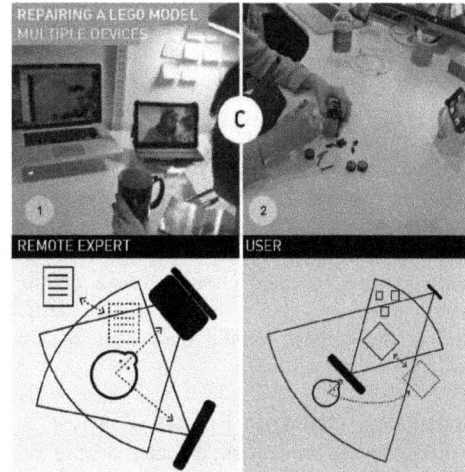

Figure 3. Repairing a Lego Model, Multiple Device Condition.

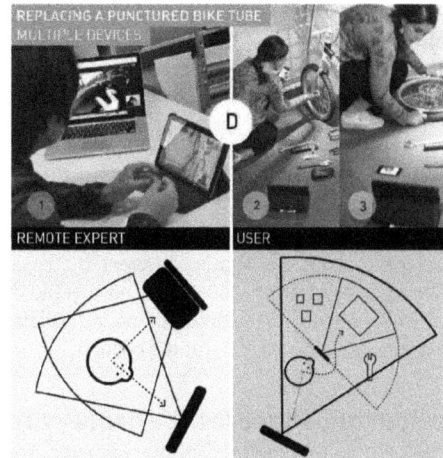

Figure 4. Replacing a punctured bike tube, Multiple Device Condition.

4.3 Multiple Devices - Repairing a Lego model

The user broadcasted the workspace details through the mobile phone, using the tablet to show an overview of her workspace and, at times, her face as well (see figure 3, C2). The remote expert had both cameras broadcasting her face and occasionally held up instructions for the user. A face-to-face connection was constant in one or both devices at all times. In this way, the remote expert viewed the user's face and workspace through the tablet, and on the computer, saw detailed views when requested. The user viewed two different broadcasts of the remote expert's face, and instructions when displayed; the remote expert consulted the instructions privately, and - on occasion - would hold them up for the user (see figure 3, C1).

4.4 Multiple Devices - Replacing a punctured bike tube

The user configured her stage so that the tablet captured the overall view of the setting and the mobile phone was used to zoom in for details (see figure 4, D2). When not needed, the user put down the phone, effectively turning off that view (see Figure 4, D3). The attention of the remote expert was focused on the overall view from the tablet, except when the zoom view was provided from the mobile phone (see figure 1, D1). The user always had the face of the remote expert displayed on the tablet and on the mobile phone, but she focused on the bicycle, with occasional glances toward the remote expert for affirmation.

5. DISCUSSION

Due to the limited number of subjects involved, the results of this study cannot be generalized; however, the behaviors of the subjects does not change considerably across the different tasks and we have observed the emergence of the same strategies within the different groups. Nevertheless, because of the natural limitation of small sample of subjects, the design issues extrapolated in the analysis should be further researched and refined.

5.1 Managing Multiple Points of View

In the Repairing a Lego model task, the additional device did not play a relevant role in the collaboration process; for the expert, it was redundant information without crucial added value. However, in Repairing a punctured bike tube, the additional device played an important role, making the remote expert better equipped to help the user because of a more comprehensive understanding of the physical space. One of the user's devices could be used to capture an overall view of the space (or maintain a face-to-face conversation when appropriate) while the other device could be used to zoom in on elements as needed; this setup provided necessary details without compromising the overall contextual view for the remote expert. This use case illuminated the need for multiple devices to adapt the stage to different workspace scales. In the large scale context, the need to focus on specific details is a fundamental issue; however, an additional point of view can help to maintain a general understanding of the context.

5.2 Configuring Cameras & Display Sizes

Current device configurations best support face-to-face conversations: the display space allocation of the different video streams allows both the user and remote expert to have the face of the other as a main stream and a picture-in-picture small window for the local monitor. However, during a physical task, one collaborator tends to show something to the other collaborator, adopting a "first-person point of view", capturing the entire setting with an overall view or broadcasting details and specifics. In this case, the user tends to be limited to the screen and works by looking through the device, as in the Lego scenario. Functionally, this is not necessary, and presents more challenges as the workspace scale escalates. And yet, the user looks through the device to understand what is drawing the remote expert's attention and thus maintain mutual awareness of the situation. In this configuration, the rear camera of the user's device is active, but the display space allocation does not change and the user must observe his/her own activity through the small picture-in-picture window. When a collaborator is presenting something to the other, it would be more efficient to have the feed of the local camera as a main video stream and the other's face in the picture-in-picture window. If both collaborators are presenting, a different display space allocation is needed to show both the local and remote feed; this allows the user to compare their situation with

information provided by the remote expert, and conversely, it allows the expert to assess the user's situation with respect to the shared information. Existing video-conference systems do not support simultaneous reconfiguration of display space in relation to active cameras on multiple devices. This seems to be an important feature to shift from a face-to-face conversation to a "subjective point of view", which facilitates references to the external environment and supports an effective collaboration on physical tasks. As mobile penetration increases and people use more devices for multiple channels, collaboration systems will have to adapt to better support complex configurations with multiple devices.

5.3 Integrating & Interacting with Content

In all the conditions, the remote expert needs a simple way to reference external documents to guide the user and clarify details. In particular, the remote expert needs a private space to browse and select content with only the relevant document broadcasted to the user. The mixing of video streams with physical or digital documents needs to be carefully considered to provide a fluid user experience. Additionally, in each condition collaborators naturally pointed at the screen to indicate even though they were aware that the technology could not relay this gesture. However, natural gestures like this should be considered as a means of annotation and interaction.

6. CONCLUSION

This study aimed to outline user behaviors around remote collaboration by examining the configuration and use of devices under different device conditions and workspace scales. As part of our future work, this study will lead to a conceptual framework to inform the design of applications in this field, going beyond the state-of-the-art in video-conferencing software. Future developments should provide users with tools to achieve the most appropriate collaboration stage through different device configurations, adding and managing multiple points of view (to address different scales of the workspace), and integrating digital and physical media into the video stream for richer experiences.

7. REFERENCES

[1] Bao, P., and Gergle, D., 2009. What's "This" You Say? The Use of Local References on Distant Displays. In CHI 2009. ACM, New York, NY, USA.

[2] Clark, H.H., & Brennan, S.E., 1991. Grounding in communication. In L. B.. Resnick, R. R. Levine, & S. D. Teasley (Eds.), Perspectives on socially shared cognition. Washington, DC: APA.

[3] Cole, H., and Stanton, D., 2003. Designing mobile technologies to support co-present collaboration. Springer-Verlag, London, UK.

[4] Gaver, W., Sellen, A., Heath, C., Luff, P., 1993. One is not enough: multiple views in a media space. In CHI 1993. ACM, New York, NY, USA.

[5] Kirk, D., Rodden, T., and Fraser, D. S., 2007. Turn It This Way: Grounding Collaborative Action with Remote Gestures. In CHI 2007. ACM, New York, NY, USA.

[6] Kraut, R., Fussell, S., and Siegel, J., 2003. Visual Information as a Conversational Resource in Collaborative Physical Tasks. In Human-Computer Interaction, vol 18.

[7] Tomasello, M., & Carpenter, M., 2007. Shared intentionality. Developmental Science, 10, 121-125.

Evaluating Performance Benefits of Head Tracking in Modern Video Games

Arun Kulshreshth
Department of EECS
University of Central Florida
4000 Central Florida Blvd
Orlando, FL 32816, USA
arunkul@knights.ucf.edu

Joseph J. LaViola Jr.
Department of EECS
University of Central Florida
4000 Central Florida Blvd
Orlando, FL 32816, USA
jjl@eecs.ucf.edu

ABSTRACT

We present a study that investigates user performance benefits of using head tracking in modern video games. We explored four different carefully chosen commercial games with tasks which can potentially benefit from head tracking. For each game, quantitative and qualitative measures were taken to determine if users performed better and learned faster in the experimental group (with head tracking) than in the control group (without head tracking). A game expertise pre-questionnaire was used to classify participants into casual and expert categories to analyze a possible impact on performance differences. Our results indicate that head tracking provided a significant performance benefit for experts in two of the games tested. In addition, our results indicate that head tracking is more enjoyable for slow paced video games and it potentially hurts performance in fast paced modern video games. Reasoning behind our results is discussed and is the basis for our recommendations to game developers who want to make use of head tracking to enhance game experiences.

Categories and Subject Descriptors

H.5.2 [**User Interfaces**]: Evaluation/methodology;
K.8.0 [**Personal Computing**]: Games

Keywords

Head Tracking; Motion control; video games; TrackIR 5; 3D interaction; user performance & experience.

General Terms

Experimentation, Measurement, Performance

1 INTRODUCTION

With the advancement of game interface technology, several new devices and gaming platforms (e.g., Microsoft Kinect,

PlayStation Move, TrackIR 5) that support 3D spatial interaction have been implemented and made available to consumers. Head tracking is one example of an interaction technique, commonly used in the virtual and augmented reality communities [2, 7, 9], that has potential to be a useful approach for controlling certain gaming tasks. Recent work on head tracking and video games has shown some potential for this type of gaming interface. For example, Sko et al. [10] proposed a taxonomy of head gestures for first person shooter (FPS) games and showed that some of their techniques (peering, zooming, iron-sighting and spinning) are useful in games. In addition, previous studies [13, 14] have shown that users experience a greater sense of "presence" and satisfaction when head tracking is present. However, these studies were conducted in simple game scenarios. We seek to systematically explore the effects of head tracking, in complex gaming environments typically found in commercial video games, in order to find if there are any performance benefits and how it affects the user experience. A thorough understanding of the possible performance benefits and reasoning behind them would help game developers to make head tracked games not only more enjoyable, but more effective. Our study is an initial step towards a foundational understanding of the potential performance benefits of head tracking in modern video games.

In this paper, we present a study investigating whether user performance is enhanced when head tracking is used over a traditional button-based controller in modern video games. We made use of the TrackIR 5 head tracking device, a PC, the Xbox 360 controller for Windows, and four carefully chosen games as a representation of modern head tracking enabled games. All these games had native support for the TrackIR 5 and had tasks that may potentially benefit from use of a head tracking device. To evaluate the players performance, we collected both quantitative data based on the tasks associated with each game and qualitative data based on post-questionnaires to evaluate perception of their performance. We used a between subjects design where the control group played the games without head tracking and the experimental group played with head tracking with both groups using the Xbox 360 controller as the input device.

2 RELATED WORK

Sko et al. [10] used head tracking for FPS games and presented a simple two-level taxonomy, which categorized head controlled based techniques into *ambient* or *control*. Ambient (or perceptual) techniques enhance the visual and/or audio feedback based on the user's head position, and control techniques are focused on the controlling the state of the game. Four interaction techniques (zooming, spinning, peering, and iron-sighting) were developed for control and two (head-coupled perspective and handy-cam) for ambient interactions. Their evaluation found that control based techniques are most useful for games which are specifically designed with head tracking in mind and ambient techniques bring more energy and realism in FPS games. However, the main focus of their work was to analyze the effectiveness of each individual technique in isolation and no quantitative measures were involved. In our study we focused on quantitatively measuring the combined affect, on user performance, of simultaneously using several techniques. Yim et al. [14] developed a low cost head tracking solution based upon the popular work of Johnny Lee [6] using Nintendo Wii Remotes. Although they did not perform a formal user study, their preliminary results show that users perceived head tracking as a more enjoyable and intuitive gaming experience.

Head gesture recognition techniques based on face tracking, which is similar to head tracking, have been studied by HCI researchers as an input to computer games. Wang et al. [13] used face tracking for head gesture recognition and developed two basic interaction techniques in two game contexts (avatar appearance & control in a third person game and dodging-and-peeking in a FPS game). Their evaluation, based on simple game prototypes they developed, showed that the test participants experienced a greater sense of presence and satisfaction with their head tracking technique. However, they did not find any differences in user performance compared to using a traditional game controller. Limited accuracy of the head tracking data based on web cam could have been the reason that they did not find any quantifiable performance benefits.

Ashdown et al. [1] explored head tracking to switch the mouse pointer between monitors in a multi-monitor environment. Although participants preferred using head tracking, their results indicate that the task time was increased with head tracking usage. Another study [11] evaluated exaggerated head-coupled camera motions for game-like object movement but did not find any performance differences with different exaggeration levels. Zhu et al. [15] used head tracking for remote camera control but did not find any benefits of using head tracking compared to keyboard based control. Additionally, they found that users with more gaming experience performed better not only in keyboard controls but also in head tracking controls.

Head tracking has been explored by virtual reality scientists to visualize and understand complex 3D structures [9]. Bajura et al.[2] used head tracking for visualizing patient ultrasound data overlapped with a patient image in real time using a head mounted display (HMD). Head tracking has also been used to control avatars in Virtual Environments (VE) [7] and it was found that although head tracking is more intuitive for view control, it does not provide any performance benefits compared to using traditional button based controllers.

None of the work mentioned above evaluated performance benefits of head tracking in complex gaming environments like in modern video games. To the best of our knowledge,

our work is the first to systematically explore user performance benefits of head tracking in commercially available modern video games for different game genres.

3 SELECTING THE GAMES

We chose the TrackIR 5 by NaturalPoint Inc. as our head tracking device because it is natively supported in many (about 130) commercially available games (a list of commercially supported games is available on the TrackIR website [8]). TrackIR 5 is an optical motion tracking game controller which can track head motions up to six degrees of freedom, but not all degrees of freedom are supported in all games, depending on the nature of interaction required for that game. Most of these games fall into three categories, racing , flight simulation, and first person shooter. We rejected the games which used head tracking for minimal tasks not related to the objective of the game. We also rejected some old games which did not support rendering at full 1080p resolution. We chose four games, Arma II, Dirt 2, Microsoft Flight and Wings of Prey, that we thought could benefit when played in head tracked environment (see Figure 1). All these games supported alternate control methods, using joystick or buttons on Xbox 360 controller, when head tracking is not available.

Arma II is a first person shooter (FPS) in which users can rotate their heads to look around in the game environment and move their heads closer to screen, in iron-sight (aim using markers on the gun) mode, to shoot distant enemies. We felt that knowledge of the ambient environment, through the use of natural gestures to look around, might help user to find enemies more easily, and zoom-in by moving closer to the screen would make the game more immersive.

Dirt 2 is a car racing game and supports head tracking only in first person view. In this game, users can rotate their heads to rotate the driver's head in the game to look around through the car windows. We expected that this would help users to see upcoming turns more easily and increase their gaming performance.

Microsoft Flight is a flight simulation game and supports head tracking in cockpit view (first person view) mode. In this game, users can also rotate their heads to look around through the windows of the cockpit. Use of head tracking would make it easier for the user to look around for any stationary objects in the flight path in order to avoid collisions.

Wings of Prey is an air combat game in which users shoot enemies while flying. This game is significantly different from Microsoft Flight because in this game you have to shoot moving targets requiring more head usage to find those targets around you. In this game, users can look around through the aircraft windows by rotating their head. The aircraft had windows to the left, right, front and top of the player. Looking around naturally would help users find surrounding enemies in the air more easily and would help them increase their performance.

4 USER STUDY

We conducted an experiment with four PC games (as discussed in the previous section) where participants played each game either with head tracking or without head tracking using the Xbox 360 controller. We examined both quantitative metrics, based on each game's goals and tasks, and qualitative metrics, based on whether participants preferred playing the games with head tracking and whether they perceived any benefits. Based on previous findings in related work and our analysis of the games, we have following hypotheses:

Hypothesis 1 (H1) : Head tracking improves user's gaming performance compared to a traditional game controller.

Hypothesis 2 (H2) : Users will learn to play games faster with head tracking on average than with a traditional game controller.

Hypothesis 3 (H3) : Users prefer playing games with head tracking since it provides a more engaging user experience.

4.1 Participants and Equipment

Forty participants (36 males and 4 females ranging in age from 18 to 30 with a mean age of 20.9) were recruited from a university population. A modified version of Terlecki and Newcombe's Video Game Experience survey [12] was used as a pre-questionnaire in which they answered questions about their previous gaming experience. The survey was modified to include questions related to previous experience, if any, with head tracking, and the games used for the study. Of the 40 participants, 6 were ranked as beginners (4 in head tracked group and 2 in non-head tracked group), 16 as intermediate (7 in head tracked group and 9 in non-head tracked group), and 18 as advanced (9 in each group). Since there were only a few beginners, we decided to combine beginners and intermediate categories into one category called casual gamers. The experiment duration ranged from 60 to 80 minutes depending on how long participants took to complete the tasks presented to them in the games and how much time was spent on the questionnaires. All participants were paid $10 for their time.

The head tracked setup (see Figure 1) used a TrackIR 5 with Pro Clip, a Samsung 50" DLP 3D HDTV, a Xbox 360 controller, and a PC (Core i7 920 CPU, GTX 470 graphics card, 16 GB RAM). These are all commodity hardware components.. For the control group, the TrackIR 5 was not used and the participant played only using the Xbox 360 controller. Note that a limitation with head tracking based game camera control is that the maximum amount of head rotation is dependent on the display screen size and distance of user from screen. Too much head rotation could lead you to look away from the screen. This is the reasoning behind our use of a large screen TV for our experiments so, even if users (sitting approximately 3 feets away from the TV screen) rotate their head slightly (about 45 degree in either direction), they would still be looking at the screen.

4.2 Experimental Task

The participants were given the task of playing through levels of the four games. For each game, they were presented with a task specific to that game and a goal for completing each task. Participants played these games in random order (counter-balanced Latin Squares design) with three attempts for each game.

Arma II: Participants played "Single player scenario: Trial by Fire" and their task was to shoot as many enemies as possible within 10 minutes. The trial ends before 10 minutes if the player gets shot by the enemy. The game was reset after each trial.

Figure 1 The experimental setup.

Table 1 Summary of metrics for each game. The metrics are used to quantify how users in the head tracked (H) and non-head tracked (NH) groups performed.

Game	Metric
Arma II	Number of enemies shot, Survival Time
Dirt2	Race completion time, Rank in the race
Microsoft Flight	Game Score
Wings of Prey	Time taken, Number of enemy planes shot

Dirt 2: The participants played "London Rally" and their task was to win the race in as little time as possible with a maximum of 10 minutes. The game was reset after each trial.

Microsoft Flight: Participants played "First Flight" and their task was to maneuver the aircraft through numerous stationary balloons and finally land on the runway. The aircraft crashes if hit by balloon or if the orientation/speed of aircraft is not right while landing. The game was reset after each trial.

Wings of Prey: The participants played single player mission "Battle of Britain: Defend Manston" and their task was to shoot down all the enemy planes before time runs out (about 5 minutes). The game ends before the time limit if the aircraft crashes or gets shot down during air combat. After each trial, the game was reset.

4.3 Design and Procedure

Our study design was based, in part, on the study by Kulshreshth et al.[5]. We chose a between subjects design to avoid any effects of learning on user performance, where the independent variable was head tracking (with or without) and the dependent variables were the various scoring metrics used in each game. We wanted some additional information about the use of head tracking in video games for those who played the games without head tracking. Thus, we chose to have those participants who played without head tracking, pick one game to try with head tracking in order to gather their reactions. Both the quantitative and qualitative data was explored collectively as well as according to the two player expertise groupings (casuals and experts).

4.3.1 Quantitative and Qualitative Metrics

For each game, we tracked quantitative data that we felt was a good indication of how well users performed. Quantitative metrics are summarized in Table 1.

Table 2 Post-game Questionnaire. Participants answered these questions on a 7 point Likert scale after playing each game. We used this data for qualitative analysis.

Postgame Questions	
Q1	To what extent did the game hold your attention?
Q2	How much effort did you put into playing the game?
Q3	Did you feel you were trying your best?
Q4	To what extent did you lose track of time?
Q5	Did you feel the urge to see what was happening around you?
Q6	To what extent you enjoyed playing the game, rather than something you were just doing?
Q7	To what extent did you find the game challenging?
Q8	How well do you think you performed in the game?
Q9	To what extent did you feel emotionally attached to the game?
Q10	To what extent did you enjoy the graphics and the imagery?
Q11	How much would you say you enjoyed playing the game?
Q12	Would you like to play the game again?

Table 3 Head Tracking Questionnaire. Participants responded to statements 1-4 on a 7 point Likert scale. Questions 5-10 were multiple choice and open ended questions to gauge the users perception of the effects of head tracking.

Head Tracking Questions	
Q1	Head Tracking improved the overall experience of the game.
Q2	I would choose to play head tracked games over normal games.
Q3	I felt that head tracking enhanced the sense of engagement I felt.
Q4	Head Tracking is a necessity for my future game experiences.
Q5	Did head tracking help you perform better in the games?
Q6	Which games did it help you in?
Q7	How did it help you in those games?
Q8	Did head tracking decrease your performance in the games?
Q9	Which games did it decrease your performance in?
Q10	How did it decrease your performance in those games?

In Arma II, survival time and number of enemies shot were tracked as performance metrics. In Dirt 2, we recorded race completion time and rank in the race. In Microsoft Flight, we recorded the game score. The player was scored on the basis of how many balloons it passed through, if proper speed was maintained while landing, and if the plane landed on runway. In case of a plane crash, this game does not show the final score, but does show the points the player gets for each task while playing. We used this to calculate the final score. In Wings of Prey, number of enemies shot, time taken and game score were tracked as performance metrics.

For the qualitative data, all participants filled out an immersion questionnaire [4] (see Table 2) upon completion of all trials of each game. Responses were measured on a 7 point Likert scale (1 = most negative response, 7 = most positive response). Upon completion of all experimental tasks, participants were given a survey to determine how head tracking affected their gaming experience (see Table 3), whether they preferred to play the games with head tracking, and if head tracking helped or hurt their performance.

4.3.2 Procedure

The experiment began with the participant seated in front of the TV and the moderator seated to the side. Partic-

Table 4 Two-way ANOVA analysis for Arma II. Significant differences based on head tracking mode.

Source	Enemies Shot	Time
HTM	$F_{1,36} = 4.205, p < 0.05$	$F_{1,36} = 5.764, p < 0.05$
EXP	$F_{1,36} = 3.577, p = 0.067$	$F_{1,36} = 3.812, p = 0.59$
HTM×EXP	$F_{1,36} = 0.3611, p = 0.440$	$F_{1,36} = 4.656, p < 0.05$

ipants were given a standard consent form that explained the study. They were then given a pre-questionnaire that focused on their gaming expertise. Participants were then presented with the games in random order (Latin Squares design). Half the participants played the games without head tracking (control group) and half played with head tracking (experimental group). The moderator would present the game and give instructions to the participant as to what they needed to accomplish in the game and what their goals were. They were also instructed on how to use the Xbox 360 controller. During the experiment, the moderator recorded quantitative data using scores from the games and a stopwatch for timing information (if not already provided by the game). After each game, the participant filled out a post-questionnaire with questions about their experiences with the game. If the participants played the four games in the non-head-tracked condition, they then selected one game to play with head tracking. All participants were given a final post-questionnaire about their experiences with head tracking.

5 RESULTS AND ANALYSIS

We broke up the participants in each group (head tracked and non-head tracked group) into casual gamers (11 participants in the head tracked group, 11 participants in the non-head tracked group) and expert gamers (9 participants in the head tracked, 9 participants in the non-head tracked group). To analyze the performance data, a two-way ANOVA was conducted that examined the effect of game-play expertise (EXP), casual or expert, and the head tracking mode (HTM), present (H) or absent (NH), on the average (of the three trials) user performance (see Table 1 for metrics used for each game). We did a post-hoc analysis using independent sample t-tests. We used Holm's sequential Bonferroni adjustment to correct for type I errors [3] and the Shapiro-Wilk test to make sure our data is parametric. We also wanted to see whether there was learning taking place in the form of game play improvement. We looked at the improvement in the performance measures for each game from the first user run to their last run using a repeated measures ANOVA. Finally we wanted to look at the participant's perception of their performance through the post questionnaires. To analyze this Likert scale data, we used the Mann-Whitney test. For all of our statistical measures, we used $\alpha = 0.05$. In all graphs error bars represents 95% confidence interval.

5.1 Arma II

Table 4 shows the results of a two-way ANOVA analysis for Arma II. Although this table shows some significance based on head tracking mode (HTM), the post-hoc analysis results were not significant. Experts in the head tracking group (H) survived significantly ($t_{16} = 31.94, p < 0.01$) longer than the experts in the non-head tracking group (NH) (see Figure 2). For score improvements, neither casual gamers nor expert

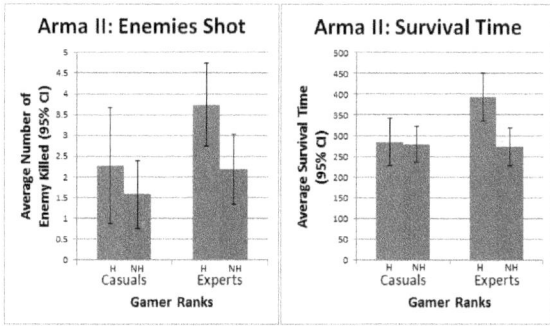

Figure 2 Arma II: Differences in the average number of enemy shot and survival time between the two head tracking modes (H: head tracked, NH: Non-head tracked) in the two gamer categories. Expert gamers performed significantly better with head tracking in terms of survival time.

Table 5 Two-way ANOVA analysis for Dirt 2. Significant differences in rank based on gaming expertise was found.

Source	Race Time	Rank
HTM	$F_{1,36} = 0.001, p = 0.980$	$F_{1,36} = 0.003, p = 0.953$
EXP	$F_{1,36} = 3.738, p = 0.061$	$F_{1,36} = 7.467, p < 0.01$
HTM×EXP	$F_{1,36} = 0.090, p = 0.765$	$F_{1,36} = 0.346, p = 0.560$

gamers showed any significant improvements, from the first trial to the last trial, in terms of number of enemies shot and survival times. For the questionnaire data, people thought that the game was too challenging ($\bar{x} = 6.5, \sigma = 0.88$) and they performed badly ($\bar{x} = 2.4, \sigma = 1.28$) in the game. When broken down based on gamer ranks, no significant differences were found on any question in the qualitative data between the two head tracking groups.

5.2 Dirt 2

A two-way ANOVA analysis shows (see Table 5) significance in the rank based on game expertise. Gamers in the expert group ($\bar{x} = 2.75, \sigma = 1.77$) scored significantly ($t_{38} = 2.794, p < 0.01$) better ranks in the race (lower is bet-

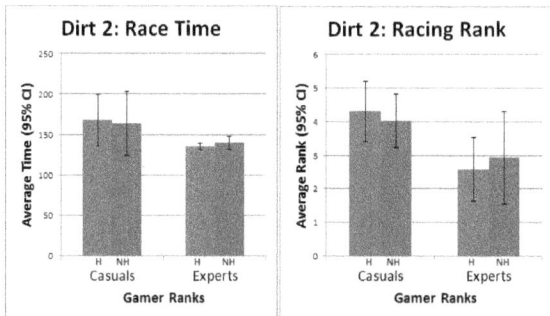

Figure 3 Dirt2: Differences in the average race time and average rank (lower is better) between the two head tracking modes (H: head tracked, NH: Non-head tracked) in the two gamer categories. Expert gamers took less time and scored better rank with head tracking.

Table 6 Two-way ANOVA analysis for Microsoft Flight. No Significance was found.

Source	Game Score
HTM	$F_{1,36} = 0.021, p = 0.886$
EXP	$F_{1,36} = 2.276, p = 0.140$
HTM×EXP	$F_{1,36} = 0.717, p = 0.403$

ter) than the casual gamers ($\bar{x} = 4.16, \sigma = 1.42$). For score improvements, casuals in the head tracking group significantly improved their racing time ($F_{2,9} = 5.354, p < 0.05$), from 188.72 seconds ($\sigma = 81.14$) in the first trial to 152.72 seconds ($\sigma = 33.72$) in the third trial, and rank ($F_{2,9} = 71.40, p < 0.05$), from 5.36 ($\sigma = 1.50$) in the first trial to 3.81 ($\sigma = 1.83$) in last trial. Casuals in the non-head tracking group significantly improved their racing time as well ($F_{2,9} = 8.449, p < 0.05$), from 171.36 seconds ($\sigma = 73.87$) in the first trial to 157.36 seconds ($\sigma = 63.75$) in the third trial, and rank ($F_{2,9} = 4.244, p < 0.05$), from 5.00 ($\sigma = 1.41$) in the first trial to 3.09 ($\sigma = 2.07$) in last trial. This translates to 19.07% improvement for head tracking group compared to 8.16% for non-head tracking group in terms of time, and 28.91% improvement for head tracking group compared to 38.20% for non-head tracking group in terms of game rank. Experts in the head tracking group did not show any significance improvements in racing time or rank. Experts in the non-head tracking group significantly improved their racing time ($F_{2,7} = 5.048, p < 0.025$), from 146.55 seconds ($\sigma = 19.04$) in the first trial to 133.22 seconds ($\sigma = 8.58$) in the third trial, but no significance was found for rank improvement.

For the qualitative data, Dirt 2 held significantly more ($Z = -2.028, p < 0.05$) attention for the head tracking group ($\bar{x} = 6.45, \sigma = 0.759$) compared to the non-head tracking group ($\bar{x} = 5.7, \sigma = 1.380$). All the participants thought they were trying their best ($\bar{x} = 6.10, \sigma = 1.277$) to play the game. Casuals in the head tracking group thought that they put in significantly more effort ($Z = -1.96, p < 0.05$) to play this game, were significantly less ($Z = -1.997, p < 0.05$) distracted, and were trying their best ($Z = -2.144, p < 0.05$), compared to the non-head tracked group. Significantly more people ($Z = -1.97, p < 0.05$) in the casual head tracking group than in the casual non-head tracked group thought that they would like to play the game again. In the case of expert gamers, the head tracking group enjoyed the graphics and imagery significantly more ($Z = -2.012, p < 0.05$) than the non-head tracked group.

5.3 Microsoft Flight

No statistically significant differences were found based on head tracking mode or the gamer ranks (see Table 6). Casuals in the head tracking group did not show any significant score improvements, but the casuals in the non-head tracked group significantly improved ($F_{2,9} = 4.865, p < 0.05$), their score from 859.09 ($\sigma = 396.11$) in the first trial to 995.45 ($\sigma = 332.00$) in their last trial. In case of experts, the head tracked group significantly improved ($F_{2,9} = 3.811, p < 0.05$), their score from 966.66 ($\sigma = 271.569$) in the first trial to the maximum possible score of 1150.0 ($\sigma = 0$) in their last trial, while the non-head tracked group significantly improved ($F_{2,9} = 8.413, p < 0.01$), their score from 761.11 ($\sigma = 356.87$) in the first trial to 1122.22 ($\sigma = 66.66$) in their

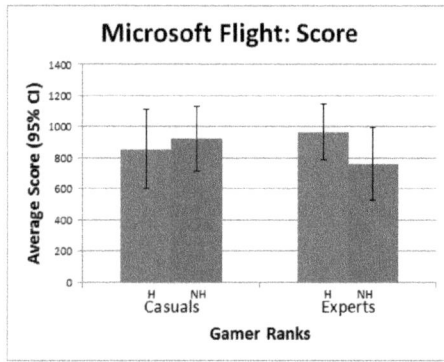

Figure 4 Microsoft Flight: Differences in the game score between the two head tracking modes (H: head tracked, NH: Non-head tracked) in the two gamer categories. Casual gamers performed slightly better without head tracking but expert gamers performed slightly better with head tracking.

Table 7 Two-way ANOVA analysis for Wings of Prey. Difference in time due to head tracking mode and number of enemies shot due to gaming expertise was found.

Source	Enemies Shot	Time
HTM	$F_{1,36} = 0.077, p = 0.783$	$F_{1,36} = 5.014, p < 0.05$
EXP	$F_{1,36} = 6.271, p < 0.05$	$F_{1,36} = 2.093, p = 0.157$
HTM×EXP	$F_{1,36} = 2.080, p = 0.158$	$F_{1,36} = 1.325, p = 0.257$

last trial. This translates to 18.97% improvement for head tracking group compared to 47.44% for non-head tracking group.

For the qualitative data, the game held the attention of all the participants ($\bar{x} = 5.925, \sigma = 1.047$) and all participants thought that they tried their best ($\bar{x} = 5.975, \sigma = 1.329$). The head tracked group enjoyed the game significantly more ($Z = -2.564, p < 0.05$) and thought that they performed significantly well ($Z = -2.689, p < 0.05$), when compared to non-head tracked group. When broken down based on gamer ranks, no significant differences were found between the two head tracking groups for casual gamers. But, for expert gamers, head tracked group enjoyed the game significantly more ($Z = -2.473, p < 0.05$) than the non-head tracked group.

5.4 Wings of Prey

A two-way ANOVA analysis of the Wings of Prey is shown in Table 7. The head tracked group ($\bar{x} = 245.56, \sigma = 34.79$) took slightly less ($t_{38} = -2.096, p = 0.043$) time compared to the non-head tracked group ($\bar{x} = 266.45, \sigma = 27.82$) but the results were not significant due to the post-hoc correction. However, experts in the head tracked group ($\bar{x} = 231.51, \sigma = 34.97$) took significantly less ($t_{16} = -2.301, p < 0.05$) time compared to the experts in the non-head tracked group ($\bar{x} = 264.85, \sigma = 25.80$) (see Figure 5). Experts ($\bar{x} = 4.12, \sigma = 2.36$) shot significantly more ($t_{38} = -2.501, p < 0.025$) enemy planes than casual gamers ($\bar{x} = 5.68, \sigma = 1.31$). For score improvement, no significant differences in terms of enemies shot or time taken were found for either casual gamers or expert gamers.

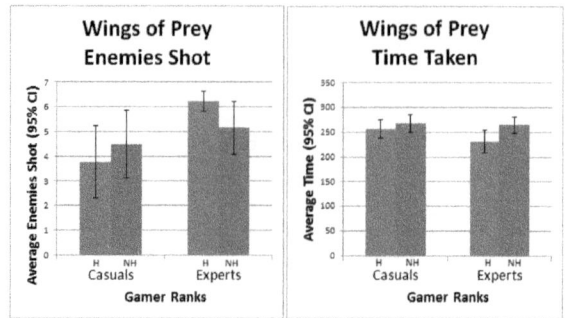

Figure 5 Wings of Prey: Differences in the average number of enemies shot and time taken between the two head tracking modes (H: head tracked, NH: Non-head tracked) in the two gamer categories. Expert gamers shot slightly more enemies and took significantly less time with head tracking.

For qualitative data, the game held the attention of all the participants ($\bar{x} = 6.05, \sigma = 1.153$) and all participants thought that they tried their best ($\bar{x} = 6.15, \sigma = 1.291$). Qualitatively, no significant differences were found between the head tracked and non head tracked groups. When broken down based on gamer ranks, there were also no significant differences.

5.5 Head Tracking Questions

Out of the 20 participants in the non-head tracked group, three chose to play Arma II, five chose to play Dirt2, three chose to play Microsoft Flight, and nine chose to play Wings of Prey. All three participants who played Arma II thought that head tracking helped them. Only one out of five participants who played Dirt 2 thought that it helped them. Two participants out of three who played Microsoft Flight thought that it helped them. Finally, six out of nine participants who played Wings of Prey thought that it helped them.

Out of the 20 participants from the head tracked group that played all games with head tracking, 19 participants thought that it gave them an advantage in at least one of the games and 13 thought that it hurt their performance in at least one of the games. Eight in Arma II, seven in Dirt 2, and only one in Wings of Prey thought that head tracking hurt their performance. No one thought that head tracking hurt their performance in Microsoft Flight.

All the participants filled out a questionnaire about their experience with head tracking (see Table 3), responding to questions Q1-Q4 on a 7 point Likert scale (1=Strongly Disagree, 7=Strongly Agree). All the participants agreed that head tracking improved their overall gaming experience ($\bar{x} = 5.05, \sigma = 1.83$) and enhanced the sense of engagement they felt ($\bar{x} = 5.30, \sigma = 1.69$). However most participants did not think that head tracking was a necessity for their future gaming experience ($\bar{x} = 3.32, \sigma = 1.93$). We did not find any statistically significant differences when data was divided across gamer ranks or head tracking modes.

6 DISCUSSION

Hypothesis testing results for each game are summarized in Table 8. Hypothesis H1 is true only for expert gamers in case of Arma II and Wings of Prey. Hypothesis H2 was always

Table 8 Summary of hypothesis (see section 4) testing results for all games in the two gamer ranks. (T=True and F=False)

Game	Casual Gamers			Experts Gamers		
	H1	H2	H3	H1	H2	H3
Arma II	F	F	F	T	F	F
Dirt 2	F	F	T	F	F	F
Microsoft Flight	F	F	F	F	F	T
Wings of Prey	F	F	F	T	F	F

found to be false which means that head tracking did not help in learning the games faster. Hypothesis H3 was true for casual gamers in Dirt 2 and expert gamers in Microsoft Flight. We noticed large variability, as indicated by large error bars in charts, in our user performance data which could be due to few factors. One factor may be different gaming abilities of the users, an expert FPS gamer may not necessarily be an expert in flight simulation or racing games. Another factor could be insufficient game training time before the experiment.

Based on our quantitative data, we can see that head tracking provided significant performance advantages only for expert gamers for Arma II (better survival time) and Wings of Prey (better time and more number of enemies shot). No other significant advantages were found in the other games we tested. Both Arma II & Wings of Prey are shooting games and in both games head tracking is useful to find enemies around the player's current position. In Arma II, gamers found it useful and natural to rotate their head to look around and move closer to the screen to zoom-in and iron-sight. In the case of Dirt 2, the user had to look forward most of the time and rotating one's head makes it difficult to focus on the road, especially at fast speeds. So, head tracking turned out to be not that useful for this game. In the case of Microsoft Flight, although the head tracking added depth perception and a sense of realism to the game, the game itself was slow paced and not difficult to play. So, users did equally well and it did not matter much if head tracking was present or not.

While examining learning effects (e.g., score improvement with each game trial), we noticed that there were significant improvements in some cases when the two groups (head tracked vs non-head tracked) were analyzed separately. However, head tracking usage did not enhance learning, when compared to non-head tracked environment, and in some cases negatively affected learning (e.g., experts in Dirt 2 learned faster without head tracking). But, experts in the head tracking group for Dirt 2 already started with a high score and did not improve much. In the case of Microsoft Flight, the casual non-head tracked group and both expert groups (head tracked vs non-head tracked) improved their score significantly. For Arma II and Wings of Prey, we did not notice any significant improvements across runs. In the case of Arma II, the head tracked group already started with a higher score than the non-head tracked group and did not improve significantly with trials. In the case of Wings of Prey, casual gamers in the head tracked group started with a lower score than the non-head tracked group and both groups did not improve much with repeated attempts. However, expert gamers had a higher score in the head tracked group than the non-head tracked group but it did not improve much with repeated attempts.

Another important factor that could affect our results is the fact that head tracking was an added feature in all the games we tested. So it was up to the user whether to take advantage of head tracking or not. While expert gamers could make better use of head tracking, casual gamers appeared to focus more on games basics and did not pay much attention to head tracking. This may explain why casual gamers performed almost equally well in both the groups (head tracked vs non-head tracked). So far head tracking devices are not as successful as motion controllers (e.g., Sony Move or Nintendo Wii). Games which make use of motion controllers usually provide in-game usage instruction (e.g. a tutorial when the game starts or hints while playing) for their effective use but we found this missing in case of head tracked games we tested. Some instructions could have helped users make better use of head tracking while playing.

Based on our qualitative data, in some games we found significant differences in the two user groups (head tracked vs non-head tracked). Head tracking was perceived to be significantly more enjoyable in Microsoft Flight. Casual users had to put significantly more efforts to play Dirt 2 with head tracking. We did not find any significant differences in Arma II and Wings of Prey. In general, almost all participants were not familiar with the games we tested, and the users played for a short period of time (60 to 80 minutes). This may explain why we did not notice significant differences in qualitative data for most games.

Additionally, our qualitative data indicates that head tracking is perceived to be more enjoyable for slow paced games and could harm user performance when used in fast paced games. Our results contradict previous findings [7, 11, 15], which indicate that although intuitive and enjoyable, head tracking does not provide significant performance benefits. The main reason for these differences could be the choice of game tasks we assigned to participants or the head tracking system used for this study. All the games we tested had native head tracking support and currently there is a limited selection of game genres (Racing, Flight Simulator, and First Person Shooter) that support head tracking, so we need to explore more head tracked based interaction techniques to be able to use them in more game genres. This could be achieved by including tasks in the games which can only be achieved by head tracked-based interaction and bonus points could be given for these tasks. This would force users to use head tracking and help them learn new head tracking based interaction techniques. This could be useful, especially, in the initial phases until head tracking becomes a very commonly used gaming accessory. Based on our findings and observations, we have the following recommendations to game designers:

- Make use of head tracking in FPS and air-combat games because these games have tasks that could benefit from head tracking usage.

- Include instructions/hints while playing games to guide gamers to make optimal use of head tracking. Most people are used to playing games with traditional button based controllers, so most of the time they forget to use head tracking. We think, instructions/hints while playing would remind them of the presence of head tracking.

- Limit head tracking usage in racing games. Head tracking usage could be distracting for racing games.

Note that our study did have some limitations. Due to the nature of experiment and time limitations, it was difficult to balance (in terms of gaming abilities) the participants across the two groups (head tracked vs non-head tracked). Although we had same number of expert users in the two groups, the casual head tracked group had more beginners than the casual non-head tracked group. This disproportion could have skewed some of our results. In addition, unlike previous work [10, 13, 14], the games we tested were complex so it may have been difficult for users to use head tracking effectively and learn how to play the games at the same time. This could have had an affect on performance results.

7 CONCLUSION AND FUTURE WORK

We have presented a study exploring the effects of head tracking on user performance in head tracking enabled modern video games. We observed that head tracking could provide significant performance advantages for certain games (Arma II and Wings of Prey) depending upon game genres and gaming expertise. Our results indicate that head tracking is useful in shooting games (FPS, air combat etc.) and it is not a good idea to use it in a fast paced racing games. However, not all users benefit equally well with head tracking. Casual gamers do not benefit significantly from head tracking, but expert gamers can perform significantly better when head tracking is present. A possible reason is that casual gamers focus more on the basic games mechanics and do not pay much attention to a more advanced feature like head tracking. Our qualitative results indicate that head tracking is more enjoyable for slow paced video games (e.g. flight simulation games) and it might hurt performance in fast paced modern video games (e.g. racing games).

Our study is a preliminary step towards exploring the effectiveness of head tracking in realistic game scenarios. Clearly, further research with more game genres and head tracking techniques is required to further validate our results. In the future, we will continue to explore how head tracking could be made more enjoyable and effective in modern video games including how to better enhance casual gamer's performance. We also plan to explore whether head tracking is a better depth cue compared to 3D stereo and the effectiveness of simultaneously using head tracking and 3D stereo in modern video games.

8 ACKNOWLEDGMENTS

This work is supported in part by NSF CAREER award IIS-0845921 and NSF awards IIS-0856045 and CCF-1012056. We would also like to thank the members of ISUE lab for their support and the anonymous reviewers for their useful comments and feedback.

9 REFERENCES

[1] M. Ashdown, K. Oka, and Y. Sato. Combining head tracking and mouse input for a gui on multiple monitors. In *CHI '05 Extended Abstracts on Human Factors in Computing Systems*, CHI EA '05, pages 1188–1191, New York, NY, USA, 2005. ACM.

[2] M. Bajura, H. Fuchs, and R. Ohbuchi. Merging virtual objects with the real world: seeing ultrasound imagery within the patient. *SIGGRAPH Comput. Graph.*, 26(2):203–210, July 1992.

[3] S. Holm. A simple sequentially rejective multiple test procedure. *Scandinavian Journal of Statistics*, 6(2):65–70, 1979.

[4] C. Jennett, A. L. Cox, P. Cairns, S. Dhoparee, A. Epps, T. Tijs, and A. Walton. Measuring and defining the experience of immersion in games. *International Journal of Human-Computer Studies*, 66,9:641–661, 2008.

[5] A. Kulshreshth, J. Schild, and J. J. LaViola Jr. Evaluating user performance in 3d stereo and motion enabled video games. In *Proceedings of the International Conference on the Foundations of Digital Games*, pages 33–40, New York, NY, 2012. ACM.

[6] J. Lee. Hacking the nintendo wii remote. *J. IEEE Pervasive Computing*, 7(3):39–45, 2008.

[7] S. Marks, J. Windsor, and B. Wunsche. Evaluation of the effectiveness of head tracking for view and avatar control in virtual environments. In *Image and Vision Computing New Zealand (IVCNZ), 2010 25th International Conference of*, pages 1–8, Nov 2010.

[8] NaturalPoint. Trackir 5. http://www.naturalpoint.com/trackir/products/trackir5/.

[9] J. Rekimoto. A vision-based head tracker for fish tank virtual reality-vr without head gear. In *Virtual Reality Annual International Symposium, 1995. Proceedings.*, pages 94 –100, mar 1995.

[10] T. Sko and H. Gardner. Head tracking in first-person games: Interaction using a web-camera. In *Human-Computer Interaction - INTERACT 2009*, volume 5726 of *Lecture Notes in Computer Science*, pages 342–355. Springer Berlin / Heidelberg, 2009.

[11] R. J. Teather and W. Stuerzlinger. Exaggerated head motions for game viewpoint control. In *Proceedings of the 2008 Conference on Future Play: Research, Play, Share*, Future Play '08, pages 240–243, New York, NY, USA, 2008. ACM.

[12] M. Terlecki and N. Newcombe. How important is the digital divide? the relation of computer and videogame usage gender differences in mental rotation ability. *Sex Roles*, 53:433–441, 2005.

[13] S. Wang, X. Xiong, Y. Xu, C. Wang, W. Zhang, X. Dai, and D. Zhang. Face-tracking as an augmented input in video games: enhancing presence, role-playing and control. In *Proceedings of the SIGCHI Conference on Human Factors in Computing Systems*, CHI '06, pages 1097–1106, New York, NY, USA, 2006. ACM.

[14] J. Yim, E. Qiu, and T. C. N. Graham. Experience in the design and development of a game based on head-tracking input. In *Proceedings of the 2008 Conference on Future Play: Research, Play, Share*, Future Play '08, pages 236–239, New York, NY, USA, 2008. ACM.

[15] D. Zhu, T. Gedeon, and K. Taylor. Keyboard before head tracking depresses user success in remote camera control. In *Human-Computer Interaction , INTERACT 2009*, volume 5727 of *Lecture Notes in Computer Science*, pages 319–331. Springer Berlin / Heidelberg, 2009.

Volume Cracker: A Bimanual 3D Interaction Technique for Analysis of Raw Volumetric Data

Bireswar Laha and Doug A. Bowman
Center for Human Computer Interaction and Department of Computer Science
Virginia Tech
2202 Kraft Drive,.Blacksburg, Virginia, U.S.A.
(blaha, bowman)@vt.edu

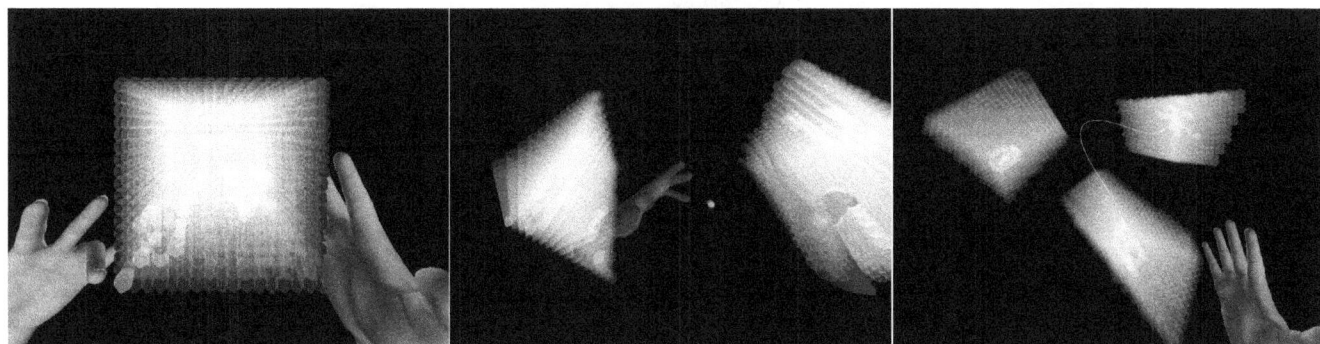

(a) A simulated volume dataset   (b) Cracking preview   (c) Cracked and connected sub-volumes

Figure 1: The Volume Cracker interaction technique.

ABSTRACT
Analysis of volume datasets often involves peering inside the volume to understand internal structures. Traditional approaches involve removing part of the volume through slicing, but this can result in the loss of context. Focus+context visualization techniques can distort part of the volume, or can assume prior definition of a region of interest or segmentation of layers of the volume. We propose a new bimanual 3D interaction technique, called Volume Cracker (VC), which allows the user to crack open a raw volume like a book to analyze the internal structures. VC preserves context by always displaying all the voxels, and by connecting the sub-volumes with curves joining the cracked faces. We discuss the design choices that we made, based on observations from prior user studies, input from domain scientists, and design studios. We also report the results of a user study comparing VC with a standard desktop interaction technique and a standard 3D bimanual interaction technique. The study used tasks from two categories of a generic volume analysis task taxonomy. We found VC had significant advantages over the other two techniques for search and pattern recognition tasks.

Categories and Subject Descriptors
I.3.6 [Computer Graphics]: Methodology and Techniques—Interaction techniques; I.3.7 [Computer Graphics]: Three-Dimensional Graphics and Realism-Virtual reality; H.5.2 [Information Interfaces and Presentation]: User Interfaces-Input devices and strategies.

Permission to make digital or hard copies of all or part of this work for personal or classroom use is granted without fee provided that copies are not made or distributed for profit or commercial advantage and that copies bear this notice and the full citation on the first page. To copy otherwise, or republish, to post on servers or to redistribute to lists, requires prior specific permission and/or a fee.
SUI'13, July 20–21, 2013, Los Angeles, California, USA.
Copyright © ACM 978-1-4503-2141-9/13/07...$15.00.

Keywords
3D interaction; 3D visualization; volume data analysis; bimanual interaction; virtual reality.

1. INTRODUCTION
Volume data comes from several domains, like medical imaging, geophysical sciences, engineering science and mechanics, and paleontological sciences. The sheer amount of volume data getting generated is increasing exponentially in these various domains [20]. It is generated through processes like computed tomography (CT), microscopic CT (micro-CT), magnetic resonance imaging (MRI), functional MRI (fMRI), positron emission tomography, and ultrasonography.

Volume data, in its raw form, is composed of voxels (x, y, z, v) in a 3D grid, instead of 2D pixels. Each voxel has one or more numeric values, representing color, density, refractive index, or other material properties. Generally, one of these properties is mapped to the transparency of the voxels (see Figure 1-a) in the rendering using some transfer function [10]. Scientists analyzing volume data often need to peer inside the volume [14, 15]. For example, a biologist may wish to follow a blood vessel through a CT scan to determine how many times it branches. This process involves finding the voxels representing the structure they are looking for, either by disregarding or removing the unwanted voxels, and then joining all the desired voxels to understand the structure. The analysis could also involve understanding in context, when the other voxels and relevant neighboring structures play an active role in the analysis [10].

The most standard method for analysis is called segmentation, in which the transfer function for mapping is adjusted manually or automatically based on some thresholds, to mark out the region of interest (ROI) in the volume accurately. Although segmentation produces very good results, it is quite time-consuming and often requires very precise selection of ROI in every slice of the volume. Thus, it would be useful to have alternative techniques that allow analysis of volume data and viewing of an ROI without requiring segmentation. Alternative analysis techniques such as axis-aligned slicing (AAS) cause users to lose context partially, and focus+context visualization and interaction techniques have several drawbacks (as discussed in section 2).

To address these problems, we propose a bimanual 3D interaction technique called the Volume Cracker (Figure 1), which preserves all the voxels, and the relative geometric shape and size of the various internal structures, but provides the flexibility to focus on any ROI chosen by the user. Our approach is inspired by the exploded views technique [4] that cracks open a volume into pre-defined selection objects, which could be refined interactively in real-time by volume painting [5]. The novel feature of our technique is that it is designed to be used with raw volume datasets, prior to any form of segmentation or any definition of selection objects or ROI. Our technique is aimed to contribute towards the suite of interaction techniques scientists are designing for interactive coarse segmentation of raw volume datasets [13].

We discuss the design and development of the Volume Cracker and present a user study comparing this tool with the desktop standard axis-aligned slicing (AAS) technique and a corresponding 3D standard arbitrary slicing (AS) technique. For evaluating the Volume Cracker, we chose different tasks from specific categories in a volume analysis task taxonomy [13].

2. RELATED WORK

Previous approaches to exploring volume data can be broadly divided into two categories. The techniques or tools in the first category remove part of the volume to reveal hidden structures inside, like orthogonal or axis-aligned slicing (AAS), in which the user controls cutting planes aligned with the three orthogonal axes, and can also obtain axial, coronal, and sagittal views along the three axes. The AAS technique has been widely used as part of various software packages like Amira[1] and 3D Slicer. Commercial 3D imaging hardware manufacturers, like Xradia[2] and GE healthcare, provide the AAS interaction as a de facto technique in their factory packaged software.

Hinckley et al. designed a bimanual asymmetric interface allowing arbitrary 3D slicing [8], based on Guiard's framework [7], using real world props. Going beyond simple cutting planes, researchers have used deformable cutting planes [12], clipping based on arbitrary geometry [26], and a filterbox tool [19]. Sculpting metaphors have also been proposed [25], and various sculpting tools like cutaway and ghost tools [5], and for erasing, digging, and clipping were explored [9]. All these techniques, although allowing the user to explore the volume in very useful ways, cause the user to lose spatial context.

This problem is addressed by the techniques of the second category, Focus+Context techniques. They seek to preserve the entire volume at all times, while letting the user focus on the ROI in various ways. One such approach is to use a 3D magnification lens metaphor, such as the Magic Volume Lens [24]. Some researchers have proposed focal-region-based feature enhancement [27] or importance-driven volume rendering [23]. Such magnifying or enhancing techniques, although highlighting

the ROI over surrounding areas in the volume, distort the volume or the ROI at least partially with respect to its neighboring structures. Also, many of these techniques are intended for use with segmented datasets. Thus they assume a partial and existing solution of the problem they are trying to address.

Other Focus+Context visualization techniques include layered browsing of volume data, promoted through an array of deformation tools [17]. These assume semantic layers in the volume data, which may not always exist [17].

Our approach relies on using the two hands of the user for interaction with a volume. Both symmetric [1] and asymmetric [7] bimanual interaction techniques have been designed, but few researchers focused on designing or standardizing bimanual techniques for volume data analysis (Hinckley et al. [8] is an exception). Ulinski [22] found that symmetric and synchronous techniques were best for selection tasks in volume data. Recently, there has been some effort in leveraging symmetric asynchronous bimanual techniques for medical data exploration [19]. Researchers are also exploring bimanual gestures for various direct touch interaction metaphors for exploring volume data [11].

3. VOLUME CRACKER DESIGN
3.1 Goals
We set out to design a new interaction technique for volume data analysis that would address the problems of existing techniques. We wanted to allow the users to view internal structures while keeping all the voxels visible and not distorting the dataset in any way, and not requiring any prior segmentation.

During our interviews with researchers and our prior empirical studies for evaluating task performance with volume data, the researchers expressed a strong desire for 3D interaction techniques to directly interact with and analyze volume datasets for various research tasks they perform on a regular basis. They were of the opinion that having a technique where they could use their hand(s) would be more natural, faster, and easier than using indirect tools. Thus, our goal was to design 3D interaction technique(s) using direct manipulation.

3.2 Design
3.2.1 High Level Metaphor Selection
We used design studio sessions in the context of a university course to seek innovative ideas for interaction techniques mapped to a set of task categories [13]. We asked participants to brainstorm ways to use two hands to carry out such tasks in the real world (e.g., searching for seeds in cotton is similar to search tasks in volume data). We also drew inspiration from techniques found in the literature [9, 17, 19] In particular, Zhou et al's magic story cube [28] inspired our use of a cracking metaphor.

This resulted in a shortlist of metaphors to analyze more closely. These included knife, cracker, peeler, hinge spreader [17], and box spreader [17] techniques. In the knife metaphor, the dominant hand cuts open slices from a volume held by the non-dominant hand. The cracker technique uses two hands to crack open a volume, like cracking open a book. The peeler uses the fingers to peel off outer layers from a volume, revealing the inner layers. The hinge spreader uses a hinge, while the box spreader uses a resizable box to open up the volume. We created paper prototypes or storyboards of each technique to understand and discuss the

---
[1] http://www.amira.com/

[2] http://www.xradia.com/solutions/index.php

affordances that each technique provides. To select the final metaphor, we looked at a set of usability criteria.

3.2.2 Usability Criteria

For the requirements of our technique, we had good reference from prior empirical studies in the literature with volume datasets [14, 15], and from our interview sessions with domain scientists, from various domains such as geophysics, paleontology, medical biology, and biomechanics. The usability criteria were, in decreasing order of importance:

1. Allow the user to understand what is hidden inside a volume
2. Allow the user to look at smaller chunks of a volume more closely, to identify the regions of interest (ROIs)
3. Allow the user to maintain the spatial context
4. Do not distort any part of the volume
5. Do not assume that the data has predefined semantic layers
6. Make the results of user actions clear and predictable
7. Allow the user to quickly reverse or cancel their actions

Of the shortlisted metaphors, the hinge spreader and the box spreader remove occluding voxels, making the ROI more clearly visible, but violating the criterion to maintain the spatial context.

The cracker, peeler, and knife metaphors preserve all the voxels in the volume, while breaking it in useful ways for the user to analyze. The peeler, however, is based on the assumption of semantic layers in the volume.

The knife technique allows cutting along specific lines through the volume, like we cut open an apple using a knife, while we hold it with the non-dominant hand. The cracker allows cracking open a volume with two hands, and also cracking sub-volumes recursively. Both these techniques satisfied the first five usability criteria. The cracker technique, however, offers the possibility of informing the user of the result of the cracking action prior to cracking (see section 3.2.3 below), through a "cracking preview," satisfying the sixth usability criterion. It was difficult to see how a knife metaphor might offer such a feature, since multiple cuts may be required to cut out a piece of the volume.

Further, while an asymmetric technique (knife) might offer more precision in the cut that we make to analyze the ROI closely, based on Guiard's framework [7], a symmetric technique (cracker) could be faster, as we use the degrees of freedom offered by two hands instead of one [16].

Based on this analysis, we chose to design and develop the cracker metaphor. The next section discusses various design decisions that we incorporated in the Volume Cracker, and how those address the various usability criteria.

3.2.3 Design Details

The basic idea of cracking emerged from the first usability criterion—to understand what is inside a volume. Intuitively, like we crack open a book, we wanted to crack open a volume with our two hands, to look at the things inside. Cracking preserves all the voxels in a volume, and does not assume layers in a volume. It also does not distort any part of the volume.

We designed a cracking preview (see Figure 1-b), which showed up as long as the midpoint between the two hands was within the volume. This was created and updated in real time by dividing the volume into two halves on either side of the plane orthogonal to the line joining the two hands, and then by displacing each voxel

Figure 2: User inspecting a dataset with Volume Cracker.

by a fixed distance along that line, towards the hand closer to the individual voxel. The preview showed how the voxels (along with the internal structures that they form) moved from one sub-volume to the other interactively as the position and orientation of the crack moved. It was designed to make the resulting sub-volumes fully predictable, and ties back to the sixth usability criterion above. Interestingly, from user feedback, we found that the cracking preview also provided a quick and dirty analysis of the various internal structures as well.

Cracking required simultaneous closing of both fists, and broke the volume into two sub-volumes as shown by the preview. The user could choose to crack recursively, until she had separated out the internal structures in blocks of ROIs, which she wanted to analyze separately. To preserve the context after cracking (as per Balakrishnan and Hinckley [1]), we displayed a line joining the two sub-volumes (third usability criterion). Separating the ROIs in connected sub-volumes served the second usability criterion— looking at smaller chunks of volume or ROIs more closely.

To address the final usability criterion, we introduced a bimanual grab function in the Volume Cracker. This allowed the users to grab connected sub-volumes, move them farther apart, or closer together, and also join them back (when their bounding boxes overlapped, and the grab was deactivated). We added visual feedback for activation of bimanual grab (blue), and joining of sub-volumes (green).

If the user cracked a sub-volume into two sub-sub-volumes, the line joining the original sub-volumes disappeared, while a new line joining the two new sub-sub-volumes appeared. The users could only rejoin connected sub-volumes, which maintained the hierarchy of sub-volumes.

The other action available in the original design was a single-hand grab on the entire dataset, cracked or otherwise, for manipulating its position and orientation directly. The fist did not need to be within the volume to activate the single-hand grab.

From demo sessions, we found that there were structures on the newly revealed surfaces of both sub-volumes that users wanted to analyze simultaneously, but they were having trouble because the surfaces were facing each other. This became another important usability criterion as even the domain scientists want to look at separate ROIs together. Also, this would help to figure out if there was an internal structure that got split in two during cracking.

We thus introduced rotations of the sub-volumes in the bimanual grab function, which gets activated right at the time of cracking. This allowed the users to grab the connected sub-volumes with both hands, and open those up like a book (while cracking) to look at the interior surfaces simultaneously. We connected the rotated sub-volumes with Hermite curves, defined and updated in real time by the normal vectors coming out of the two hands at any point during a bimanual grab (see Figure 3-c).

We initially allowed the users to reposition and reorient the sub-volumes however they wanted. This easily got confusing because if a structure is broken in two parts, it will be almost impossible to understand it as a whole if the divided structures get rotated about the axis running longitudinally through the unbroken structure, as in that case, the outlines of the structure on the broken faces would align improperly against each other.

In the final design, therefore, we use constraints to preserve the relative orientation of the structures between the two sub-volumes. We limit the movements of the sub-volumes to be along a plane and rotations of the sub-volumes to be around the normal vector to this plane (Figure 3-c). We define the plane at the time of cracking, as the plane containing the vector joining the two hands, and the vector joining the center of the original volume to the viewpoint. We selected these vectors, as at the time of cracking, the resulting plane allows the user to open up the sub-volumes like a book, so that the interior surfaces can face the user. This also serves the seventh usability criterion much better, as the users can quickly reverse the action of cracking if desired.

To avoid confusion, the cracking preview only shows where the crack will be, and not how the sub-volumes can be rotated after cracking. In other words, the preview shows what sub-volumes will be created, and then the separation and rotation of the sub-volumes is done after cracking. Although this means the cracking preview does not show the final state of the sub-volumes after cracking, the user can still quickly reverse the action if desired.

We use head tracking in combination with the Volume Cracker, since it helps the user to get different viewpoints very easily around a volume [15], and serves the first three usability criteria well. We also use stereoscopic display for better depth perception.

4. EVALUATION
4.1 Goals and Hypothesis
Our primary goal was to find out whether the Volume Cracker (VC) would improve quantitative task performance for volume data analysis, as compared to standard techniques. Thus, our first research question was:

1. How does VC perform as compared to a standard 2D and a standard 3D interaction technique for volume data analysis?

Further, we also wanted to gather qualitative insights on the usability and the design of VC, represented by our second research question:

2. How usable and easy to learn is VC?

Corresponding to the two research questions, we had two hypotheses:

1. *VC will produce significantly better task performance than other standard techniques for volume data analysis.* The design choices that we made while designing VC were all geared towards making volume analysis task performance faster and more accurate.

2. *VC will have comparable usability and learnability to existing techniques for volume data analysis tasks.* Based on the real-world metaphor of cracking with human hands, we believed VC would be easy to learn and intuitive to use.

To test our hypotheses, we designed an experiment to evaluate the VC and compared it against two existing interaction techniques for volume data analysis.

4.2 Preliminary Evaluation by Experts
Before running a more formal study, we invited four domain experts to evaluate VC. They included: a biomechanics professor who analyzes micro-CT scans of beetles and snakes, a medical biology doctoral student who works with micro-CT and nano-CT scans, a molecular biology doctoral student working with volume datasets generated from proteins, and an engineering science and mechanics doctoral student working with volume datasets.

We demonstrated a VC prototype to the experts. They appreciated being able to crack open a volume and segregate any region of interest to analyze the internal structures. All of them gave us examples of analysis tasks from their research domains where they felt the technique would be an improvement over the standard tools and techniques they use regularly.

We also verified with them that the rendering of our simulated volume datasets (see section 4.4) were comparable to the real datasets they are used to. We made the simulated datasets as large as we could (17^3 voxels) without sacrificing real-time interactivity, which is needed for VC to work smoothly. They opined that if we observed any benefits in the speed of task completion by using VC with these datasets, it would further improve with real volume datasets. Based on their feedback and input, we created structures inside the simulated datasets similar to the ones in real datasets, and we used realistic analysis tasks from a volume analysis task taxonomy [13].

4.3 Study Design
There are several existing interaction techniques for volume data analysis (see section 2). The wide variety of available techniques makes it difficult to evaluate the benefits of a new design in an absolute sense, but it highlights the need for empirical studies to compare the designs. We chose to compare VC against the most widely used desktop 2D interaction technique, and a widely known 3D bimanual interaction technique [3, 8].

We called the desktop 2D interaction technique the "axis-aligned slicing (AAS) technique." In AAS, the user looks at four views of the same data simultaneously. One is a 3D view of the volume. The user can slice it along three orthogonal axes, the views along which are called the axial, sagittal, and coronal views.

We termed the 3D interaction technique the "arbitrary slicing (AS) technique." AS is currently used by several 3D volume visualization software packages like 3D Visualizer [3]. In the AS, the user can rotate the volume data to any arbitrary 3D orientation. The user also has a slicing or cutting plane, which can also be rotated to any orientation, and can be used to slice through the volume to look at any arbitrary cross section of the volume.

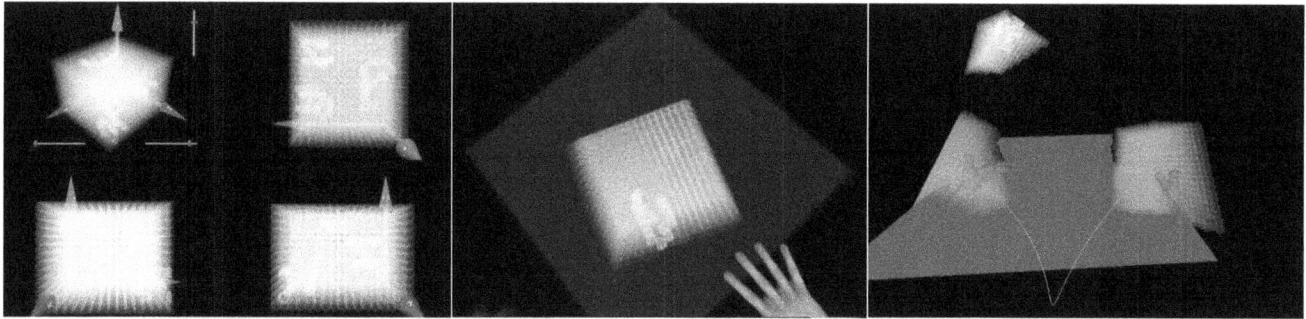

(a) Axis Aligned Slicing (AAS) technique   **(b) Arbitrary Slicing (AS) technique**   **(c) Volume Cracker (VC) technique**

Figure 3: The three interaction techniques we compared in our study.

4.4 Implementation

We implemented each of the three techniques in Vizard[3]. Because of implementing techniques like VC that manipulate individual voxels, we chose to create simulated volume datasets in the shape of a cube with 17^3 simulated voxels (represented by spheres). We varied the transparency between the various simulated voxels just like in real volume datasets. We verified with domain scientists that these datasets were comparable to the ones they use (see 4.2).

In our AAS technique (see Figure 3-a), we created four views, showing the simulated volume from four different viewpoints. The top left view showed a perspective view; the top right view looked down the vertical axis; the bottom left view looked down the left horizontal axis; the bottom right view looked down the right horizontal axis. We placed three sliders in the top left view, for slicing along the three axes. The three sliders and the corresponding cutting planes could be used in combination, by clicking and dragging with a wireless desktop mouse, placed on a table in front of the display. The handle of each slider bar spanned 20x10 pixels. None of the participants reported or appeared to have any trouble selecting them with the mouse pointer.

In our AS technique (see Figure 3-b), the user could grab using her left hand. She had a cutting plane attached rigidly to a six-degree-of-freedom (6DOF) tracked IS-900 wand, held in her right hand. The plane removed the voxels from the simulated volume that were on the rear side of the plane. The user could also make the cutting plane static with the wand, and use the left hand grab to analyze the various cross sections easily. Mapping the cutting plane to a wand held in the user's hand allowed the user to manipulate the plane easily to orientations difficult to achieve with just the human right hand.

The VC technique used in our study (Figure 3-c) was implemented as described in section 3.

We ran the evaluation with a rear projected Visbox-X2 display, a 10 by 7.5 foot display wall with passive stereo capabilities provided by Infitec. An Intersense's IS-900 tracking system provided 6DOF position and orientation tracking of the head and hands of the users in the AS and VC techniques, with a hand tracker for the left hand, and a wand held in their right hand. We used a 5DT data glove for detecting the grab action with the left hand. The right hand grab action in the VC technique was mapped to the trigger button click of the wand.

We used the same display (see Figure 2) in our study for all three techniques. We used stereoscopic rendering and head tracking in

AS and VC. However, we used monoscopic rendering with no head tracking in AAS, trading off the experimental control for ecological validity. Since three of the four views in AAS showed just 2D slices, it is unlikely that stereoscopic rendering, and head tracking would have made much impact.

4.5 Participants

We recruited 17 unpaid voluntary participants, of whom three were pilot participants, one had equipment problems, and one retired due to sickness. The final study thus had 12 participants, of whom two were female. Their ages ranged from 19 to 33 years, with an average of 22 years. All the participants were graduate or undergraduate students, either native or fluent in English, and self-reported no prior background in volume data analysis (see selection of novices vs. experts in section). The ordering of the three techniques (AAS, AS, VC) was counterbalanced, giving six different orderings. We had two participants with each ordering.

4.6 Tasks

Researchers are designing an abstract volume data analysis task taxonomy incorporating tasks from various domains under one umbrella [13]. The experts we invited in our lab for a qualitative evaluation of the VC reflected upon some of these task categories (see 4.2). Based on their suggestions, we initially chose four categories in which we hypothesized VC would improve task performance. After running three pilot participants, and informally testing the tasks ourselves with the three techniques, we chose two task types for the final study.

The first was a search task. In a real volume dataset, scientists search for blood vessels, joints in a tracheal network, bones, soft floating tissues, tumors, and many other structures [14]. We chose to use letters from the English alphabet as an abstraction for such structures. This allowed us to recruit novice participants (see 5.1). We believed this task was valid, because a task defined by experts, and used in a prior study of volume data analysis [15] also asked participants to describe the shape of an internal structure as a letter from the alphabet. In each dataset, we created 13 letters, of various size and thickness, randomly oriented, and distributed in the simulated volume. Of the 13 letters, four letters were the same. The participants were told that there were at least two, but no more than six of that particular letter, and were asked to find all the instances of that letter.

The second task was a pattern recognition task. Domain scientists often seek patterns in different parts of volume datasets. For this they try to match complex shapes and clusters—they correlate and compare them to shapes in other parts of the dataset. To simulate this task, we created three closely matching coiled structures, all randomly oriented in 3D. We made the structures

---

[3] http://www.worldviz.com/products/vizard

overlapping and interweaving in 3D, like in real volume data. One of these was a little different from the rest. The task was to find the odd one out.

We did not repeat the datasets between techniques to avoid learning effects. We also wanted to have two trials for each task, for each technique. Thus, we created six datasets for search tasks, and six more for pattern recognition tasks. We also created a training dataset with many letters and two coiled structures.

4.7 Procedure

The study was approved by the Institutional Review Board of our university. After arrival, the participant signed an informed consent form, and filled out a background questionnaire. Then she was given a short introduction of the motivation behind the study, and went through a training session in the technique that would be used first. During the training, she spent three minutes practicing a search task, and three minutes practicing a pattern recognition task, with the training dataset. Next, she used the first technique to complete two search tasks and two pattern recognition tasks, each with different datasets. We created multiple simulated datasets of the same complexity level to avoid any learning effects between the techniques, and the datasets were counterbalanced between the participants and techniques. She was provided three minutes to complete each task. The experimenter used a stopwatch to record the time taken to complete each task. The same experimenter recorded the time for each participant, and we assumed that any time measurement errors were distributed evenly among the participants and techniques. The same experimenter recorded the response of each participant for each search task. For the pattern recognition task, the experimenter directly recorded whether the answer was correct or incorrect.

During the search task, the participants were asked to confirm their answer if they sounded unsure of what they were answering. This was done to make sure that the novice participants were not making passing guesses at what apparently looked like the structures they were searching for, but it also avoided over-counting. The experimenter reminded the participant before every search task that the letters could be big or small, and thick or thin.

After completing the tasks with the first technique, the participant had a short round of training with the second technique, with the training dataset. Then she completed the two search tasks and two pattern recognition tasks with the second technique. The participant then repeated the cycle with the final technique. Following that, the participant completed a post-questionnaire capturing her feedback on ease of use, ease of learning, and preference, all rated on a 1-7 scale for each technique, in addition to a few other usability and strategy-related questions for VC. The experimenter also recorded the participant's responses to different usability and design-related questions in a free-form interview.

From the pilot participants, we gathered useful strategies for the three techniques, which we passed on to the participants in the

main study, in a way to give them a little bit of expertise that they wouldn't have. For the search task with VC, we recommended that the participants crack through the middle of the simulated volume to reduce the clutter of the dataset. For the pattern recognition task with the VC, we recommended that the participants separate the three structures into three sub-volumes, for easier comparison. For the AS, we recommended that they orient the plane towards the back of the simulated volume, so that the structures or letters towards the front became more distinguishable. We also suggested that they keep the plane static, parallel to the view, and through the middle of the dataset, and then use head tracking to look at both sides of the sliced dataset. With the AAS, we recommended using all three sliders together.

4.8 Results

The score metric was of ordinal numeric type, while the time was continuous numeric. The quantitative metrics in the post questionnaire (ease of use, ease of learning, and liking) were all of ordinal numeric type. For the time metric, we ran a one-way analysis of variance (ANOVA). For the other metrics, we ran an ordinal logistic regression based on a Chi-square statistic. If we found significant difference between the techniques, we employed post-hoc Tukey's HSD tests (for differences in least square means) for the time metric, and the two-sided Wilcoxon Signed rank test (with Bonferroni corrections), for all other metrics.

4.8.1 Search Tasks

The score metric for the search tasks had responses ranging from zero to four. We took the difference of the participants' response from four, which gave us the error produced by the participants. We found a significant effect of technique ($\chi^2_{df=2}$ = 25.6202; p < 0.0001) on error. Post-hoc tests indicated that the errors decreased significantly from AAS to AS (p=0.0348), AAS to VC (p=0.0003), and AS to VC (p=0.0027), as illustrated by the graph in Figure 4-a. The mean errors of participants with the three techniques are in Table 1.

We also found a significant effect of techinque (F(2, 69) = 3.3915; p = 0.0394) on time. A post-hoc test indicated that VC was significantly faster than AAS for search tasks, as seen in Figure 4-b. There was no significant difference between the AAS and AS, or the AS and VC pairs. Mean times are in Table 1.

Table 1. Mean errors, scores, and time taken for the task types

Interaction Technique	Search Task Mean Error	Search Task Mean Time (seconds)	Pattern Task Mean Score	Pattern Task Mean Time (seconds)
AAS	1.833	175.00	0.2917	149.46
AS	1.208	164.08	0.7500	150.88
VC	0.583	154.45	0.8750	168.92

4.8.2 Pattern Matching Tasks

The score metric for the pattern recognition task was either 1 (correct) or 0 (incorrect). We found a significant effect of technique

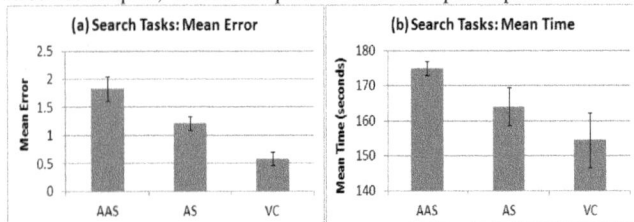

Figure 4: Performance metrics for search tasks.

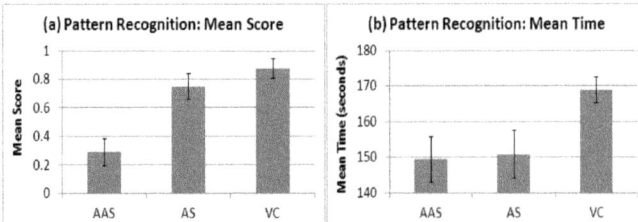

Figure 5: Performance metrics for pattern recognition tasks.

$(\chi^2_{df=2} = 20.1322; p < 0.0001)$ on score. Post-hoc tests indicate that the score increased significantly from AAS to VC (p=0.0003), but neither AS and VC nor AAS and AS scores were significantly different (see Figure 5-a; mean scores in Table 1).

We found a significant effect of technique on time (F(2, 69) = 3.5537; p = 0.0340), although post hoc tests found no significant difference in the time taken between the different techniques (also see Figure 5-b). Mean time spent is in Table 1.

4.8.3 Post Questionnaire Results
The participants reported no significant difference between the techniques for ease of use or ease of learning. However, the participants reported a significant difference $(\chi^2_{df=2} = 17.5265; p = 0.0002)$ in their preference for the three techniques—they liked VC significantly more than AAS (p=0.0411).

5. DISCUSSION
Looking back at our research questions, we have found evidence that partially supports and partially refutes our first hypothesis that VC improves task performance over standard techniques for search tasks and pattern recognition tasks. For the search tasks, VC had the lowest mean error and was also the fastest, which strongly supports the first hypothesis for the search tasks.

For the pattern recognition tasks, VC had the highest absolute score (0.875), but was the slowest, which could have been due to a speed-accuracy tradeoff. With VC, participants took quite some time to crack the volume such that the three structures were in separate sub-volumes. We believe the time spent on this would reduce with more practice. The AAS had significantly lower times of completion because several participants gave up on the pattern recognition task with AAS, as they felt it was really difficult. The graphs plotting the mean scores and errors (Figure 5-a, Figure 4-a) indicate that in the AAS the participants scored very close to the score that would have resulted from random chance (2.0 for search error, 0.33 for pattern recognition score).

We believe that the specific design choices that we made (section 3.2.3) supporting our different usability criteria (see section 3.2.2), contributed to the observed benefits of the VC technique, like the basic function of cracking a volume in two halves served to instantly reduce the clutter inside the volume, so that several participants could identify all the letters inside correctly in as little as 40 seconds. Most of them took the remaining time just to join the sub-volumes back, break at some other point, and recount to confirm to themselves, before giving a final answer.

For the pattern recognition task with the VC technique, once they had broken the volume to separate out the shapes in distinct sub-volumes, it was quite easy to determine the right answer. Out of 24 trials, they were incorrect in only 3 cases. Looking back closely at the results, we found that in two of those three incorrect cases they ran out of time. Also, we constrained the bimanual movement only on a plane as described in section 3.2.3. For the pattern recognition task, if we removed the constraints, the participants could actually rotate the sub-volumes so that they could align the coiled structures to verify visually if they matched.

The post-questionnaire results support our second hypothesis. The participants liked VC significantly better than the standard AAS technique. Even though the VC technique challenged the participants with more gestures to recall and use (single-handed grab, crack, bimanual grab, join) than both the AAS (orthogonal slicing) and the AS technique (unconstrained slicing, single-handed

grab) combined, the participants reported no significant difference in learning or usability for the three techniques. VC was easy to learn, it was preferred by participants, and it had good performance in most cases. We believe that the use of a real world metaphor that was natural to the users contributed to these results.

Participant comments included concerns about the lack of precision while cracking, blocking of the view by the hands, and difficulty in understanding the depth of the hands. The lack of precision might have also contributed to the slow task performance with VC. We are planning to address these issues in the next iteration of VC, by using an asymmetric interface, and reducing visibility of the 3D models of hands.

5.1 Novice vs. Expert Participants
We initially evaluated our design with experts (see 4.2), but chose to run the main study with novice participants (see 4.5). This decision is in line with arguments made by researchers running empirical studies for evaluating task performance with volume datasets [6, 14, 15]. There are not very many expert users of volume datasets, and researchers find it hard to locate domain scientists as study participants. The field of micro-CT is relatively new, domain scientists have little experience in analyzing volume data [21], and training activities are actively being pursued [18]. Laha et al. found that none of the experts in their study self-reported as *experts* in the background survey questionnaire [15].

We could argue that experts might perform better than novices with the AAS technique. But the results of our study provides evidence that AAS at the least requires a lot of training for *search* tasks, much more than what is needed for AS and VC. Also, as discussed in 4.7, we gave the novices useful interaction strategies in each technique in a way to give them a little bit of expertise when they began to use each technique.

5.2 Simulated Datasets vs. Real Datasets
Using simulated volume datasets for evaluation studies is not ideal, but given our rendering hardware constraints, we believed it to be a reasonable choice. We kept the size of the datasets as big as possible (17^3) without sacrificing real-time interactivity, but they were much smaller than real data $(256^3$ or higher). We verified that the design of the simulated datasets closely corresponded to real datasets by evaluating them qualitatively with scientists from four different domains (see 4.2). We designed the simulated structures inside these datasets to be similar to those from real data, with internal objects coiling and overlapping in 3D. All four scientists who verified the structures opined that they closely resemble structures from real datasets that they work with. They were also of the opinion that the results we found would translate to their individual domains, but also encouraged us to find ways to work with real datasets. Currently, we are working on rendering real datasets in such a way to access and manipulate individual voxels interactively as needed by the VC, to prototype and evaluate VC with real datasets.

6. CONCLUSIONS AND FUTURE WORK
The contribution of this paper is a bimanual interaction technique for generating exploded views of volumes [4], which works directly on raw volumetric datasets, prior to any form of segmentation or definition of selection objects or ROI. We discussed in detail the various decisions that we made while designing the Volume Cracker, and reported the results of a user study comparing VC with the AS and the AAS techniques. We found that VC had significant advantages over both of these for search and pattern recognition

tasks. We have contributed a deeper understanding of the usability criteria for volume data analysis interaction techniques, and a proven exemplar design satisfying those criteria.

We are currently working on creating an asymmetric interface for VC, based on Guiard's framework [7], to increase the precision. The literature suggests preference of symmetric designs over assymetric [2], and vice versa [1] for different task types, and factors affecting task performance. But we need more evidence for performance, and preference of one design over the other. We plan to evaluate the new VC design with real volume datasets, using the task categories from an abstract task taxonomy [13].

We have just started exploring the design space of 3D interaction techniques useful for volume data analysis. As we do not have standardized techniques mapped to the various tasks that domain scientists perform, we need to design, develop, and evaluate further novel 3D interaction techniques for volume data analysis. A bigger goal is to map the various techniques together in a suite of tools for coarse but interactive volume segmentation [13].

7. ACKNOWLEDGEMENTS

The authors wish to thank Jake Socha, Kriti Sen Sharma, Sharmistha Mitra, and Suvojit Ghosh (all from Virginia Tech) for the expert evaluation of the Volume Cracker, and the anonymous reviewers for improving the paper in various ways.

8. REFERENCES

[1] Balakrishnan, R. and Hinckley, K., "Symmetric bimanual interaction," in *Proceedings of the SIGCHI conference on Human Factors in Computing Systems*, pp 33-40, 2000.

[2] Balakrishnan, R. and Kurtenbach, G., "Exploring bimanual camera control and object manipulation in 3D graphics interfaces," in *ACM CHI conference*, pp 56-63, 1999.

[3] Billen, M. I., Kreylos, O., Hamann, B., Jadamec, M. A., Kellogg, L. H., Staadt, O., and Sumner, D. Y., "A geoscience perspective on immersive 3D gridded data visualization," *Computers & Geosciences*, 34(9):1056-1072, 2008.

[4] Bruckner, S. and Groller, M. E., "Exploded Views for Volume Data," *IEEE Transactions on Visualization and Computer Graphics*, 12(5):1077-1084, 2006.

[5] Bruckner, S. and Groller, M. E., "VolumeShop: an interactive system for direct volume illustration," in *IEEE Visualization*, pp 671-678, 2005.

[6] Forsberg, A., Chen, J., and Laidlaw, D. H., "Comparing 3D vector field visualization methods: A user study.," *IEEE Transactions of Visualization and Computer Graphics*, 15(6):1219-1226, 2009.

[7] Guiard, Y., "Asymmetric division of labor in human skilled bimanual action: The kinematic chain as a model," *Journal of motor behavior*, 19:486-517, 1987.

[8] Hinckley, K., Pausch, R., Goble, J. C., and Kassell, N. F., "Passive real-world interface props for neurosurgical visualization," in *Proceedings of the SIGCHI Conference on Human Factors in Computing Systems*, pp 452-458, 1994.

[9] Huff, R., Dietrich, C. A., Nedel, L. P., Freitas, C. M. D. S., Comba, J. L. D., and Olabarriaga, S. D., "Erasing, digging and clipping in volumetric datasets with one or two hands," in *ACM international conference on Virtual reality continuum and its applications*, pp 271-278, 2006.

[10] Kaufman, A. E., "Volume visualization," *ACM Computing Surveys*, 28(1):165-167, 1996.

[11] Klein, T., Guéniat, F., Pastur, L., Vernier, F., and Isenberg, T., "A Design Study of Direct-Touch Interaction for Exploratory 3D Scientific Visualization," *Computer Graphics Forum*, 31(3):1225-1234, 2012.

[12] Konrad Verse, O., Preim, B., and Littmann, A., "Virtual resection with a deformable cutting plane," in *Proceedings of simulation und visualisierung*, pp 203-214, 2004.

[13] Laha, B. and Bowman, D. A., "Interactive Coarse Segmentation and Analysis of Volume Data with a Suite of 3D Interaction Tools," presented at the IEEE VR Workshop on Immersive Volume Interaction, 2013.

[14] Laha, B., Bowman, D. A., and Schiffbauer, J. D., "Validation of the MR Simulation Approach for Evaluating the Effects of Immersion on Visual Analysis of Volume Data," *IEEE Transactions of Visualization and Computer Graphics*, 19(4):529-538, 2013.

[15] Laha, B., Sensharma, K., Schiffbauer, J. D., and Bowman, D. A., "Effects of Immersion on Visual Analysis of Volume Data," *IEEE Transactions on Visualization and Computer Graphics*, 18(4):597-606, 2012.

[16] Leganchuk, A., Zhai, S., and Buxton, W., "Manual and cognitive benefits of two-handed input: an experimental study," *ACM Transactions on Computer-Human Interaction*, 5(4):326-359, 1998.

[17] McGuffin, M. J., Tancau, L., and Balakrishnan, R., "Using deformations for browsing volumetric data," in *IEEE Visualization*, pp 401-408, 2003.

[18] Mishra, S., Sensharma, K., Lee, S. J., Fox, E. A., and Wang, G., "SLATE: Virtualizing multiscale CT training " *Journal of X-Ray Science and Technology*, 20(2):239-248, 2012.

[19] Mlyniec, P., Jerald, J., Yoganandan, A., Seagull, F. J., Toledo, F., and Schultheis, U., "iMedic: a two-handed immersive medical environment for distributed interactive consultation," in *Medicine Meets Virtual Reality 18: NextMed*, 163:372-378: IOS Press, 2011.

[20] Ritman, E. L., "Micro-computed tomography-current status and developments," *Annual Review of Biomedical Engineering*, 6:185-208, 2004.

[21] Stock, S. R., *Microcomputed tomography: Methodology and applications*: CRC Press, 2008.

[22] Ulinski, A. C., "Taxonomy and experimental evaluation of two-handed selection techniques for volumetric data," Department of Computer Science, The University of North Carolina, 2008.

[23] Viola, I., Kanitsar, A., and Groller, M. E., "Importance-Driven Volume Rendering," in *Proceedings of the conference on Visualization*, pp 139-146, 2004.

[24] Wang, L., Zhao, Y., Mueller, K., and Kaufman, A. E., "The magic volume lens: an interactive focus+context technique for volume rendering," in *IEEE Visualization*, pp 367-374, 2005.

[25] Wang, S. W. and Kaufman, A. E., "Volume Sculpting," in *ACM Symp. on Interactive 3D Graphics*, pp 151-156, 1995.

[26] Weiskopf, D., Engel, K., and Ertl, T., "Interactive clipping techniques for texture-based volume visualization and volume shading," *IEEE Transactions on Visualization and Computer Graphics*, 9(3):298-312, 2003.

[27] Zhou, J., Hinz, M., and Tonnies, K. D., "Focal region-guided feature-based volume rendering," in *First International Symposium on 3D Data Processing Visualization and Transmission*, pp 87-90, 2002.

[28] Zhou, Z., Cheok, A. D., Pan, J., and Li, Y., "Magic Story Cube: an interactive tangible interface for storytelling," in *Proceedings of the ACM SIGCHI International Conference on Advances in computer entertainment technology*, pp 364-365, 2004.

Direct 3D Object Manipulation on a Collaborative Stereoscopic Display

Kasım Özacar
kozacar@riec.tohoku.ac.jp

Kazuki Takashima
takashima@riec.tohoku.ac.jp

Yoshifumi Kitamura
kitamura@riec.tohoku.ac.jp

Research Institute of Electrical Communication, Tohoku University
2-1-1 Katahira, Aoba, Sendai, Miyagi
980-8577, Japan

ABSTRACT

IllusionHole (IH) is an interactive stereoscopic tabletop display that allows multiple users to interactively observe and directly point at a particular position of a stereoscopic object in a shared workspace. We explored a mid-air direct multi-finger interaction technique to efficiently perform fundamental object manipulations for single user (e.g., selection, rotation, translation and scaling) on IH. Performance of the proposed technique was compared with a cursor-based single pointing technique by a 3D docking task. The results showed that direct object manipulation with proposed technique provides greater benefits on user experience in a collaborative environment.

Categories and Subject Descriptors

H.5.1 [**Information interfaces and presentation**]: Multimedia Information Systems. –Artificial augmented and virtual realities. H.5.2 [**Information interfaces and presentation**]: User Interfaces. –Method devices and strategies.

General Terms

Performance, Design, Human Factors

Keywords

3D user interface, Stereoscopic display, Mid-air interaction, Multi-finger manipulation.

1. INTRODUCTION

3D displays, which present 3D virtual environments, have become widespread due to increased availability of visualizing 3D objects. Besides the benefit of visualizing 3D content, a combination with direct multi-finger interactions can offer fast, easy interactions with 3D content [1,4]. In addition, 3D multi-user supported displays are widely used in collaborative environments. It is because they allow multiple users to work together and manipulate shared virtual contents [3,9]. As a result, a combination of a 3D display and direct multi-finger interaction can promote users' experience in terms of collaboratively viewing and manipulating 3D objects. Consequently, users can have the similar experience of working with a physical object when they work with a virtual object. To accomplish this, an important requirement of the display is to allow multiple users to view collaboratively, select and manipulate 3D objects in a same physical space. For example, information about a directly-touched

3D object (e.g., whose action touched it, which finger he/she used, the position of the object, the finger's movement direction etc.) must be recognized by all the users. This leads to a natural and mutual attention on the structural information of the object.

Despite many research studies on 3D user interfaces and 3D displays, such requirement for a natural collaborative working space has not been provided due to potential limitations of existing display configurations. Although half-silvered mirror stereoscopic displays with head tracking offer directly touching 3D content by overlapping between virtual and physical spaces, they are not suitable for multiple users' interactions because of their narrow viewing angle [4,5]. Hachet et al. [4] proposed and evaluated the system that combines a multi-touch surface and stereo visualization. A user can interact on a touchscreen using 9 Degree-Of-Freedom (DOF) widgets to perform RTS interactions with floating objects above the separated surface. Hilliges et al. [5] introduced Holodesk, an interactive system that combines a semi-transparent mirror and Kinect depth sensing device. They proposed a 3D-physics-based interaction describing users directly merging their hands in the virtual world to grasp virtual objects as if they were real. On the other hand, Grossman et al. [3] designed bimanual gesture-based techniques on a hemispherical volumetric display where users collaboratively share 3D content from a 360-degree viewing angle. However, users cannot place their fingers or hands inside the content visualized space for direct manipulation of 3D objects due to the covered glass of the display. Kitamura et al. [6] developed *IllusionHole* (IH) to satisfy the requirement, where multiple users can directly point at stereoscopically rendered objects with their fingers from any direction. This feature has not been explored in terms of finger tracking and object manipulation with multiple fingers, but it would be a promising feature for designing natural and highly interactive collaborative workspaces.

Researchers have investigated the effect of manipulation distance on user performance in stereoscopic virtual environments. Mine et al. [8] found direct manipulation to be easier than the manipulation at a distance on a stereoscopic display. Djajadiningrat et al. [2] found no difference in performance for direct manipulation and manipulation at distance of 20 cm in a fish-tank VR setup. However, participants preferred direct manipulation over manipulation at a distance. In addition, touching a virtual object in stereoscopic displays suffers from visual conflicts. Valkov et al. [10] analyzed the visual conflicts and gave some recommendations for direct touching of stereoscopic displays.

Therefore, we focused on direct multi-finger object manipulation while collaboratively sharing the 3D objects among users for IH display system. We designed and evaluated the direct interaction technique with optical finger tracking, where one of the users around the display manipulates virtual objects by mid-air finger-

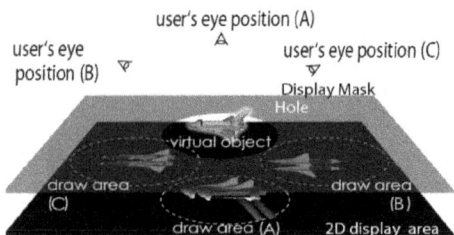

Figure 1. Configuration of drawing areas for 3 users: A, B, and C.

based gestures, and the others collaboratively recognize the manipulations. Performance of the designed technique for the basic object manipulations was evaluated by comparing with a baseline single pointing technique in a controlled experiment based on several docking tasks with 6 DOFs (3 axes translations, 1 axis rotation and 1 uniform scaling). The contribution of this paper is two-fold. First, we implement direct multi-finger object manipulations on a stereoscopic display. This can be used to build a new 3D cooperative working environment where 3D images coexist with physical work space. Second, our study empirically shows benefit to this direct 3D object manipulation by comparing indirect single pointing on IH.

2. DESIGNING DIRECT MULTI-FINGER INTERACTIONS

2.1 Overview

This study explores direct multi-finger object manipulation on 3D virtual objects based on the IH stereoscopic display. IH basically consists of a display and a display mask, which has a hole in its center. Each user can observe the stereoscopic image pairs shown in an individual area through the hole without seeing the image drawing areas of the other users (See Figure 1). Because IH's virtual space exactly corresponds to the physical space, the stereoscopic image pairs for each user around the table is at exactly the same position. The display mask hole allows these image pairs to be directly touched. Therefore, any manipulation of a virtual object can be performed and viewed by any of the users. Here, we implemented the direct multi-finger interaction technique (direct multi-finger method) to select, manipulate and release the objects.

2.2 Direct Multi-finger Object Manipulation

All gestures for manipulations are determined by either one or two fingers of a user, the position of which is tracked by optical markers on the tips of their fingers. The positional data of the fingers of the user are subsequently mapped actions on the 3D virtual environment where the objects are. 3D position of the object is computed by using the users' eye position, and the distance between the display mask and 2D display area. Figure 2.a shows the markers fastened on user's finger tips for the direct multi-finger manipulation.

2.2.1 Selection and Release

Theoretically, the selection with direct method is triggered when the position of the virtual object and the user's fingertips overlap. In operation, the users have different perception and eye disparity, therefore, a small upward gap between the manipulated object and fingers is used. When one or two fingers touch the object, a yellow circle appears around the object as visual feedback. Here, a timer is used to release the object with not using any button. When the user holds his fingers for a certain time (around 1.5

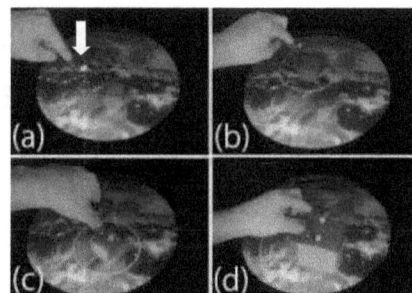

Figure 2. Direct object manipulations with multi-finger interaction.

seconds), the visual feedback disappears, and then selection terminates. This time period is determined by pilot studies.

The white arrow in Figure 2.a shows a finger above the hole that has not started the interaction.

2.2.2 Translation

3-dimentional translation is performed either by moving one finger freely or two fingers without changing the distance between each other. Figure 2.b shows the selected object being translated horizontally from the original position shown as Figure 2.a.

2.2.3 Rotation

Rotation is initiated by touching the object with two fingers (only one axis of rotation about the upright z axis). We did not focus on the yaw and pitch rotation because they often fail finger tracking by optical marker occlusion. This is not a technical limitation of the display. It can be solved by using an occlusion-free finger tracking system. Therefore, this study shows that fundamental benefits to user manipulation from optical trackers could be obtained. Rotation is triggered when the user rotates his/her two fingers around an object's center. Figure 2.c shows rotation with two fingers. The gesture for rotation is imitated from common multi-touch interfaces with two fingers. During the rotation, translation and scaling can be performed simultaneously.

2.2.4 Scaling

The size of a selected object is smoothly uniformly extended or shrunk by moving fingers closer together or further apart. During the scaling, rotation and translation also can be performed. Figure 2.d shows a combination of the scaling and rotation.

2.3 Sharing Object Manipulation

IH allows multiple users to observe and directly point at 3D objects without using any marker. By implementing finger tracking, the users can collaboratively manipulate the object. In this implementation, one of the users can manipulate the object, the others view the manipulation from their own viewpoints in real-time. Figure 3.a demonstrates a result where a user is performing the manipulation while two other participants stand on the right and left side of the display, observing stereoscopic image pairs throughout the hole from their own point of view (See

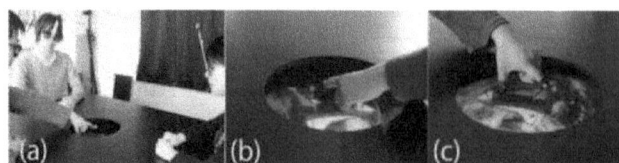

Figure 3. A user directly interacts with an object and others look from their direction (a). The appearance of the object from the user at the left side (b) and the right side (c).

Figure 3.b and 3.c). Here, the users are allowed to move around IH during the observation. If the distance between the users falls below a threshold, the system interpolates their position and creates a unified image drawing area to prevent users' individual viewpoint overlapping.

3. EVALUATION

In order to investigate its fundamental interactivity, we compared the direct multi-finger method (direct manipulation) with an indirect single-point method (manipulation at a distance). Twelve volunteers (8 males and 4 females) participated the experiment with ages between 22 and 34 (mean age 23). They had no previous experience in using any large stereoscopic display. The participant who performed the manipulation stood in front of the horizontal 60-inch diagonal IH [7] which uses passive stereoscopy and has the mask hole with diameter of 26 cm. Refresh rate of the screen is constant 60 Hz per eye of each user, even if the number of users increases.

3.1 Indirect Single-point Interaction

The reason of designing this competitor was that it could be a common interface with totally opposite concept to our proposed input method. For example, although directly touching a stereoscopic object with fingers is natural, it potentially has visual conflict [10]. On the other hand, using a cursor to perform distant object manipulation has fewer selection errors [8]; however, it has not offer natural interaction in 3D environments. This pros and cons must be discussed in order to see fundamental interactivity of the proposal interaction for object manipulation in a collaborative environment. Figure 4.a shows the indirect single point method which was designed based on a mouse button and a 3-dimensional single cursor with a 3-point optical trackable. A green cursor is displayed in 3D space (See Figure 4.b) and its movements correspond to movements of the 3D mouse. Selecting is triggered by merging the cursor inside the object. When the object is selected, a yellow circle appears. If the user holds the mouse for a short time, the yellow circle disappears. Translation is performed corresponding to 3D movement of the 3D mouse. A 1:1 movement ratio of method to cursor movement was used. To perform the rotation, the user rotates the 3D mouse about the upright z axis. The desired amount of rotation can be performed either at once, or in a few steps smoothly. Scaling is performed by rolling the mouse's wheel as the common usage for zoom in/out, which is rolled forward to enlarge and backward to make the object small.

3.2 Experimental Design

The participants were asked to complete a 3D docking task implying five DOFs (x-y-z translation, rotation about the upright z-axis, and uniform scaling). In each task, two cubes (different colors on each side, see Figure 2) were displayed in the hole. One cube could be manipulated and the other was transparent indicating desired position, scale, and rotation. Task completion was based on users' sense of proportion for approximate difference between the transparently represented target and the

manipulated object. The goal of the participants was to place the

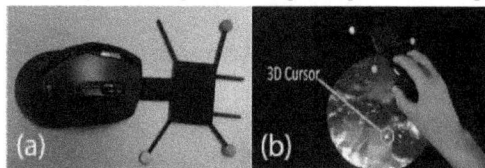

Figure 4. Indirect single-point input methods (a) and its usage (b).

object at the transparent object's coordinates, to include proper rotation, translation and scaling. Here, we are interested in observing the difference on interaction time and errors between both methods for each user, rather than in their absolute values. Since all the participants used both methods, this would not change the differences between the results. On the other hand, if we used a threshold to define the matching between the target and the manipulated object, the task could be over even if the users were not satisfied (i.e. the manipulated object still did not seem to be in the right position), hindering our ability of measuring the real accuracy of the system. Position, size, and orientation of the target were changed between tasks to fit the size of the mask hole. Participants practiced two types of method for five minutes before the actual trials. A repeated-measures design was used with the within-participants. Independent variables were methods (direct multi-finger, indirect single-point), target size (object size x1.6 and x1.0), target distance (13 and 18 cm) and rotation angle (0, 90, and 180 degrees). The order of the two methods was counterbalanced among participants. All participants were shown the same set of target positions, angles, and sizes of the objects. Each participant completed 8 combinations of docking tasks with 4 repetitions, resulting in 64 trials in total. For each task, the system measured task completion time and errors in terms of position, scale, and rotation parameters. Participants were allowed to perform multiple selections and releases in a task. Task completion time was denoted as the total elapsed time between all selections and releases for each task. If a participant released the object by mistake, he/she could select it again to complete the task. At the end of the experiment, they answered a questionnaire based on a seven-point Likert scale. The entire experiment took approximately 50 minutes per participant.

3.3 Results and Discussion

A 2-sample t-Test was used to compare the two input methods because we were primary interested in the comparison. Experimental results are shown in Figure 5 with error bars which indicate standard errors. In the task completion time, direct multi-finger input was significantly faster than indirect single-point input ($t (119) = -2.56$, $p < 0.05$, see Figure 5.a). One reason may be that participants were familiar with the interface because multi-finger interaction is similar to multi-touch surface interaction. Moreover, the closely coupled visual and motor workspace on the hole of IH may have achieved greater performance. Although nearly all the participants could correctly target, scale and rotate the object with both inputs, they said that indirect single-point

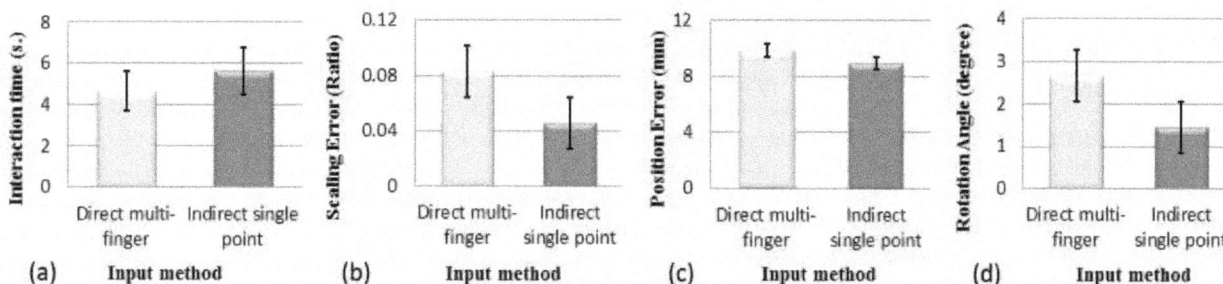

Figure 5. Experimental results.

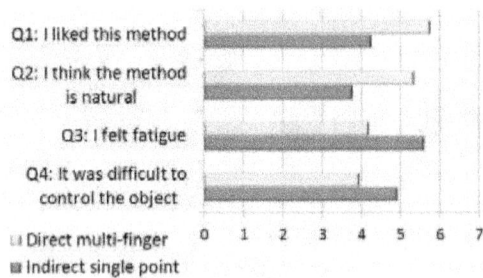

Figure 6. General Feelings

input felt more tiresome. Size, angle and position errors between the manipulated and target object for each input also were recorded. While there was a significant difference between the inputs in terms of scaling errors in favor of indirect single input (t (119) = 3.05, $p >$ 0.05), see Figure 5.b), no significant difference was seen in terms of position errors (t (119) = 0.749, $p > 0.05$) and rotation errors (t (119) = -0.179, $p > 0.05$, see Figure 5.c and Figure 5.d). While there were quite small scaling errors, the reason was probably that scaling with a mouse wheel was more sensitive than the multi-finger pinch in/out gestures and because some jitter movements occurred when the participants scaled the object with fingers. Most of the participants reported that selection with the direct multi-finger method was notably easier. However, the markers attached to the fingertips were easily occluded while rotating the object.

Ratings of general feelings are shown in Figure 6. Ten participants preferred direct multi-finger input and gave many positive comments about it. They liked direct multi-finger manipulation with an average of 5.8 (Q1), which demonstrates satisfying overall docking tasks. The score for the naturalness is 5.3 (Q2). They also said that the direct multi-finger manipulation was less tiresome (Q3). Most of the participants pointed that the cursor-based selection with indirect single input was difficult (Q4). In both inputs, the participants were mainly able to manipulate the shown object, including selecting and releasing objects freely. However, the failure of position tracking arises from marker occlusions which disturb their natural interaction. The indirect single-point input has less occlusion error by about half. This is because the device was held up in the air during the interaction and had less tracking fails. However, this caused fatigue in the participants' hands. Additionally, most of the participants did not like the scaling the object with mouse wheel. Although selection with cursor is an easy method in 2D environments, it's apparently hard to select an object with 3D cursor in virtual space. Rather, when a user touches the object by finger, it can be easily selected. Directly touching a virtual object is easier than a 3D cursor-based interaction, especially for object selection. The reason may be that the 3D objects are displayed within arm's reach, and since a 3D cursor is usually used for manipulation at a distance, it is not a natural way.

In contrast, after the selection with direct multi-finger interaction, a small upward gap between the manipulated object and fingers seems acceptable due to the insufficient tracking accuracy and individual difference of eye disparity of each user. Moreover, if the displayed object is blocked by the manipulating finger(s) and hand, this will result in decreased visibility and interactivity. In other words, directly mapping between the finger movements and manipulated object is more important than directly touching the object. This allows users to observe the displayed 3D content from their own viewpoint. Since hands might block the view of the users who observing the manipulations, especially in case the manipulated object is small, indirect method could be useful.

On the other hand, if the user scales and translates the object too much, stereoscopic image pairs in other users' individual area also scale and translate too much. This causes one user's individual image drawing area to be seen by other users.

Using more accurate and higher DOF direct methods would offer more natural and faster interaction. This is an interesting research topic and should be investigated further. Future work could include the investigation of the effect of higher DOFs, direct multi-finger object manipulations for multiple users, and more complex tasks that involve manipulations and sharing awareness at the same time.

4. CONCLUSION

In this paper, we designed and evaluated direct multi-finger 3D object manipulation on IllusionHole. IllusionHole is a stereoscopic tabletop display that provides multiple users to interactively observe and directly point at a particular position of stereoscopic objects in a shared workspace. We designed a direct multi-finger interaction to perform fundamental manipulations of 3D objects (e.g., translation, rotation and scaling). It was evaluated and compared with a baseline cursor-based single pointing technique in a controlled study with 3D docking tasks. The study showed that direct object manipulation provides better user experience on a collaborative stereoscopic environment.

ACKNOWLEDGEMENTS

This work was supported in part by Strategic Information and Communications R&D Promotion Programme (SCOPE) of the Ministry of Internal Affairs and Communications, Japan.

REFERENCES

[1] Bowman D. A., Kruijff E., LaViola J. J., and Poupyrev I. 3D User Interfaces: Theory and Practice, 2004.

[2] Djajadiningrat J. P. Cubby: What you see is where you act. Interlacing the display and manipulation spaces. PhD thesis, Delft University of Technology, 1998.

[3] Grossman T., Wigdor D., and Balakrishnan R. Multi-finger gestural interaction with 3D volumetric displays, In *Proc. of* UIST '04, 61-70.

[4] Hachet, M., Bossavit, B., Coh´e, A., and de la Rivi`ere, J. B. Toucheo: multi-touch and stereo combined in a seamless workspace, In *Proc. of* UIST '11. 587–592.

[5] Hilliges O., Kim D., Izadi S., Weiss M., Wilson A. HoloDesk: Direct 3D interactions with a situated see-through display, In *Proc. of* CHI '12, 2421-2430.

[6] Kitamura Y., Konishi T., Yamamoto S., and Kishino F. Interactive stereoscopic display for three or more users. In *Proc. of* SIGGRAPH '01, 231-240.

[7] Kitamura Y., Nakayama T., Nakashima T., and Yamamoto S. The IllusionHole with polarization filters. In *Proc. of* VRST '06, 244-251.

[8] Mine M. R., Brooks F. P., Jr., and Sequin C. H. Moving objects in space: exploiting proprioception in virtual-environment interaction. In *Proc. of* SIGGRAPH '97, 19–26.

[9] Takemura, H. and Kishino, K. Cooperative work environment using virtual workspace, In *Proc.* CSCW '92, 226-232.

[10] Valkov, D., Steinicke, F., Bruder, G., and Hinrichs, K. 2D touching of 3D stereoscopic objects, In *Proc. of* CHI'11, 1353-1362.

FocalSpace: Multimodal Activity Tracking, Synthetic Blur and Adaptive Presentation for Video Conferencing

Lining Yao, Anthony DeVincenzi, Anna Pereira, Hiroshi Ishii
MIT Media Lab
75 Amherst St. E14-348P
Cambridge, MA 02142 USA
+1 87 253 9354
{liningy, anna_p, tonyd, ishii} @media.mit.edu

ABSTRACT

We introduce FocalSpace, a video conferencing system that dynamically recognizes relevant activities and objects through depth sensing and hybrid tracking of multimodal cues, such as voice, gesture, and proximity to surfaces. FocalSpace uses this information to enhance users' focus by diminishing the background through synthetic blur effects. We present scenarios that support the suppression of visual distraction, provide contextual augmentation, and enable privacy in dynamic mobile environments. Our user evaluation indicates increased memory accuracy and user preference for FocalSpace techniques compared to traditional video conferencing.

Categories and Subject Descriptors

H.5.2 [**User Interface**]: Graphic user interface (GUI), Screen design, user-centered design.

Keywords

Diminished reality; video conferencing; synthetic blur; focus; attention; focus and context; depth camera.

1. INTRODUCTION

During face-to-face conversations, without conscious thought, our eyes move in and out of different focal depths, fading out irrelevant background imagery. However, in the case of videoconferencing, this natural behavior is reduced by the inherent constraints of a "flat screen" [9]. The background, which can be distracting and contain unwanted noise, remains in focus.

While gaze and sound have been explored as potential cues [16][17] to prevent visual distractions and enhance focus in video conferencing, we were inspired by artists in cinematography who direct people's attention through Depth of Field (DOF). Previous research has shown that differences between sharp and blurred portions of an image can affect user attention [11]. In FocalSpace (Figure 1), focus is placed on pertinent information and the remainder is blurred, giving users visual indicators for selective attention.

To emphasize pertinent information, we constructed a dynamic layered space that allows participants to perceive different layers, including foreground and background, in different focus.

Figure 1. FocalSpace: active speaker in focus, inactive speakers dimmed 50%, and synthetic blur applied to background.

The focused foreground includes participatory and non-participatory individuals, activities such as sketching, and artifacts, including props and projection walls. Through depth sensing and hybrid tracking of multimodal cues, the system can dynamically identify the foreground and apply the blur filter. These types of visual effects are known as "Diminished Reality" [12].

Our contributions include:

• Application of activity detection to videoconferencing through multimodal tracking of audio, gesture and users' proximity to surfaces.
• Introduction of contextual synthetic blur to steer attention towards relevant content, in the spirit of "Diminished Reality".
• Proposed design scenarios including filtering visual detritus, augmentation with contextual graphics, and privacy in mobile environments.
• User evaluation that indicate increased memory accuracy and preference for FocalSpace techniques over traditional video conferencing.

2. RELATED WORK

2.1 Diminished Reality

Several different approaches of blur and focus have been used as Diminished Reality in data visualization and on screen display to direct people's attention. One example is a geographical information system with 26 layers that fades in and out through blur and transparency [2]. A digital chess tutoring system shows each chess piece in different blur level to indicate strategy step by step [11], and a file browser was developed to show the age of files through continuous blur [11].

2.2 Image Filters for Video Conferencing

"Multiscale communication"[14] was proposed with several video-based communication systems using image filters aimed at increasing engagement. In one example, blur was applied to the entire video, not portions of interest. In addition, image filters have been shown to effectively eliminate details while enhancing others. Blur has, for example, been explored to enhance users' sense of presence and portrayal [13].

2.3 "Focus + Context"

Some related work has demonstrated techniques for segmenting foreground from background in video conferencing, such as zooming [9] and gazing tracking and repositioning the focus [17]. Aforementioned systems treated speakers with gaze directed at them, either one or multiple, as foreground. Kinected Conference [4] introduced voice as a cue to trigger focus on speakers. Our system builds on this previous work, while introducing multiple cues such as gestures, proximity and voice, to track semantic activities beyond "talking heads". To enable the dynamic tracking, "Layered Space Model" is proposed.

2.4 Foreground Sensing Technology

One approach of foreground sensing technology is to pre-capture the background so that image elements that differ are calculated and considered as foreground [5]. However, it requires a pre-calibration process. Face recognition cannot detect other foreground elements beyond human faces. The availability of depth sensing devices [1]for situated environments and their expected imminent integration in mobile devices make the approach scalable and applicable to a wide range of usage scenarios.

3. SYSTEM DESCRIPTION

Our system was adapted to a traditional conference environment with simple readily available components (Figure 2). Three depth cameras are placed in front to optimally capture 3 sides of a meeting table in a conference room. The optional peripheral setup contains satellite-webcams pointing to predefined areas to access high-resolution images of the specified regions.

Figure 2. Three depth cameras and microphone arrays in front of a video screen

3.1 Hybrid Tracking of Multimodal Cues

Depth map and human skeleton data given by the Kinect camera are used to track different cues [10]. A microphone array embedded in the Kinect can track the audio cues from the horizontal sound angles of users talking in front of the device. Calibration matches each column of on-screen pixels with the sound angle. If pixels from a person match with the sound angle (10 cm buffer), the person is considered "active speaker" and brought into focus. To prevent unexpected transitions, such as from a natural pause in speech, there is a two-second delay before focus-to-blur transitions.

The system also detects certain gestures, such as "hands up". The hand raising detection is based on skeletal tracking and acceleration rate of the hand joint.

In order to detect how far away an active speaker is from a certain location, proximity cue was tracked using depth maps of the target location and the participants. If the average depth distance between the two was smaller than 20cm, we considered the participant to be approaching or working at a predefined location. Additionally, in order to detect participants' hands approaching an arbitrary object, such as a sketchbook, the object is color marked, thus the spatial location of the marked object can be tracked through depth camera.

Proximity between participants' hands and the marked object is tracked in real time.

3.2 Image Filter

The tracked foreground participants are taken in and out of focus computationally. By applying the Fragment GLSL shader [15] to the background pixels twice, horizontally then vertically, Gaussian blur filter is generated for the video. The extent of blur is a user-adjustable parameter, currently allowing blur to be set in steps up to a ten-pixel radius. The system also allows multiple areas of focus and blur at the same time.

4. INTERACTION TECHNIQUES

4.1 Dynamic Layered Space

In order to segment the scene based on activity, we divide the remote space into two discrete layers (Figure 3), the foreground and the background. Conference participants and objects of interest exist within the foreground layer. Further, the foreground layer contains active and inactive foreground: pertinent images, such as the active speaker and active drawing surfaces, are considered active foreground. Active foreground is presented in focus. The remainder is inactive foreground that is focused, but dimmed 50%. The background layer contains the less relevant visual elements behind the foreground. Synthetic blur effects are applied to diminish the salience of the background.

Figure 3. Dynamic Layered Space: Divided into foreground and background layers.

4.2 Multimodal Activity Detection of Semantic Events

Three cues, voice, gesture and proximity, are tracked to determine the active foreground (Figure 4). In addition, remote listeners can manually select the focus.

Audio Cue is used to detect the active speaker. The current speaker is typically the most prominent foreground in group meetings [17][2]. Once the current speakers are detected, they are placed into active foreground and automatically focused on.

Gesture is detected to understand user intent. The ability to track gestures enables the system to behave as a meeting leader, by tracking people raising their hands, and putting the waiting person into focus simultaneously with the active participant.

Since many kinds of communication make use of illustrations and presentation, the system also supports a Proximity Cue. The system tracks the active participants and activates focus on the corresponding surfaces, when users interact with a drawing surface or projection board.

Figure 4. Voice, Gesture and Proximity Cue

In addition, participants who wish to define an area, person, or object of interest at their discretion, can use a user-defined selection mode. Objects are presented as object hyperlinks with common user interface behaviors such as *hover* and *click* states.

5. USER SENARIOS

5.1 Filtering Visual Detritus

Earlier work proposed the idea of utilizing blur effect on the video rather than the "talking heads" area to direct audience's attention [4]. Based on our Layered Space Model, FocalSpace interprets and updates the background in a more dynamic way. For certain scenarios, such as a busy working environment or noisy cafeteria, the background layer refers to the unwanted visual and auditory clutter behind speakers. While during other meetings involving frequent sketching and body movement, the background will exclude both participants and working artifacts, such as sketchbooks and whiteboards. By removing the unwanted background visual distraction we are able to increase communication bandwidth and direct participants' focus on the foreground activity.

5.2 Adaptive Presentation

FocalSpace diminishes unnecessary information and leave the space for adding additional more relevant information to the foreground layer.

Extending the former work of augmentation of "talking heads" with depth sensing [4], FocalSpace provides spatially registered, contextual augmentations of pre-defined objects. With an additional camera, we are able to display a virtual representation of a surface where a remote user is drawing. This technique allows remote users to observe planar surfaces in real time that would otherwise be invisible or illegible. We demonstrate sketching on flip charts, paper and a digital surface (Figure 5).

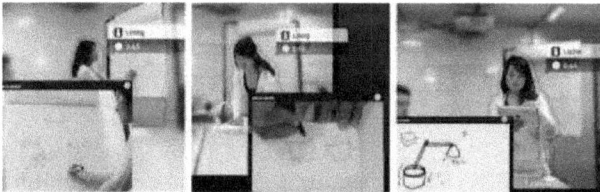

Figure 5: Contextual augmentation of local planar surfaces.

5.3 Privacy for Mobile Environments

We also developed a prototype to explore the FocalSpace concept to more flexible environment using mobile devices (Figure 6). Video stream is captured in front of a situated depth camera and sent over to the phone interface via screen sharing tool [8]. Given the ongoing development of wearable depth sensing technology [7], we envision scenarios where people sit in a coffee shop and send their video streams with blurred background to the remote side using their phones.

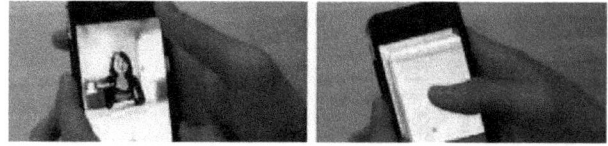

Figure 6: Focus is sent to the mobile interface via network.

6. USER STUDY

As an initial evaluation of FocalSpace we performed a user study of one fundamental aspect of FocalSpace: blur and focus. We investigate how video conferencing with blur and focus compares to video conferencing without, referred to as traditional conferencing. In the study we test two alternative hypotheses:

H_1: FocalSpace increases participant content retention.

H_2: FocalSpace has increased user preference.

As previously highlighted, few user evaluations of video conferencing with diminished and augmented reality exist. We believe that an important first step is to quantify the advantages of FocalSpace and diminished reality. We believe that FocalSpace will increase user focus and therefore memory. Hence, we focus on user memory in our user study. In future work, we plan to follow up with investigations of our previously discussed interaction techniques.

6.1 Methods

In this user study, 16 participants, 8 female, watched two six-minute prerecorded videos emulating video conferences with and without FocalSpace effect. In order to keep the consistency of distraction level and content intensity, prerecorded videos were used instead of real time interactive video conferencing. Both of the videos showed conversations between two users with similar content and generality. Experimental conditions were counterbalanced. The FocalSpace video was recorded with the synthetic blur effect based on audio cues, with the blur level set to three-pixel radius. The traditional video had no special effects.

Content questionnaires evaluated accuracy of user memory. Seven multiple-choice questions were evenly distributed along the timeline of the conversation. The final score was the average percent correct per video. In addition, participants were interviewed on usability and user experience.

Differences in total percent correct score for both FocalSpace and traditional video were analyzed with a two tailed paired t-test. Error bars were reported as standard error of the mean (SEM).

6.2 Results and Discussion

Left of Table 1 shows that participants scored significantly more questions correct watching the FocalSpace conference compared to the traditional conference ($p < 0.01$). Participants retained more content information watching the FocalSpace conference system compared to the traditional system. Participants also skipped significantly ($p = 0.01$) more questions on the traditional video content questionnaire (26) compared to the FocalSpace questionnaire (7). A post-hoc analysis of the FocalSpace content questionnaire showed an increasing trend of questions answered correctly over time ($R^2 = 0.71$). This positive trend implies two key points. First, FocalSpace requires an adjustment period, as users missed more questions in the beginning. It also implies that if the experiment had continued for a longer duration, participants might have performed even higher on the FocalSpace content questionnaire.

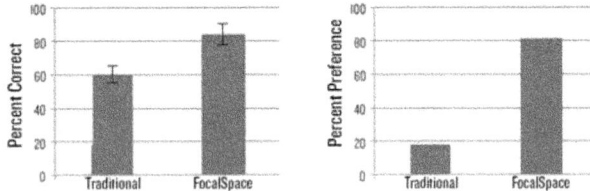

Table 1: (Left) Percent Correct; (Right) Percent Preference

In addition, participants reported their preferred video conferencing system (Right of Table 1). FocalSpace was significantly more preferred compared to a traditional system ($p = 0.02$). During the interview, seven participants explicitly mentioned that the background movements in the non-blurred video were "distracting." However, though the distractions were the same between videos, no participants mentioned the background movements as distracting in the FocalSpace video. Other comments included a preference towards the FocalSpace because he felt like he was "talking one on one."

Another discussion point of the interview was situations where people might find FocalSpace useful based on the test and previous personal video conferencing experience. Suggested scenarios include: "meetings in a chaotic and distracting environment," "long business meetings with heavy load for concentration," "interviews and lectures that are important and need focus," "larger group video conferencing when active faces are hard to identify," "meetings with participants who are non-native speakers or whose voices are weak," and "meetings with identical faces or voices in the same group." However, blur effect concerns were raised, mostly in casual chatting and complex remote collaboration. For example, one user mentioned that for personal chatting, the blur effect might lead to misunderstandings. People also worried about accidentally blurring important information in a dynamic creative environment. Concerns surround unwanted effects of blurring that could be mitigated in future design parameters of FocalSpace.

In summary, we reject both the null hypotheses. FocalSpace has significantly higher participant memory retention and preference compared to traditional video conferencing.

7. FUTURE WORK

We are interested in exploring the use of gaze tracking for local video conferencing parties to detect focus areas. While our current system focuses on tracking cues and raising users' attention on certain areas, gaze tracking gives a stronger emphasis on areas that users have already been looking at, which can be a complementary approach to FocalSpace.

Our interviews indicated users' preference towards a more flexible environment, such as coffee shops or a home setting, using mobile devices. Additional development of enabling technology [7] is a necessary step in this direction.

In addition, by storing the rich, semantic information collected from both the sensors and user activity, we can begin to build a new type of search-and-review interface. With such an interface, conversation could be categorized and filtered by participant, topic, object, or specific types of interaction. Recalling previous teleconference sessions would allow users to adjust their focal points by manually selecting different active foregrounds, enabling them to review different perspectives on past events.

8. CONCLUSION

This paper presents an interactive video conferencing system called FocalSpace. By incorporating depth imaging into a teleconference system, we have demonstrated a method to effectively reduce perceptual clutter by diminishing unnecessary elements of the environment. We believe that by observing the space we inhabit as a richly layered, semantic object, FocalSpace can be valuable tool for other applications domains beyond video conferencing system.

9. REFERENCES

[1] Chatting, D. J., Galpin, J. S., and Donath, J. S. Presence and portrayal: video for casual home dialogues. In MULTIMEDIA '06. ACM, 395–401.

[2] Colby, G., and Scholl, L. Transparency and blur as selective cues for complex visual information. In SPIE 1460. Image Handling and Reproduction Systems Integration, 114.

[3] Criminisi, A., Cross, G., Blake, A., and Kolmogorov, V. Bilayer Segmentation of Live Video. In CVPR '06. IEEE Computer Society, 53-60.

[4] DeVincenzi, A., Yao, L., Ishii, H., and Raskar, R. Kinected conference: augmenting video imaging with calibrated depth and audio. In CSCW '11. ACM, 621-624

[5] Follmer, S. Raffle, H., Go, J., Ballagas, R., and Ishii, H. Video play: playful interactions in video conferencing for long-distance families with young children. In IDC '10. ACM, 49-58.

[6] Harrison, C., Benko, H., and Wilson, A. D. OmniTouch: wearable multitouch interaction everywhere. In UIST '11. ACM, 441-450.

[7] Hirsch, M., Lanman, D. Holtzman, H., and Raskar, R. BiDi screen: a thin, depth-sensing LCD for 3D interaction using light fields. In SIGGRAPH Asia '09. ACM, 159-165.

[8] iDisplay. Retrieved May 8, 2013, from SHAPE: http://www.getidisplay.com

[9] Jenkin, T., McGeachie, J., Fono, D., and Vertegaal, R. eyeView: focus+context views for large group video conferences. In CHI EA '05. ACM, 1497-1500.

[10] Kinect for Windows SDK. Retrieved May 8, 2013, from Microsoft: http://www.microsoft.com/en-us/kinectforwindows/

[11] Kosara, R., Miksch, S., and Hauser, H. Semantic Depth of Field. In INFOVIS '01. IEEE Computer Society, 97.

[12] Mann, S. "Through the Glass, lightly". IEEE Technology and Society, 31 (3). 10-14.

[13] McCay-Peet, L., Lalmas, M., and Navalpakkam, V. On saliency, affect and focused attention. In CHI '12. ACM, 541-550.

[14] Roussel, N., Gueddana, S. Beyond "Beyond Being There": Towards Multiscale Communication Systems. In MM'07. ACM, 238-246.

[15] OpenGL. Retrieved May 8, 2013 http://www.opengl.org/

[16] Okada, K., Maeda, F., Ichikawaa, Y., and Matsushita, Y. Multiparty Videoconferencing at Virtual Social Distance: MAJIC Design. In CSCW'94. ACM, 385-393.

[17] Vertegaal, R., Weevers, I., and Sohn, C. GAZE-2: an attentive video conferencing system. In CHI EA '02. ACM, 736-737.

Effects of Stereo and Head Tracking in 3D Selection Tasks

Bartosz Bajer
York University
bartb@cse.yorku.ca

Robert J. Teather
York University
rteather@cse.yorku.ca

Wolfgang Stuerzlinger
York University
wolfgang@cse.yorku.ca

ABSTRACT

We report a 3D selection study comparing stereo and head-tracking with both mouse and pen pointing. Results indicate stereo was primarily beneficial to the pen mode, but slightly hindered mouse speed. Head tracking had fewer noticeable effects.

Categories and Subject Descriptors

H.5.2 [Information Interfaces and Presentation]: User Interfaces – input devices, interaction styles.

Keywords

Pointing; Fitts' law; ISO 9241-9; virtual reality

1. INTRODUCTION

Stereoscopy and head tracking are commonly used in virtual reality systems to improve immersion, but results indicating the value of these in selection tasks are somewhat mixed [1, 2, 4]. We present a study evaluating these technologies for a ray-casting, and a mouse-based pointing. One might expect that mouse pointing would not benefit from these additional depth cues, as it is predominantly 2D. However, it is an example of "projected" pointing [5], i.e., 3D screen-plane selection via target projections. Both the cursor and targets are affected by stereo and head tracking, which may improve pointing, even with a mouse. Our study investigates this.

2. EXPERIMENT

Thirteen participants volunteered for the study, a 3D version of the ISO 9241-9 [3] reciprocal tapping task. We used a stereo-capable PC with a NaturalPoint *OptiTrack* system to track the head and pen. The software displayed 3D interpretation of the ISO 9241-9 reciprocal tapping task, (Figure 1, right) set in a 10 cm deep box matching the 22" display size. Participants were instructed to select the highlighted target using the current pointing technique. Target height relative to the screen varied from +8 cm to 0 cm in 1 cm increments. The first target in the circle (the top-most highlighted target in Figure 1, right) was the highest (+8 cm), and the opposite target was the lowest (0 cm). All other targets had a height between these two extremes. Mouse pointing used a mono cursor, while the pen used ray-casting. Participants completed all combinations of pointing technique (mouse/ray), stereo (on/off), and head tracking (on/off).

3. RESULTS

Stereo significantly increased pen movement time $(F_{1,11} = 106.36, p < .001)$, by 30% with mono display. There was a significant interaction between head tracking and target height for pen movement time $(F_{15,165} = 3.11, p < .005)$, larger height

differences were slower with head-tracking. This same effect was present for stereo as well $(F_{15,165} = 3.31, p < .001)$. Surprisingly, stereo slightly *increased* mouse movement time by about 5% $(F_{1,11} = 10.51, p < .01)$.

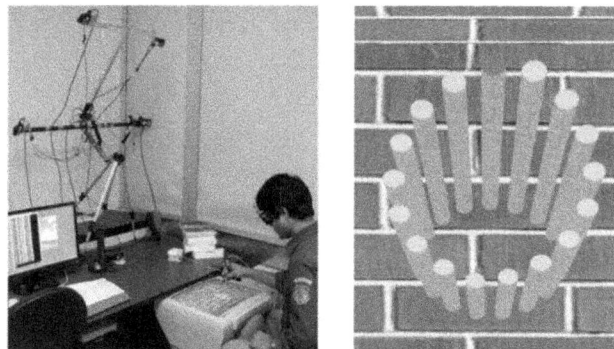

Figure 1. (Left) Apparatus. (Right) 3D version of ISO 9241-9 [3] task used, requiring depth with each motion.

4. CONCLUSIONS

Overall, the effect of stereo display was stronger in our study than that of head-tracking. Surprisingly, stereo negatively affected the mouse, yielding slower target acquisition times. Head-tracking also yielded worse completion times with larger height differences. This may be because participants required extra head-motion to properly view the scene in these cases.

5. REFERENCES

1. Arsenault, R. and Ware, C., Eye-hand co-ordination with force feedback, in *Proceedings of the ACM Conference on Human Factors in Computing Systems - CHI 2000*, 408-414.

2. Boritz, J. and Booth, K. S., A study of interactive 3D point location in a computer simulated virtual environment, in *Proceedings of the ACM Symposium on Virtual Reality Software and Technology - VRST 1997*, 181-187.

3. ISO 9241-9 Ergonomic requirements for office work with visual display terminals (VDTs) - Part 9: Requirements for non-keyboard input devices. International Standard, International Organization for Standardization, 2000.

4. Teather, R. J. and Stuerzlinger, W., Guidelines for 3D positioning techniques, in *Proceedings of the ACM Conference on FuturePlay 2007*, 61-68.

5. Teather, R. J. and Stuerzlinger, W., Pointing at 3D target projections using one-eyed and stereo cursors, in *ACM Conference on Human Factors in Computing Systems - CHI 2013*, 159-168.

Towards Bi-Manual 3D Painting: Generating Virtual Shapes with Hands

Alexis Clay[1]   Jean-Christophe Lombardo[2]   Julien Conan[1]   Nadine Couture[1,3]

[1]ESTIA, [3]LaBRI
Technopole Izarbel
F-64210 Bidart,France
{a.clay, j.conan, n.couture}@estia.fr

[2]INRIA Sophia Antipolis
2004 Route des Lucioles
F-06560 Sophia Antipolis, France
jean-christophe.lombardo@inria.fr

ABSTRACT

We aim at combining surface generation by hands with 3D painting in a large space, from 10 to ~200 m^2 (for a stage setup). Our long-term goal is to phase 3D surface generation in choreography, in order to produce augmented dance shows where the dancer can draw elements in 3D (characters, sets) while dancing. We present two systems; a first system in a CAVE environment, and second system more adapted to a stage setup. A comparison of both systems is provided, and an exploratory user experiment was performed, both with laypersons and dancers.

Author Keywords

Virtual Painting; CAVE; surface generation; digital arts; augmented dance; Movement based Interaction.

ACM Classification Keywords

H.5.1, H.5.2 [Information interfaces and presentation]: Virtual Reality, User Interfaces; J.5 [Computer Applications]: Arts and Humanities—Arts, fine and performing.

INTRODUCTION

We focus on allowing a user/artist (dancer) to create 3D shapes, in order to combine plastic creation with a choreographed movement. We mainly inspired ourselves from two systems from the literature. Schkolne *et al.'s SurfaceDrawing* [2] allows the user to generate 3D surfaces directly from his hands, using data gloves; Keefe *et al.'s CavePainting* [1] uses a large space (a CAVE) for painting 3D strokes. Our systems combine free-hands interaction with a large action/perception space.

INTERACTIONS AND SYSTEMS

The main interaction proposed in our system is to draw a 3D shape with any of his hands. The line from the beginning of the palm to the middle finger's tip is used as a generative line, extruded through movement to give a 3D surface. Users bend the thumb to begin drawing, and relax it to stop. Users can choose a color for each hand. The first system was developed for a CAVE, where users are

tracked using infrared markers. This setup is fully immersive, but only the drawer can perceive the 3D scene. The second system uses a single screen with back projection, a motion capture suit and datagloves. This setup can be used on stage, and the 3D can be rendered for an audience's point of view instead of the dancer's. However, the MEMS sensors in the suit do not allow direct positional tracking, rendering the system less precise and robust than the CAVE system.

USER EVALUATIONS

We first conducted an exploratory user study with four laypersons, and then with two dancers as experts in space evaluation and manipulation. The four laypersons were asked to draw a Mickey Silhouette, a desert Island, and a tunnel surrounding them. Users were generally pleased with the experienced. First-time users tended to look at the screen, and produced 2D drawings. More experienced users moved to produce 3D drawings, using the screen only as a feedback. Two dancers tried the two prototypes. They explored its possibilities and showed a great interest in combining it with choreography. As for laypersons, dancers' first reaction was to focus on the strokes, in order to obtain beautiful lines; they then focused on their own movements, and only checking punctually on the visual display.

CONCLUSION

Further work involves mainly developing the systems and collaborating with dancers to produce augmented shows. These shows act as both technical and artistic validation, as system failure is not an option. The authors would like to thank the dancers Gaël Domenger and Gildas Diquero.

REFERENCES

[1] Keefe, D. F., Feliz, D. A., Moscovich, T., Laidlaw, D. H., and LaViola, J. J. 2001. CavePainting: a fully immersive 3D artistic medium and interactive experience. In *Proceedings of the 2001 Symposium on interactive 3D Graphics* (I3D '01), New York, NY, 85-93.

[2] Schkolne, S., Pruett, M., and Schröder, P. 2001. Surface drawing: creating organic 3D shapes with the hand and tangible tools. In *Proceedings of the SIGCHI Conference on Human Factors in Computing Systems* (Seattle, Washington, United States). CHI '01. ACM (2001), New York, NY, 261-268.

User-defined SUIs: An Exploratory Study

Alexis Clay[1], Anissa Samar[2], Maroua Ben Younes[2], Régis Mollard[2], Marion Wolff[2]

[1] ESTIA
Technopole Izarbel
F-64210 Bidart,France
a.clay@estia.fr

[2] Université Paris Descartes / ESTIA-PEPSS
45 rue des Saints-Pères 75006 Paris, France
{anissa.samar, maroua.ben-younes}@etu.parisdescartes.fr
{regis.mollard, marion.wolff}@parisdescartes.fr

ABSTRACT

In this poster we present an exploratory bottom-up experiment to assess the user's choices in terms of bodily interactions when facing a set of tasks. 29 subjects were asked to perform basic tasks on a large screen TV in three positions: standing, sitting, and lying on a couch, without any guidance on how to perform them. As such, we obtained spontaneous interaction propositions for each task. Subjects were then interviewed on their choices, and their internal representation of information and its dynamics. A statistical analysis highlighted the preferred interactions in each position.

Author Keywords
Natural user interface, interaction design, HCI.

ACM Classification Keywords
H.1.2 [**Information Systems**]: User/Machine Systems

INTRODUCTION

De facto standard space user interactions exist for a few tasks (reach for an icon, swipe). These interactions, although well-engineered, are forced onto the user. We designed a bottom-up experiment to have users spontaneously suggest interaction techniques to perform specific tasks when manipulating a large screen television. We created and validated a database of most frequently used gestures. We also asked the subjects to verbalize on their choices of techniques, on their internal representation of the information, on the link between their suggested technique and the visual display, and how they would envision the resulting feedback.

MATERIALS AND METHODS

In a preliminary study, we selected four criteria from scientific literature [1],[2],[3] : efficiency, feedback, fun and engagement of the user. We used MSPowerpoint in a Wizard of Oz setup to fake TV manipulation. We then defined 5 basic tasks: 1) bring up a menu (make a mosaic of channels appear), 2) Select an icon (a channel in a mosaic presentation), 3) navigate through content (change channel), 4) modify a continuous parameter (sound volume), and 5) engaging/disengaging from the system.

The last task is interesting as SUIs suffer from the user being "always engaged". A script featuring those tasks in 3 different positions (standing, sitting, and lying on a couch) was written. The experiment was led on 29 users (14 women and 15 men). Users were positioned about 3m away from a projection screen. No guidance was given on how to accomplish the tasks (as such, some subjects favored the voice modality). Subjects were interviewed during and after the experimentation.

RESULTS

We coded and listed all movements, selected the most frequent ones, and analyzed the links between those movements and TV commands. Although results show a predilection for typical interactions (resp. point and swipe for tasks 2 and 3), some interesting discrepancies occur according to the user's position. For example, user tend to favor a clap for engaging/disengaging the system when standing or sitting, while they prefer a "stop" sign (hand in front of the chest) when lying. Some users performed unexpected interactions, e.g. heavily favoring voice over movement. For each interaction, users verbalized on their internal representation of information and their process of interaction, leading us to a few hypotheses that will be developed in the future.

CONCLUSION

We isolated favored SUIs for the tasks we defined. We will validate those in a larger-scale evaluation. Our future works involve analyzing in details user's interviews and set up experiments to validate the hypotheses we withdrew from those.

REFERENCES

[1] Bianchi-Berthouze, N. (2011). Understanding the role of body movement in player engagement (Research Report). UCLIC, University College London

[2] Daniel, T. (2008). Les usagers des bornes interactives en lieux publics, 1988-2008 évolutions des usages (Rapport de recherche 5, Juin 2008). MORSOUIN

[3] Groenegress, C. (2010). Whole-body interaction for the enhancement of presence in virtual environments (Rapport de recherche, 8 Avril 2010). EVENT Lab.

Bimanual Spatial Haptic Interface for Assembly Tasks

Jonas Forsslund
Stanford University

Sara C. Schvartzman
Stanford University

Sabine Girod
Stanford University

Rebeka Silva
US Department of Veterans
Affairs

Kenneth Salisbury
Stanford University

Categories and Subject Descriptors

H.5.2 [**User Interfaces**]: Haptic I/O

Keywords

Haptics; Bimanual Interaction; 3DUI

1. INTRODUCTION

We have created a novel virtual assembly tool that uses two haptic devices for bimanual manipulation. The project is focused on the manipulation of fractured jaw bones for patient-specific surgical planning, but can be extended to any assembly task of organic shaped objects (Figure 1).

Spatial input devices that support virtual object manipulation through direct mapping are easier and more natural to use for tasks that are fundamentally in 3D, like assembly tasks. Employing both hands further provides a frame of reference which improves spatial understanding of the manipulated objects [2].

Few studies have been carried out on the importance of haptic feedback for bimanual interactions, but it has been showed meaningful even for unimanual tasks [4]. We are showing a demo of our work in progress to bring high-fidelity haptic rendering to bimanually operated spatial interfaces. As bimanual direct manipulation interaction improves performance even without collision response, we hypothesize that haptic feedback improves it further.

2. METHODS

The implementation of a bimanual spatial haptic application presents certain challenges in two different ways: (i) because of the reduced symbolic input options (we assume only one button per spatial device), certain actions that would be easily commanded using a keyboard have to be commanded using only the haptic devices, (ii) interaction with the virtual world requires a series of algorithms such as collision detection and haptic rendering. The methods listed next provide solutions to the presented challenges:

- Selection and Manipulation: We use the button of the haptic devices to select objects when the manipulandums are in contact with virtual objects. The movement is controlled by the direct manipulation of the haptic devices. The user is also able to group objects together, to manipulate them as a single object.

Figure 1: Assembly of fractured jaw bones.

- Navigation: Changing the point of view is done using both haptic devices. We have implemented the "handle-bar metaphor"[3] to move and rotate the scene by moving the extremes of a virtual bar.

- System Control: A hybrid keyboard/mouse graphical user interface combined with spatial input devices for easy selection of key viewpoints and scenes.

- Haptic Rendering: The collision detection and haptic rendering has been implemented following Barbic's approach [1] for high resolution models. Other methods can be selected in the GUI for evaluation.

3. ADDITIONAL AUTHORS

Sonny Chan and Brian Jo (Stanford University)

4. REFERENCES

[1] J. Barbic. *Real-time reduced large-deformation models and distributed contact for computer graphics and haptics.* PhD thesis, 2007.

[2] D. A. Bowman, E. Kruijff, J. J. LaViola, and I. Poupyrev. *3D User Interfaces: Theory and Practice.* Addison Wesley Longman Publishing Co., Inc., 2004.

[3] P. Song, W. B. Goh, W. Hutama, C.-W. Fu, and X. Liu. A handle bar metaphor for virtual object manipulation with mid-air interaction. In *CHI 2012.*

[4] S. Ullrich, T. Knott, Y. C. Law, O. Grottke, and T. Kuhlen. Influence of the bimanual frame of reference with haptics for unimanual interaction tasks in virtual environments. In *3D User Interfaces (3DUI), 2011.*

Fusing Depth, Color, and Skeleton Data for Enhanced Real-Time Hand Segmentation

Yu-Jen Huang
USC Institute for Creative
Technologies
whuang@ict.usc.edu

Mark Bolas
USC Institute for Creative
Technologies
bolas@ict.usc.edu

Evan A. Suma
USC Institute for Creative
Technologies
suma@ict.usc.edu

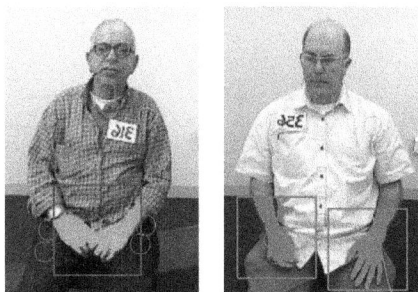

Figure 1: Example results of our hand segmentation approach. Green circles represent the original skeleton tracking data, and the rectangles indicate the search area within the depth and color images.

Categories and Subject Descriptors

I.3.6 [**Computer Graphics**]: Methodology and Techniques—*Interaction techniques*

Keywords

hand tracking, hand segmentation

1. INTRODUCTION

As sensing technology has evolved, spatial user interfaces have become increasingly popular platforms for interacting with video games and virtual environments. However, existing skeleton tracking middleware created for the consumer-level motion tracking devices, such as those developed by Microsoft and OpenNI, tend to focus on coarse full-body motions, and suffers from several well-documented limitations when attempting to track the positions of the user's hands and segment them from the background. In this paper, we present an approach for more robustly handling these failure cases by combining the original skeleton tracking positions with the color and depth information returned from the sensor.

2. METHODS

In our approach, we start by acquiring the skeleton tracking data for the elbows and hands (in our tests we used the Microsoft Kinect for Windows SDK). We informally observed that the elbows are substantially more reliable than the reported hand positions. Therefore, we used the elbows as a reference for defining a rectangular search area where the hands would most likely be located. Although the hand tracking data is often inaccurate, it still provides a likely initial guess that we used to set the length/width of the search area. If the distance between the estimated hand positions is within a predefined threshold, we define one large, single search area instead of two separate ones. This allows our approach to more robustly handle cases where the hands are held together.

The next step in our approach is to more precisely locate the hands using both the color and depth images returned from the sensor. In the color image, we applied an explicit RGB boundaries skin cluster to classify the skin pixels in the search area that were obtained in the previous step [1]. Using the depth image, we make use of the existing Kinect segmentation implementation, which separates the user from the background but does not differentiate between specific parts of the body. We take the intersection of the two pixel sets, thereby eliminating erroneous false positives to provide a more robust overall segmentation. We then apply a connected component labeling algorithm to remove small impossible objects. The results of our hand segmentation algorithm are shown in Figure 1.

3. CONCLUSION

In this paper, we described an approach for enhanced hand segmentation using the Microsoft Kinect. By combining the existing skeleton tracking data with the depth and color image streams, we achieve a more robust segmentation from both the background and other parts of the user's body.

4. ACKNOWLEDGEMENT

This work is supported by DARPA under contract (W911NF-04-D-0005 and the U.S. Army Research, Development, and Engineering Command. The content does not necessarily reflect the position or the policy of the Government, and no official endorsement should be inferred.

5. REFERENCE

[1] V. Vezhnevets, V. Sazonov, and A. Andreeva. A survey on pixel-based skin color detection techniques. In *Proc. Graphicon*, volume 3, pages 85–92, 2003.

A Virtually Tangible 3D Interaction System using an Autostereoscopic Display

Takumi Kusano
Saitama University
255 Shimo-Okubo Sakura-ku,
Saitama City Saitama, Japan
kusano@is.ics.saitama-u.ac.jp

Takehiro Niikura
University of Tokyo
Hongo 7-3-1 Bunkyo-ku,
Tokyo, Japan

Takashi Komuro
Saitama University
255 Shimo-Okubo Sakura-ku,
Saitama City Saitama, Japan
komuro@mail.saitama-u.ac.jp

ABSTRACT

We propose *a virtually tangible 3D interaction system* that enables direct interaction with three dimensional virtual objects which are presented on an autostereoscopic display.

ACM Classification Keywords

H.5.2 [**User Interfaces**]: Interaction styles; I.3.7 [**Three-Dimensional Graphics and Realism**]: Virtual reality.

General Terms

Design.

Author Keywords

3D user interface; tabletop system; interactive game.

1. INTRODUCTION

In conventional touch panel interfaces, operation and presentation are restricted on a two dimensional plane. On the other hand, studies on interaction systems in a 3D space have been conducted. As an example, *tangible user interfaces* using physical objects have been studied [1]. However, they require application-specific system design and lack versatility. Meanwhile, 3D interaction systems using the VR technology have been developed [2]. However, there are problems that the user has to wear glasses and that practical applications have not been proposed.

With the background above, we propose *a virtually tangible 3D interaction system* that enables direct interaction with 3D virtual objects which are presented on an autostereoscopic display. In addition, we show implementation examples of two types of interactive games as practical applications.

2. SYSTEM

The virtually tangible 3D interaction system that we propose in this study consists of an upwardly-placed multi-view autostereoscopic display and a camera installed above the display. A user can interact with 3D virtual objects which are presented on the display. The user can view more natural stereoscopic images

by drawing 3D scenes from the correct viewpoint. Collision detection between the hands and virtual objects is performed by using images which are captured by the camera. When collision with virtual objects occurs, they move according to the touch position and penetration depth. This gives the user a sense of touching real objects. We use a high-speed camera to reduce latency and to present a feeling of high reality. In addition, we made it possible for the user to interact with a number of virtual objects by implementing simultaneous collision detection with multiple objects and cross- interaction between the virtual objects. Thus, the proposed system realizes direct bare-hand interaction with 3D virtual objects without glasses.

3. APPLICATIONS

Since the system can present higher object reality and gives the fun of operating a lot of objects simultaneously, it is suitable for amusement and education system for children. We implemented two types of interactive games, taking advantage of the features of our system and characteristics of an autostereoscopic display.

Figure 1. Interactive games

The first one is the game that the player carries objects to goals with careful attention not to fall off the pathway (Figure. 1, left). There are some holes on the floor, and when objects go out of the way, the objects fall into the holes and return to the starting points. The visual effect of falling objects utilizes stereoscopic view behind the display plane, which gives good stereoscopic effect to the player.

The second one is the casino game using a lot of coin-shaped objects (Figure. 1, center and right). The player bets a pile of coins by bringing it to specific areas. After judged by a roulette, the floor of the miss areas open and the coins fall. Since objects with the variety of heights exist at a time, the player recognizes different heights of objects, and feels better stereoscopic effect.

4. REFERENCES

[1] Jorda, S., et al. 2007. The reacTable: Exploring the Synergy between Live Music Performance and Tabletop Tangible Interfaces. In *Proceedings of TEI '07*, Feb., ACM, 139–146.

[2] Benko, H., et al. 2012. MirageTable: Freehand Interaction on a Projected Augmented Reality Tabletop. In *Proceedings of CHI '12*, May, ACM, 199–208.

Up- and Downwards Motions in 3D Pointing

Sidrah Laldin
York University
slaldin@cse.yorku.ca

Robert J. Teather
York University
rteather@cse.yorku.ca

Wolfgang Stuerzlinger
York University
wolfgang@cse.yorku.ca

ABSTRACT

We present an experiment that examines 3D pointing in fish tank VR using the ISO 9241-9 standard. The experiment used three pointing techniques: mouse, ray, and touch using a stylus. It evaluated user pointing performance with stereoscopically displayed varying height targets above an upward-facing display. Results show differences in upwards and downwards motions for the 3D touch technique.

Categories and Subject Descriptors

H.5.2 [Information Interfaces and Presentation]: User Interfaces – input devices, interaction styles.

Keywords

Pointing; Fitts' law; ISO 9241-9; virtual reality.

1. INTRODUCTION

We present a pointing experiment based on previous work [3], comparing the mouse (an established performance benchmark, see e.g., [2, 4]) to two pen techniques. One required touching targets, while the other used remote pointing via ray casting. We had two goals: 1) to investigate effects of target height (relative to the display) and 2) to evaluate the effect of movement direction. We previously [3] observed such effects, but did not analyze them.

2. EXPERIMENT

Twelve volunteers participated in our study. We used a fish-tank VR system with a NaturalPoint *OptiTrack* system to track the head and pen. The software displayed a 3D version of the ISO 9241-9 [1] task, (Figure 1, left). Participants selected the highlighted target using the current pointing technique.

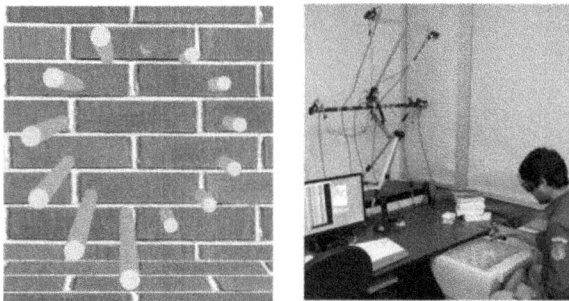

Figure 1. (Left) The pointing task. (Right) The setup.

In every target circle, half of the targets were at one depth, and the rest were at another, using all 2 cm increments between 8 and 0 cm relative to the display surface. Every motion required depth, either moving down toward the screen, or up away from the screen. Mouse pointing used a mono screen-plane cursor. The first pen mode used ray-casting, while the second required participants directly touch targets with the tip of the pen.

3. RESULTS

There were significant main effects for both technique ($F_{2,11} = 65.8$, $p < .05$) and height difference ($F_{3,11} = 7.4$, $p < .05$) on movement time. Touch was worst overall, especially for larger height differences (i.e., 6 to 8 cm differences), while mouse was fastest. Motion direction (upward vs. downward motion) did not affect movement time. Throughput, calculated according to ISO 9241-9 [1], showed a significant interaction between movement direction and technique ($F_{2,11} = 5.5$, $p < .05$) – upwards motions with the touch condition were worse than downwards motions. The other two techniques were not affected by this. A similar effect was found for error rate. There was a significant effect between motion direction and technique ($F_{2,11} = 7.54$, $p < .05$) for error rate: Touch error rate decreased significantly from around 30% to around 23% for *downward* motions, while the other two techniques both improved significantly for *upward* motions.

4. CONCLUSIONS

Performance with downward touch motions may be higher, as participants can visually overlap the pen tip with the target, and move down until hitting the target. Moving *upwards* (away from the display) is more difficult, possibly because of conflicting occlusion and stereo cues. Mouse pointing likely performed best because it allows 2D pointing at target projections, which scale larger for closer targets. This may explain why error rates were lower for upward motions with the mouse and ray [4]; the pointing task was effectively easier due to this scaling effect.

5. REFERENCES

1. ISO 9241-9 Ergonomic requirements for office work with visual display terminals (VDTs) - Part 9: Requirements for non-keyboard input devices. International Standard, International Organization for Standardization, 2000.

2. Soukoreff, R. W. and MacKenzie, I. S., Towards a standard for pointing device evaluation, perspectives on 27 years of Fitts' law research in HCI, *International Journal of Human-Computer Studies 61*, 2004, 751-789.

3. Teather, R. J. and Stuerzlinger, W., Pointing at 3D targets in a stereo head-tracked virtual environment, in *IEEE Symposium on 3D User Interfaces*, 2011, 87-94.

4. Teather, R. J. and Stuerzlinger, W., Pointing at 3D target projections using one-eyed and stereo cursors, in *ACM Conference on Human Factors in Computing Systems - CHI 2013*, 159 - 168.

Autonomous Control of Human-Robot Spacing:
A Socially Situated Approach

Ross Mead
University of Southern California
3710 McClintock Ave., RTH 423
Los Angeles, CA 90089-0781
(213)-740-6245
rossmead@usc.edu

Maja J Matarić
University of Southern California
3650 McClintock Ave., OHE 200
Los Angeles, CA 90089-1450
(213)-740-4520
mataric@usc.edu

ABSTRACT
To enable socially situated human-robot interaction, a robot must both understand and control *proxemics*, the social use of space, to employ communication mechanisms analogous to those used by humans. In this work, we investigate speech and gesture production and recognition as a function of social agent spacing during both human-human and human-robot interactions. These models were used to implement an autonomous proxemic robot controller. The controller utilizes a sampling-based method, wherein each sample represents inter-agent pose, as well as agent speech and gesture production and recognition estimates; a particle filter uses these estimates to maximize the performance of both the robot and the human during the interaction. This functional approach yields pose, speech, and gesture estimates consistent with related literature. This work contributes to the understanding of the underlying pre-cultural processes that govern proxemic behavior, and has implications for robust proxemic controllers for robots in complex interactions and environments.

Categories and Subject Descriptors
I.2.9 [**Artificial Intelligence**]: Robotics – *operator interfaces*. H.1.2 [**Models and Principles**]: User/Machine Systems.

Keywords
Human-robot interaction, proxemics, probabilistic models.

1. INTRODUCTION
To facilitate socially situated human-robot interaction (HRI), a robot must often employ multimodal communication mechanisms analogous to those used by humans: speech production (via speakers), speech recognition (via microphones), gesture production (via physical embodiment), and gesture recognition (via cameras or motion trackers). This research focuses on answering the question: How do speech and gesture influence spatially situated communication between humans and robots in social encounters? Within that question there are several others: How does the pose between a robot and a person affect speech and gesture recognition for each of them? How can a robot adjust its communication mechanisms to maximize human perceptions of its social signals?

In [1], we proposed a probabilistic framework for autonomous human-robot spacing that considered the sensory experience of each agent (human or robot) in a co-present social encounter. In this work, we present the results of a preliminary data collection to formally investigate this framework and model the relationship between spatial, speech, and gesture parameters to develop a socially situated autonomous spatial controller for HRI.

2. APPROACH
We conducted a data collection to inform models of pose, speech, and gesture parameters for humans and robots in our probabilistic framework [1, 2]. This data collection was designed to expose: (1) how people place themselves with respect to each other and a robot; (2) how inter-agent spacing influences human speech and gesture production (output); and (3) how inter-agent spacing influences speech and gesture perception (input) for both humans and robots.

Models resulting from this data collection were implemented as an autonomous spacing controller for a sociable robot. The robot considers (samples) possible interagent poses, estimating how all interacting agents would likely perceive and produce social stimuli (speech and gesture) if the interaction occurred with the robot at that pose—these estimates are maintained in a "particle". For each sampled pose, the corresponding speech and gesture input/output levels [2] are inferred based on the model as if the interaction were to occur at that pose; the pose is then assigned a weight based on the likelihood ("desirability") of an interaction actually occurring with these parameters. The pose, speech, and gesture parameters with maximum weight are selected as the robot goal state.

Models and controllers are available in the Social Behavior Library in the USC Interaction Lab ROS repository (https://code.google.com/p/usc-interaction-software.ros).

3. REFERENCES
[1] Mead, R. and Matarić, M.J. 2012. A probabilistic framework for autonomous proxemic control in situated and mobile human-robot interaction. *Proc. of the 7th ACM/IEEE Int'l. Conf. on Human-Robot Interaction.* Boston, MA, 193-194.

[2] Mead, R. 2012. Space, speech, and gesture in human-robot interaction. *Proc. of the 14th ACM Int'l. Conf. on Multimodal Interaction.* Santa Monica, CA, 333-336.

SUI'13, July 20–21, 2013, Los Angeles, California, USA.
ACM 978-1-4503-2141-9/13/07.

Real-time Image-based Animation Using Morphing with Skeletal Tracking

Wataru Naya
Hokkaido University

Kazuya Fukumoto
Hokkaido University

Tsuyoshi Yamamoto
Hokkaido University

Yoshinori Dobashi
Hokkaido University

ABSTRACT

We propose a real-time image-based animation technique for virtual fitting applications. Our method uses key image finding from a database which uses skeletal data as a search key, and then create in-between images by using image morphing. Comparing to conventional method using 3DCG rendering, our method achieves higher frame rate and realistic textile representation. Unlike [1], data size and search time are reduced with database optimization.

Categories and Subject Descriptors

H.5.1 [Multimedia Information Systems]: Animations Artificial, augmented, and virtual realities

General Terms

Design

Keywords

Image-based animation, Morphing, Virtual fitting

1. PROPOSED METHOD

Figure 1 shows a process of the method. The method involves database generation and run-time rendering subsystems. The former is run once as a preprocessing step to create a database of various cloth images, structural data and feature point data. We use Kinect to get the cloth images and the skeletal data to create the database. To extract feature points for the morphing process, contours of clothes and joint locations are projected onto the image plane from 3D positions.

The rendering subsystem is a service application to compose fitting images for the user. At run-time, user images and skeletal data are first extracted using Kinect. By comparing skeletal data in the database, the most similar posture is extracted from the frame. Postures can be compared simply based on skeletal data by normalizing the acquired data to a model with a uniform scale for distance between individual joints.

If inter-frame continuity is important, the number of possible human postures is large, which makes the database large. This issue can be solved by generating intermediate clothing images using morphing techniques. As discussed in [2], the shapes of the interpolated images are greatly distorted if linear interpolation with 2D feature points is used. We propose a morphing method in which the shape of the interpolated images is kept naturally using 3D human skeletal data. First, the skeletal data closest to the target is interpolated from the two sets of skeletal data attached to the pair of images. Here, skeletal data are morphed using spherical coordinates. The positions of target image feature points are then determined from the feature points of the two images by using this interpolated skeletal data. Feature point coordinates of the target image are linearly interpolated in polar coordinates, with the origin of the system situated at each joint. Next, cloth images are triangulated based on the set of feature points. Each pixel value in corresponding triangles for the target image is determined by blending pixel values of the two images. After superimposing the interpolated images onto user images, we can produce clothes animations that changes according to the movement of the subject in real time.

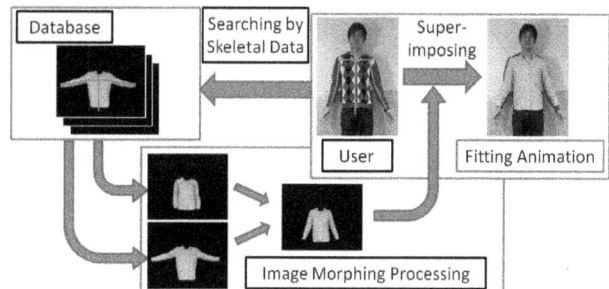

Figure 1. Process of the method

2. PAGE SIZE

The results are shown in Figure 2. It can be seen that clothing images matching the user's posture were generated and superimposed. The average processing time was 18.1 ms per frame for images of $1,440 \times 1,120$ pixels.

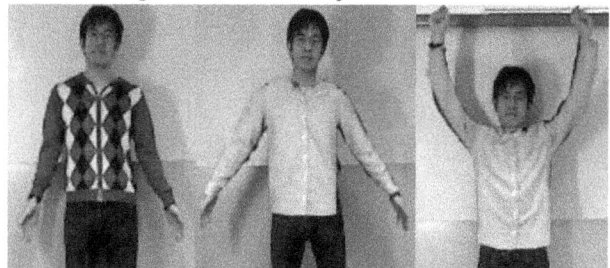

Figure 2. User image and superimposed images

3. CONCLUSIONS

I the arms and torso are overlapping, feature points can't be found by our method. Thus, this system can't create images of these poses. One solution to this is to extract edges of the overlapping region using depth data obtained from a sensor.

4. REFERENCES

[1] Z. Zhou, B. Shu, S. Zhuo, X. Deng, P. Tan, and S. Lin. Image-based clothes animation for virtual fitting. In SIGGRAPH Asia 2012 Technical Briefs, No. 36, 2012.

[2] M. Alexa, D. Cohen-Or, and D. Levin. As-rigid-as-possible shape interpolation. In SIGGRAPH '00, pp. 157-164, 2000.

Augmenting Multi-Touch with Commodity Devices

Francisco R. Ortega
Florida International University
10555 W. Flagler St., EC-3981
Miami, FL., 33174
+1 (305) 348-6072
forte007@fiu.edu

Armando Barreto
Florida International University
10555 W. Flagler St., EC-3981
Miami, FL., 33174
+1 (305) 348-3711
barretoa@fiu.edu

Naphtali Rishe
Florida International University
11200 SW 8th St, ECS-243
Miami, FL., 33199
+1 (305) 348-1706
ndr@acm.org

ABSTRACT

We describe two approaches to augment multi-touch user input with commodity devices (Kinect and wiiMote).

Categories and Subject Descriptors

D.2.2 [**Design Tools and Techniques**]: User Interface Interactions.

General Terms

Algorithms, Design, Human Factors.

Keywords

Multi-touch; 3D User Interfaces; Human-Computer Interaction.

1. INTRODUCTION

Seeking the development of efficient 3D user interfaces, we proposed augmenting multi-touch displays for 3D navigation with our current work in progress. Multi-touch interaction for 3D environments has been explored before for domain specific [1]. There have been many attempts to augment the multi-touch displays. For example, Z-Touch [5] captures a depth map to add the z-axis to the touch display. The Z-Touch has limitations and it is not a commodity device. Augmenting the touch with a force sensor has also been tried [3]. Our approach involves commodity devices to augment multi-touch. Other previous works have used mice and keyboard in surface displays and XBOX Kinect to augment touch [2,4].

2. PROPOSED APPROACH

We are using a desktop 3M Multi-Touch 22'' display, Microsoft Windows Kinect, and wiiMote with MotionPlus. We used the touch data, the Kinect depth stream, the wiiMote and Motion Plus accelerometer data (a_x, a_y, a_z) and the gyroscope data (roll and pitch only), as shown in Figure 1.

Our first attempt was to use the Kinect. The problem with the Kinect[6] is that when the user is close to the display, the depth stream becomes part of the background. We believe that using the Intel Perceptual Computing camera will yield better results. Our

second approach was to use the wiiMote with the Motion Plus to get extra sensory devices for the z-axis. While we know that the wiiMote is not ideal to combine with touch, the test allowed us to set us into the direction of augmenting with 9-axis Micro-Electro-Mechanical Systems (MEMS) attached to one or two hands in form of a watch. We can see that augmenting the touch with MEMS will yield a better interaction.

Figure 1. 3D Navigation Setup.

3. CONCLUSION

While it may be possible to find intuitive gestures for multi-touch displays, is the fusion of devices that may give a complete Natural User Interaction (NUIs).[1]

4. REFERENCES

[1] Chi-Wing, F., Wooi-Boon G., and Junxiang Ng, A. 2010 "Multi-touch techniques for exploring large-scale 3D astrophysical simulations," Proceedings of the 28th international conference on Human factors in computing systems.

[2] Hartmann B, Morris, M. R., Benko, H., and Wilson, A. D. 2009. "Augmenting interactive tables with mice & keyboards," presented at the the 22nd annual ACM symposium, New York, New York, USA. p. 149.

[3] Heo, S. andLee, G. 2011. "Force gestures: augmenting touch screen gestures with normal and tangential forces," pp. 621–626.

[4] Lai, H. 2011."Using Commodity Visual Gesture Recognition Technology to Replace or to Augment Touch Interfaces," presented at the 15th Twente Student Conference on IT.

[5] Takeoka, Y., Miyaki, T., and Rekimoto, J. 2010. "Z-touch: an infrastructure for 3d gesture interaction in the proximity of tabletop surfaces," pp. 91–94.

[1] This work was sponsored by NSF grants HRD-0833093, CNS-0959985, and GAANN fellowship.

Effectiveness of Commodity BCI Devices as Means to Control an Immersive Virtual Environment

Jerald Thomas
Dept. of Electrical Engineering
University of Minnesota Duluth
thoma891@d.umn.edu

Steve Jungst
Dept. of Electrical Engineering
University of Minnesota Duluth
jungs001@d.umn.edu

Pete Willemsen
Dept. of Computer Science
University of Minnesota Duluth
willemsn@d.umn.edu

ABSTRACT

This poster focuses on research investigating the control of an immersive virtual environment using the Emotiv EPOC, a consumer-grade brain computer interface. The primary emphasis of the work is to determine the feasibility of the Emotiv EPOC at manipulating elements of an interactive virtual environment. We have developed a system utilizing the Emotiv EPOC as the main interface to a custom testing environment comprised of the Blender Game Engine, Python, and a VRPN system. A series of experiments that measure response time, reliability, and accuracy have been developed and the current results are described.

Our poster presents the current state of the project including preliminary efforts in piloting the experiments. These findings provide insight into potential results from experimentation with active subjects and prove to be promising.

Categories and Subject Descriptors

H.5.1 [**Multimedia Information Systems**]: Artificial, augmented, and virtual realities; H.5 [**Miscellaneous**]: Brain Computer Interfaces

Keywords

Brain Computer Interface, Virtual Reality, Immersive Environment

1. INTRODUCTION

With possibilities of virtual reality making a profound entrance into the consumer market in the near future comes a strong need for a natural and more sustainable method of interacting with and controlling the virtual environment. This article presents our initial investigation into the effectiveness of using a consumer-grade BCI device, the Emotiv EPOC, to augment the aforementioned interface and manipulation technologies. The chief goal of our efforts is to understand the effectiveness of the Emotiv EPOC along with its limitations. We believe this information can be used to improve consumer-level BCI devices if they are to be used as either a sole means of interaction or asupplementary means of interaction with a virtual environment.

Research and experimentation in BCI devices for controlling and manipulating spatial information has been investigated within a variety of contexts, from controlling a video game to setting up general frameworks for using BCI devices [1, 2, 3]. However, these efforts focus on using research or medical-grade BCI devices, controlling non-immersive virtual environments, as compared to consumer-grade BCI devices controlling an immersive virtual environment. Also, many of these works use the BCI to control the virtual user, for example to move around the environment, instead of to manipulate exocentric virtual objects or the environment itself [2, 3]. These works have produced many good results, showing that there is potential use of BCI devices in virtual environments. With evidence that BCI devices can be used in these contexts, our efforts focus on determining how well consumer-grade devices, such as the Emotiv EPOC can be used within immersive virtual environments.

Our experiments represent an inital investigation aimed at understanding the questions surrounding effective use and training of consumer-grade BCI devices within virtual environments. The experimental design focuses on testing three attributes: response time, reliability, and accuracy. For the purposes of our experiments we have specified rigirous benchmarks for each of the attributes. If we are able to repeatably achieve these standards, we will conclude that the Emotiv EPOC is capable of being a sole means of control of an immersive virtual environment.

2. ACKNOWLEDGMENTS

This project has been funded by the University of Minnesota Undergraduate Research Opportunity Program and facilitated by the UMD SIVE lab.

3. REFERENCES

[1] J. Bayliss and D. Ballard. A virtual reality testbed for brain-computer interface research. *Rehabilitation Engineering, IEEE Transactions on*, 8(2):188 –190, jun 2000.

[2] R. Scherer, F. Lee, A. Schlogl, R. Leeb, H. Bischof, and G. Pfurtscheller. Toward self-paced brain computer communication: Navigation through virtual worlds. *Biomedical Engineering, IEEE Transactions on*, 55(2):675 –682, feb. 2008.

[3] F. Velasco-AÌĄlvarez, R. Ron-Angevin, L. da Silva-Sauer, and S. Sancha-Ros. Brain-computer interface: Comparison of two paradigms to freely navigate in a virtual environment through one mental task. In *Broadband and Biomedical Communications (IB2Com), 2010 Fifth International Conference on*, pages 1 –5, dec. 2010.

Author Index

www.ingramcontent.com/pod-product-compliance
Lightning Source LLC
Chambersburg PA
CBHW081550220326
41598CB00036B/6625

9 781450 325172